SHARING GOD'

SHARING
GOD'S PASSION

PROPHETIC SPIRITUALITY

Paul Hedley Jones

Paternoster:
thinking faith

Copyright © 2012

18 17 16 15 14 13 12   7 6 5 4 3 2 1

This edition first published 2012 by Paternoster
Paternoster is an imprint of Authentic Media Limited
52 Presley Way, Crownhill, Milton Keynes, MK8 0ES
www.authenticmedia.co.uk

British Library Cataloguing in Publication Data

A catalogue record for this book is available from the
British Library

ISBN 978-1-84227-745-4

Cover design by David Smart
Cover art by Sheona Beaumont (www.shospace.co.uk)
Printed and bound by CPI Group (UK) Ltd., Croydon, CR0 4YY

Abbreviations

Abbreviations used in endnotes:

AB	Anchor Bible
BSac	*Bibliotheca Sacra*
CBQ	*Catholic Biblical Quarterly*
CTJ	*Calvin Theological Journal*
ExAud	*Ex Auditu*
HAR	*Hebrew Annual Review*
HTR	*Harvard Theological Review*
HUCA	*Hebrew Union College Annual*
ITC	International Theological Commentary
JAAR	*Journal of the American Academy of Religion*
JBL	*Journal of Biblical Literature*
JSNT	*Journal for the Study of the New Testament*
JSNTSup	Journal for the Study of the New Testament: Supplement Series
JSOT	*Journal for the Study of the Old Testament*
JSOTSup	Journal for the Study of the Old Testament: Supplement Series
NIB	New Interpreter's Bible
NIBC	New International Bible Commentary
OBT	Overtures to Biblical Theology
OTL	Old Testament Library
SP	Sacra Pagina
TOTC	Tyndale Old Testament Commentary
TNTC	Tyndale New Testament Commentary
TT	*Theology Today*
TynBul	*Tyndale Bulletin*
VT	*Vetus Testamentum*
WBC	Word Biblical Commentary
ZAW	*Zeitschrift für die Alttestamentliche Wissenschaft*

For Joy Jones

Contents

Foreword

Gather a group of people together in one place and it won't be long before you notice that they share stories with one another. From the trivial—what happened on the bus this morning—to the profound—how we have encountered God—we tell stories. Some may be brief; others will be longer. Some will trigger similar tales; others will be the last word on the topic. Although some models of preaching have encouraged us to see faith as something nourished principally through propositional statements, it is not something that fits well with our own models of communication. Truth, as we share it with each other, is embodied in narrative, though at the same time we often see the need for explanatory comments, so an emphasis upon proposition or explanation is not out of place. But we are a storied people.

Anyone who reads the Old Testament (and to a lesser extent the New) will not be surprised by this. Although Israel knew a variety of strategies for speaking of what it was to know God, a huge portion of the Old Testament comes to us in the form of story. Although the Old Testament writers knew the value of fiction (see Nathan's story to David in 2 Samuel 12.1–4), for the most part they present us with history as a narrative. But this is never a 'complete' history—it is a presentation of that part of Israel's story that allows us to see how God is at work within it. Like us, the Old Testament is storied, and it shares truth with us embodied in narrative. Although there is less narrative in the New Testament, Jesus also understood the value of a story, and of course the Gospels and Acts are presented as a story, and there is also a narrative structure to the book of Revelation. Readers of the Bible are always being shaped by story.

As such, the revival in interest in narrative and its contribution to theology in recent years is something to be welcomed. Narrative is not, one might say, the whole story. But it is a significant component of how the Bible communicates with us and shapes us as readers. In doing so, we are also drawn to a storied understanding of spirituality because one of the virtues of a narrative approach is that it does not leave spirituality as something purely theoretical but rather as something earthed in real, lived experience. There is, of course, no one mode of spirituality within the Old Testament, and a narrative approach enables us to see how different modes work themselves out in the different life settings in which people find themselves. Prophetic spirituality is one of those modes, and an important one for the church to recover for our own age. Leading us through some of the stories the Old Testament tells before bringing us to the New, Paul Jones here enables us to grasp the diversity of prophetic spirituality while also showing how its narrative presentation means it is always rooted in real experience. We are thus here reminded (or for some introduced) to an important mode of biblical spirituality and continually shown that it never exists apart from a life of faith. We can be grateful to Paul Jones for both the richness and clarity of his exploration.

David G. Firth
St John's College, Nottingham

Acknowledgements

There are some similarities between writing a book and having a baby. Since the deadline for this book and the due date for our baby girl happened to fall within a week of each other, numerous parallels have been at the forefront of my mind in recent months, leading up to today, our daughter's due date, as I sit down to write this acknowledgement.

The conception of the ideas in this book can be traced back to the fertile ethos of Regent College in Vancouver, where interdisciplinary approaches to learning are strongly encouraged. The combining of narrative-critical readings, biblical theology and spiritual theology in *Sharing God's Passion* certainly owes much to Regent's influence, and I am indebted to two of my teachers in particular, Iain Provan and David Diewert, for introducing me to the delights of narrative-critical method and the beauty of the Hebrew language.

It was on the long flight from London to Melbourne on the way to my mother's funeral in January 2009 that I began writing, and a gestation period of two years followed as my understanding of prophetic spirituality began to take shape and develop. Research and writing took place on three different continents and I am indebted to various people along the way for their support. During our time in Argentina, Hans Breekveldt gave me open access to his books and commentaries so that I was able to make more progress than I had anticipated while we were living and working in Salta and Benito Juárez. The following six months in Australia were also very fruitful and we are grateful to various members of the Clark family for their outstanding generosity in providing the means for us to feel settled in Melbourne. I was also able, during those months, to spend some meaningful time with my family and an ever-growing throng of nieces and nephews. The remainder of the book has been written here in England, nearer to my in-laws, who have always treated me like a brother and son. I am especially grateful to my mother-in-law for spending many a late night reading drafts and making helpful suggestions. Gestation doesn't just happen; there have been days of uncontainable enthusiasm, days of fruitless frustration and everything in-between, and I owe much to those who have shaped my thinking and offered feedback at various points.

The past few months can best be described as fairly intensive labour, and I simply don't have a sufficient grasp of the English language to adequately thank my wife, Anakatrina, for her loving support. She has consistently inspired me to become the man God would have me be, and encouraged me to write the best book I possibly can. I am truly blessed to have such a wonderful, understanding soulmate.

With the final stage of delivery, my greatest hope is that this book will bring glory to Jesus and enthusiasm to his church. Of course, this is only possible because a publishing house has put faith in this author's work, and I would like to especially thank Mike Parsons, my editor at Paternoster, for his gracious manner and empowering words.

Finally, I dedicate this book to my mother. Her twenty-four-year battle with rheumatoid arthritis wreaked a terrible havoc on her body and it was only after enduring some trials of my own that I began to understand how her weak physical condition fuelled her relentless spiritual fervour. I know that God's words to the apostle Paul were a great source of comfort and strength to her, words that speak of a dynamic that lies at the heart of prophetic spirituality:

My grace is sufficient for you, for my power is made perfect in weakness (2 Cor 12.9a).

Paul Hedley Jones
9 May 2011

1

Introduction: Sharing God's Passion

I will walk among you and be your God,
and you will be my people (Lev 26.12).

God's Good Intentions

What does God want more than anything? What motivates him to speak, to act and to make himself known to us? As the Bible tells it, from 'the beginning' (Gen 1.1) to the final 'Amen' (Rev 22.21), God desires to live in creation among us, his creatures. Biblical scholars have identified various themes that wind their ways through the biblical story, but whether we speak of God establishing his *kingdom* on earth or renewing *creation*, or of the *covenant* vows between God and humanity, God's underlying passion is the same: to live among the people he created.

An idyllic intimacy between God and humanity is expressed in the opening scenes of Genesis where God walks among the first humans 'in the garden in the cool of the day' (Gen 3.8). Adam and Eve come into a world where fellowship with their Maker is fundamental, and like a stream springing forth from Eden, God's primary passion continues to flow steadily throughout the rest of the biblical story.[1]

> I will walk among you and be your God, and you will be my people (Lev 26.12).
>
> And I will live among the Israelites and will not abandon my people Israel (1 Kgs 6.13).
>
> 'Shout and be glad, O Daughter of Zion. For I am coming, and I will live among you,' declares the LORD. 'Many nations will be

joined with the LORD in that day and will become my people'
(Zech 2.10–11a).

The Word became flesh and made his dwelling among us. We
have seen his glory, the glory of the One and Only, who came from
the Father, full of grace and truth (Jn 1.14).

For we are the temple of the living God. As God has said: 'I will
live with them and walk among them, and I will be their God, and
they will be my people' (2 Cor 6.16b).

And I heard a loud voice from the throne saying, 'Now the
dwelling of God is with men, and he will live with them. They will
be his people, and God himself will be with them and be their
God' (Rev 21.3).

Now one might assume that if the Bible begins and ends with
God's desire to live among his people, then that is precisely what
will happen—without any ifs or buts. (Surely God gets what God
wants!) But the biblical account is not that simple or straightforward. Despite the clarity of God's good intentions, and in spite of
his unlimited capacity to make things happen, the Bible reads as
an epic power-struggle between God and humanity. One of the
reasons for this struggle is that God has included among all his
generous gifts to humanity the gift of freedom.

People are able to make genuine, free choices of their own. On
one level, this may sound perfectly obvious, but the implications
are actually quite staggering: human beings can resist the good
intentions of God. And one does not need to read far into the
Bible to discover a repeated pattern of resistance against God's
will; the first eleven chapters are more than adequate.

Free to Resist (Genesis 1–11)

In Genesis 2–3 human beings are entrusted with the preservation
of *earth* and *life*,[2] but their deliberate act of mistrust resists God's
expressed will for them. When an alternative to trusting obedience is offered—presented in Genesis 3 as a suggestion from the

snake to try the forbidden fruit[3]—Adam and Eve take it. But their disobedience to God also drives a rift between the two of them. Having demonstrated a lack of faith in God (that his rules are for the best), they begin to also treat one another with suspicion. Their first reflex upon feeling shame for the first time is to hide in order to control their level of exposure and vulnerability (a common response in human psychology, although fig leaves would be considered rather unsophisticated these days). This primal story of resistance sets off a chain of events in which God's good intentions appear to spin even further out of his control.

In Genesis 4, Adam and Eve's firstborn son, Cain, is overcome with rage when God looks upon his brother Abel's offering with favour.[4] God warns Cain of the sickness that crouches at his door, threatening to consume him, but like his parents, Cain disregards God's command—and kills his brother in cold blood. It is important to note that the story does not depict sin as something irresistible to the human will. If anything, emphasis falls on the critical importance of human *decision* in the moment of temptation. Cain is instructed by God to choose well, and his options are laid out before him quite clearly: 'If you do what is right . . . But if you do not do what is right . . .' Cain's jealousy is not depicted as an irresistible force that *makes* him sin against his own will. Rather, he stands at a crossroads where he must pause, consider, and choose: what is right, or what is not right.[5] The rebellious disposition (sin) that led to his parents' alienation from paradise is now described as a ferocious animal, biding its time at Cain's door, ready to consume him at the first opportunity. Sin would sap Cain of life and leave him wandering aimlessly (Gen 4.12), but such an outcome is not inevitable; 'Sin is crouching at your door; it desires to have you, *but you must master it*' (Gen 4.7).[6] It is of enormous significance that in these narratives Yahweh does not intervene to twist the arms or manipulate the minds of potential offenders. He gives warning and offers counsel, but his decision to entrust human beings with the liberty to choose for themselves is never withdrawn, regardless even of the consequences for Abel. God has created a world where his will is not the only determining factor.

The decline of humanity continues as Lamech takes the divine promise made to Cain and applies it to his own life:

If Cain is avenged seven times,
  then Lamech seventy-seven times (Gen 4.24).

Lamech's declaration captures the extraordinary depths of human arrogance, but even as he boasts progress, the narrator makes an opposite assertion, describing human beings no longer as images of God (Gen 1.27), but as images of their human fathers (Gen 5.3). Lamech's idea of progress is more like a 'fall', but he is not the only one at fault. Wickedness has become the norm for all humankind, so that '*every* inclination of the thoughts of his heart was *only* evil *all* the time' (Gen 6.5). Yahweh's response to this reality is expressed in no uncertain terms:

> The LORD was grieved that he had made man on the earth, and his heart was filled with pain. So the LORD said, 'I will wipe mankind, whom I have created, from the face of the earth—men and animals, and creatures that move along the ground, and birds of the air—for I am grieved that I have made them' (Gen 6.6–7).

These verses are troubling. First of all, some of us are uncomfortable with such candid acknowledgements of God's emotional capacity (including comments about the state of 'his heart'). But if that doesn't bother us, we are almost certainly shocked to discover God's quick-fix solution to the spreading virus of sin: 'I will wipe mankind . . . from the face of the earth'! As we consider how God's hopes for his creation might be recovered and sustained, these verses are neither encouraging nor hopeful. God's answer is simply to begin again! Worse still, Yahweh does not take any other point of view into account—nor does he hesitate to act on his word. The rains came down, and the floods came up.

But even the harshest divine judgements in Scripture tend to have a silver lining. God intends to begin again with Noah, 'a righteous man, blameless among the people of his time' (Gen 6.9). A fresh start[7] for humanity sounds promising, but unfortunately, hope—represented in the story by an olive leaf—withers quickly as Noah's family follow the same downward spiral as Adam's, adding drunkenness and disgrace to disobedience and murder. If families are indeed the bedrock of society,[8] these primal tales of dysfunctional families in Genesis establish shaky foundations indeed.

The introductory chapters of Genesis (1–11) conclude with a final spectacle that accentuates humanity's opposition to God's intentions. The command for Noah (like Adam) to 'be fruitful and increase in number [and] fill the earth' (Gen 1.28; 9.1,7) is directly challenged in Genesis 11 by the whole world's attempt to converge in one place. The narrative emphasizes this conflict of wills by juxtaposing human ambition with the divine response:

Come, let us build ourselves a city, with a tower that reaches to the heavens, so that we may make a name for ourselves and not be scattered over the face of the whole earth (Gen 11.4).	Come, let us go down and confuse their language so they will not understand each other (Gen 11.7).

The twice-used introductory phrase, 'Come, let us . . .' pits human intentions against God's; humanity reaches up as God comes down. Also, the story's conclusion, 'the LORD scattered them over the face of the whole earth' (Gen 11.8–9), directly quotes and counters the human initiative to 'not be scattered over the face of the whole earth' (Gen 11.4). God wants humanity to spread and cover the earth, but since people have gathered with the expressed purpose of sticking together, God (re)acts to (re)enforce his good intentions; yet another conflict of wills between the Creator and his creatures.

The persistent rebellion of God's image-bearers throughout Genesis 3–11 shows how sin undoes God's creative purposes. These chapters reveal the way things are in the world; people often use their God-given freedom to choose what is contrary to God's hopes for them. We are, all of us, shadowed by the lurking beast that took Cain (1 Pet 5.8), and the authors of Genesis were not the only ones to see the danger.

Late in the seventh century BC, just prior to Judah's exile, the prophet Jeremiah envisioned the earth in its chaotic, preformed state as a direct consequence of human rebellion against God.

'My people are fools;
　they do not know me.

They are senseless children;
    they have no understanding.
They are skilled in doing evil;
    they know not how to do good.'

I looked at the earth,
    and it was formless and empty;
and at the heavens,
    and their light was gone.
I looked at the mountains,
    and they were quaking;
    all the hills were swaying.
I looked, and there were no people;
    every bird in the sky had flown away.
I looked, and the fruitful land was a desert;
    all its towns lay in ruins
    before the LORD, before his fierce anger (Jer 4.22–26).

In the words of one of Israel's poets, creation is *unmade* by Israel's sin. The Hebrew phrase *tohu vabohu* ('unformed and unfilled') occurs only twice in the Bible, in Genesis 1.2 and Jeremiah 4.23, describing in both instances a world devoid of order. Jeremiah speaks of the devastating effect Israel's resistance against Yahweh has on the covenantal glue holding God's world together.

But whether we are reading from the opening chapters of Genesis or from the dark visions of Israel's prophets, we are faced with the same question: How can God's desire to live among his people ever be fulfilled while human beings are so deeply infected by the disease of sin? No one has to think very hard about how to follow their heart's selfish desires; such behaviour comes quite naturally to us. So what hope is there?

If we answer this question (as we often do) by jumping immediately to Jesus, we not only skip over the entire Old Testament (more than 75 per cent of the Christian Bible) but we also inevitably fail to understand the bigger story that Jesus brings to its triumphant climax. At any rate, we need not make a giant leap from Genesis 11 to the gospels in order to discover God's response to the human disease of sin. We may simply pick up where we left off—at Genesis 12.

A Grand Plan

As sin proceeds to permeate the created order, casting shadows where God had commanded light, Yahweh begins a large-scale operation for the redemption of what he has made. It is not surprising that God acts decisively to restore his good intentions. What is remarkable is that in spite of infinite resources and limitless power, Yahweh does not rescue humanity on his own. Instead, he sets out to establish a working relationship with the very creatures who defy him—a most daring enterprise! But then, God never intended to do everything *for* us. Since day one (or day six, when Adam was entrusted with the task of choosing names for the animals), free human choices have been an integral part of God's design. Apparently it has been God's intention from the beginning for human beings to co-create with him and share responsibility for the world. Walter Brueggemann has expressed the point well:

> God is not simply giver of Torah or doer of spectacular saving deeds in history, though he does such deeds. What God does first and best and most is to *trust men with their moment in history*. He trusts his men to do what must be done for the sake of his whole community.[9]

The first of such men in God's redemptive purposes is a Babylonian fellow named Abram, to whom God promises thousands of descendants who will in turn bless the rest of the world (Gen 12.2–3).[10] As the wheels of God's grand plan grind into motion, it becomes apparent that God will stop at nothing to restore good relations with humanity. In Genesis 15.8–21, God even swears on his own life that the covenant with Abraham will be honoured.[11] Abraham's descendants will multiply and God's desire to dwell among his people will come to fruition—as surely as God lives!

God's decision to make his character known to the whole world through one nation's obedience puts Israel directly in the spotlight, but this does not mean that Israel's special calling is for her own benefit. On the contrary, 'God has God's world in focus. God's exclusive move in choosing Abraham/Israel is not an end in itself, but a divine strategy for the sake of a maximally inclusive end.'[12] The final goal is that God may dwell in our midst, acknowledged by every nation as the only true God. But the means to this 'maximally inclusive end' is Israel. She is the light in the darkness appointed to draw the whole world's gaze. The implications of this are profound; God has bound *himself*, together with his hopes for the world, to be personally affected by Israel's choices in what can best be described as 'a high risk mission strategy'.[13]

Although Abraham's descendants do indeed multiply as promised, the opening chapter of Exodus reports that they have become enslaved in Egypt, where they are building a kingdom for someone other than Yahweh (Exod 1.7f.). As Moses boldly collaborates with God, however, the bondage of Egypt is swallowed up in the Red Sea and the Israelites are freed to begin the extraordinary task of establishing God's kingdom on earth.

But then something terrible happens, and we are compelled to ask whether it was a wise move for Yahweh to collaborate with human beings in this project of redemption while the disease of sin still runs rampant. Israel's first act of freedom is one of betrayal.

As Moses meets with God on Mount Sinai—ironically, to receive the Law that will set Israel apart as God's people—the Israelites proceed to worship an idol of their own making. Possibly even more disturbing than their idolatry is God's reaction, which is blatantly reminiscent of the flood narrative. Once again, God expresses regret and threatens to wipe out this rebellious people in order to start again with a single, righteous man (Exod 32.10; see Gen 6.7–8). The problem is, if God wishes to insist on respecting human freedom but cannot tolerate rebellion, what alternative is there to this endless cycle of creation and destruction? How can God's hopes for Israel and the world ever be fulfilled in the face of such stiff-necked resistance? Will God eventually find that he must resort to outright manipulation of his human partner? Will he give up on the project altogether and leave us to our own devices? Or is there yet another means of negotiating the strain between God's good intentions and human resistance?

History in Whose Hands?

A range of events in the Old Testament suggests that there is no clear-cut solution to the quandary of divine purpose versus human resistance. At one end of the spectrum, readers are confronted with stories about God pulling the strings of human hearts in a way that seems unfair and manipulative, of God intruding upon human history in a manner too powerful to resist. The archetypal example is Pharaoh's hardened heart that leads to the liberation of the Hebrews under Yahweh's direction:

> Then the LORD said to Moses, 'Go to Pharaoh, *for I have hardened his heart and the hearts of his officials* so that I may perform these miraculous signs of mine among them that you may tell your children and grandchildren how I dealt harshly with the Egyptians and how I performed my signs among them, and that you may know that I am the LORD' (Exod 10.1–2).[14]

Is it fair that God hardens Pharaoh's heart in order to prove his power and make himself known to Israel? We will leave this question unanswered for now[15] and consider another. In 2 Samuel 24.1, the narrator informs readers that the nation of Israel was punished severely because King David took a census, but a census which God incited the king to take in the first place. As the prophet Gad proceeds to mediate the harsh judgement that follows, we cannot help but question a 'justice' that invokes both the sinful act *and* its punishment.[16] Yet another possible instance of divine coercion occurs in 1 Kings 22, where Micaiah reveals that God has allowed a lying spirit to deceive King Ahab's prophets in order to bring the selfish and disobedient king to his death. Can God really claim to be respecting human freedom when he manages affairs in this way?[17]

At the opposite end of the spectrum, human beings snatch the reins from God's grasp. Various narratives present this reality throughout the biblical story, though perhaps none is quite as vivid as the enacted parable[18] of Jeremiah 13.1–11. Jeremiah is given a threefold instruction: (a) to buy and wear a new linen belt (symbolizing the nation of Israel); (b) to leave it between some

rocks by a river (which of course dirties and ruins the belt); and
(c) to dig it up and take note of its filthy condition. When God
explains the sequence of actions to Jeremiah, there is a stark contrast between what God *hoped for* and what transpired. The
punchline comes in Jeremiah 13.10–11:

> 'These wicked people, who refuse to listen to my words, who fol-
> low the stubbornness of their hearts and go after other gods to
> serve and worship them, will be like this belt—*completely useless!*
> For as a belt is bound round a man's waist, so I bound the whole
> house of Israel and the whole house of Judah to me,' declares the
> LORD, 'to be my people for my renown and praise and honour. *But
> they have not listened.'*

God had hoped to 'wear' Israel with pride, as someone might
show off a new garment to enhance their reputation, but instead,
the nation dirtied his name through disobedience and was ren-
dered 'useless'. It would appear that Israel's failure to *listen* (and
obey) resulted in a distortion of God's plans.

In another, more isolated event, God makes this remarkable
admission to King Ahab: 'You have set free a man I had determined should die' (1 Kgs 20.42). Now there are not many interpretive possibilities for what God means to say here! God had
something very specific in mind (the death of Ben-Hadad) and
Ahab's decision countered God's will. Yahweh's respect for
human freedom in this instance meant that neither Ahab's hand
nor anyone else's could be coerced. Rather, God is presented as
being 'most unpleasantly surprised'[19] and at the behest of human
decisions.

Between these extremes of God's coercive control and effective
human resistance, there are plenty of other instances where Israel
must come to a decision on her own. Moses' speech, presenting
Israel with the choice between life and blessing or death and
curses, is but one example:

> This day I call heaven and earth as witnesses against you that I
> have set before you life and death, blessings and curses. Now
> choose life, so that you and your children may live (Deut 30.19;
> echoed by Moses' successor in Josh 24.15–25).

In the same vein, Elijah also asks:

> How long will you waver between two opinions? If the LORD is God, follow him; but if Baal is God, follow him (1 Kgs 18.21).

Both instances include some attempt (through speech or signs) on the part of the prophet to stress the urgency of the decision, but it is Israel who gives the final verdict.

The seven biblical texts just mentioned vary quite widely in their particulars, but one element is common to all of them: a prophet of Yahweh. Where the balance is strained between human decision and divine intention, prophetic intervention is never far afield. Throughout Scripture, the prophets show up at every critical juncture, pulling the people of God into line with his intentions for them. It is not that they possess a blueprint of some predetermined, perfect plan; rather, God directs biblical history *through* the prophets even as he permits events that were not 'supposed' to happen. The marriage of God's purposes with human freedom is monitored and facilitated by the prophets, even as biblical history is juggled back and forth between human and divine hands.

Since it is our task as Christians to get on board with what God is doing in the world, the prophets provide excellent role-models, for they were especially privy to God's ways. Terence Fretheim's study, entitled *The Suffering of God*, stresses this special privilege of God's messengers:

> The prophet becomes a party to the divine story; the heart and mind of God pass over into that of the prophet to such an extent that the prophet becomes a veritable embodiment of God.[20]

This is a substantial claim, but one with ample support, as we shall see in the following chapters. As Yahweh's passions are inscribed upon the prophets, they become instruments in his hands, through whom he breathes divine sentiments of grief (1 Sam 15.11), jealousy (Exod 34.14), rejoicing (Isa 62.5), and love (Hos 3.1). In many respects they are precursors to Jesus of Nazareth, whose prophetic ministry brings about the fulfilment of God's passion to dwell on earth among his people. While they may not have embodied God's *perfect* Self-revelation as Jesus did, the prophets were certainly on the same continuum as visible, personal manifestations of God to his defiant partner Israel. So if we wish to know what it looks like for a human life to share God's passion, we can do no better than to turn to the prophets.

Prophetic Paradigm

The image of Moses atop Mount Sinai, poised between heaven and earth, between God's good intentions for creation and the human predisposition towards sin, accurately captures the essence of the prophetic vocation. But before we return to Moses on Mount Sinai in chapter 2, it will be helpful to survey his life in order to better understand how this remarkable figure casts the mould for others who would become prophets like him (Deut 18.18).

When Moses forgoes tending sheep in the Midian desert to represent a previously unknown god in a campaign against the ruthless political power of Egypt, a new element in God's governance of human history comes into play. Moses becomes God's earthly counterpart (Exod 7.1),[21] embodying God's concerns to accomplish his will. Upon hearing the cries of the Hebrew slaves, God remembers his covenant with Abraham and informs Moses that he has 'come down to rescue them from the Egyptians' (Exod 3.8). But the sudden shift from *Yahweh's* desire to save—'I have come down to rescue them'—to the command identifying *Moses* as the one to 'Go!' takes us (and Moses) by surprise. The aging shepherd initially stammers and objects, as do many prophets in their moment of summons,[22] but it is precisely this fusion of divine initiative with human agency that typifies the prophetic vocation. 'So now, go. I am sending you to Pharaoh to bring my people the Israelites out of Egypt' (Exod 3.10). God is anguished over Israel's distress, but it is Moses who will provide his image in Pharaoh's courts (**Daniel:** chapter 13) through spoken word and enacted signs (**Hosea:** chapter 10).

Having been sent, Moses soon feels neglected when God does not appear to act on his promises (Exod 5.22–23). In fact, Pharaoh's harsh treatment of Israel worsens as a result of the prophet's presence. But as Moses is soon to discover, things must sometimes get worse before they can get better (**Isaiah:** chapter 11). In due course, as a consequence of Moses' obedience, God's word becomes an event, the exodus, through which Yahweh demonstrates his Lordship over false gods (**Elijah:** chapter 7). As Yahweh does what he says he would do, Moses is made privy to the hardening of Pharaoh's heart 'behind the scenes' (**Micaiah:** chapter 8) as well as to miraculous signs and wonders 'on the stage'. Moses' daring encounters with Pharaoh typify the prophetic ethic of confrontation (**Samuel:** chapter 4) and the persuasive power of prophetic speech (**Nathan:** chapter 5) as he delivers God's judgement on human arrogance (**Ahijah:** chapter 6). The result is a conclusive display of God's glory, for the eyes of Israel and the nations (Exod 15.13–16).

Moses' prayers convey a deep faith in God's capacity to save, and on Mount Sinai it becomes apparent that prophetic wisdom plays a significant role in discerning God's will and acting in collaboration with God to bring it about (**Deborah:** chapter 3). In the wilderness, his humility permits him face-to-face intimacy with God (Num 12.1–8; **John:** chapter 14), but it is not a humility of weak-willed resignation that finds expression in a no-questions-asked obedience. Prophets were rarely content to settle for first offers; more typical was their bold push beyond, even in dialogue with the world's Maker (**Moses:** chapter 2, and in a negative light, **Jonah:** chapter 9). As Israel's paradigmatic prophet, Moses genuinely wrestles with God, balancing self-assertion with self-abandonment.[23]

The rest of Moses' life, spent in the wilderness with Israel, would teach him that a close walk with God does not guarantee an easy life. On the contrary, Moses' devotion to God was ultimately expressed in a radical, suffering obedience (**Jeremiah:** chapter 12).

These spiritual seeds, planted in the life of Moses, grew and developed in the lives of his prophetic heirs. Just as each of the prophetic virtues we are going to explore in chapters 2 to 14 can be traced back to Moses, each also finds its fulfilment in **Jesus** (chapters 15 and 16) and his **church** (chapter 17). But before we turn our attention fully to the prophets in their various contexts, let us consider why it is appropriate to apply their particular way of relating to God and the world, their prophetic spirituality, to our own lives.

I Wish You Were All Prophets!

If we define prophecy as 'human speech on behalf of God,'[24] then God's decision to entrust Israel with his 'ten words' (the Commandments) was tantamount to a prophetic calling on a national level. Indeed, that is what the Law-giving at Mount Sinai was all about; God entrusted his words to Israel and then asked her to behave in ways that would 'speak' those words to the rest of the world:[25] 'Be holy, because I am holy.' But if Yahweh entrusted the entire nation with the prophetic task of being his ambassadors in the world, why did the prophets exist within Israel as *individuals*?

Why indeed? The question is a good one, and it has often been overlooked that one of the primary reasons Israel had (individual) prophets was the nation's fear of getting too close to God.[26] At Mount Sinai, the terrified Israelites had asked Moses to become their go-between.

> When the people saw the thunder and lightning and heard the trumpet and saw the mountain in smoke, they trembled with fear. They stayed at a distance and said to Moses, 'Speak to us yourself and we will listen. But do not have God speak to us or we will die' (Exod 20.18–19; see Deut 5.22–31).

Israel's request (which God approved) is followed by a summary statement in Exodus 20.21 that captures the essence of Moses' prophetic call: 'The people remained at a distance, while Moses approached the thick darkness where God was.'[27] By speaking with God face to face on behalf of the nation, Moses' mediatory role comes full circle. 'In the presence of God he takes the part of the people. In the presence of the people he takes the part of God.'[28] But as well as explaining how one man came to bear the weight of God's words to Israel, Israel's response to the theophany sheds some light on Moses' remarkable statement in Numbers 11.29.

Only days after leaving Sinai (and a year since leaving Egypt), with the leadership of God's people squarely upon his shoulders, Moses came close to collapsing under the weight of Israel's whining (Num 11.1,4). In his distress he hurled a series of questions at

Yahweh, begging for intervention and even confessing that he would prefer to be smitten by God than to face his own ruin at the hands of the Israelites! In response, God proposed to disperse his Spirit upon seventy selected elders to alleviate the pressure on Moses. As Yahweh's Spirit came upon the elders gathered at the tent of meeting, they began to prophesy, although we are not told exactly what they said or did. The narrative is more interested in Joshua's reaction to two elders who were evidently in the wrong place at the right time and who had begun prophesying in the camp rather than in the tent of meeting.

This was the first time since Israel received the Commandments that anyone besides Moses had prophesied, and since the responsibility for speaking God's words had hitherto fallen solely to Moses, it is perhaps not surprising that Joshua responded as he did; 'Moses, my lord, stop them!' (Num 11.28) Joshua's efforts to protect the prophetic office from unauthorized use were surely understandable, but Moses was neither alarmed nor offended by what had happened. On the contrary, he responded with crystal clarity—and with some exasperation, no doubt!

> Are you jealous for my sake? I wish that *all* the LORD's people were prophets and that the LORD would put his Spirit on them! (Num 11.29)

Moses' first concern, far from claiming exclusive rights for those gathered at the tent of meeting, was that seventy prophets would not be enough![29] It would appear from his response that being in the 'right' place geographically (i.e. the tent of meeting) was not a problem in Moses' mind. Nor was it an issue for Yahweh, who obviously deemed the two men worthy of his Spirit regardless of their location.

The story has two implications for our study of prophetic spirituality. First, prophetic status appears to have less to do with *physical* proximity to God (e.g. on Mount Sinai or in the tent of meeting) and more to do with one's *moral* or *spiritual* proximity to God.[30] And second, Moses' comment about all of God's people being prophets is probably an expression of his wish that the Israelites were capable of fulfilling their prophetic vocation without him having to function as the middleman.

The notion of Israel's role in Yahweh's purposes having a prophetic dimension is one that continues to expand throughout the Old Testament, especially in the preaching of the prophets. In fact, some of God's clearest statements about his purposes for Israel personify the entire nation as a prophet. Take, for instance, Isaiah 49.1–9, which describes God's missional people by combining the designation 'servant of Yahweh' (frequently used of Moses) with Jeremiah's call to be 'a prophet to the nations'.

Before I formed you in the womb I knew you, before you were born I set you apart; I appointed you as a prophet to the nations (Jer 1.5).	'And now,' the LORD says – he who formed me in the womb to be his servant . . . 'I will also make you a light for the Gentiles, that you may bring my salvation to the ends of the earth' (Isa 49.5a–6b).

Since the Servant figure in Isaiah[31] is explicitly identified as Israel (Isa 49.3), allusions to Moses and Jeremiah imply that the prophets were exemplary for the whole people of God and that Israel's vocation was *prophetic* as it was *priestly* (Exod 19.6).[33] It is hardly surprising that Isaiah's portraits of the Suffering Servant combined the office of a prophet, the nation of Israel, and a Messianic figure into a single personification. For as we shall see, Israel's calling to bless the nations through obedience to the covenant was preached most rigorously by her prophets and ultimately fulfilled by her representative Messiah.

Finally, without simply collapsing Israel and the Christian church into one as people(s) of God, there are obvious continuities[34] between these families striving to bring their Father 'renown and praise and honour' among the nations (Jer 13.11). Note the parallels between God's call on Israel through the prophet Moses and his call on the church through the apostle Peter.

You yourselves have seen what I did to Egypt, and how I carried you on eagles'	But you are a chosen people, a royal priesthood, a holy nation, a people belonging to

wings and brought you to myself. Now if you obey me fully and keep my covenant, then out of all nations you will be my treasured possession. Although the whole earth is mine, you will be for me a kingdom of priests and a holy nation (Exod 19.4–6a).

God, that you may declare the praises of him who called you out of darkness into his wonderful light. Once you were not a people, but now you are the people of God; once you had not received mercy, but now you have received mercy (1 Pet 2.9–10).

God's people of Old and New Testaments share the summons to image God in creation by testifying to their salvation through an obedience that proves genuine faith (Rom 6.15–23). As Gentiles who have been 'grafted in' (Rom 11.19), the church also adopts Israel's calling to make God known to the world. For even after all that has been accomplished through Jesus' life, death and resurrection, the charge to enhance God's reputation in the world remains the same (Acts 1.8). But we will return to this theme in the final chapter, where twelve Spirit-filled apostles demonstrate that sharing God's passion is still the prophetic task of his people.

Storied Spirituality

As one enters the storied world of Scripture, new possibilities arise through the intersection of the textual world (on the page) with the reader's world (off the page). Indeed, the goal of reading biblical stories is that the texts may 'overcome, as it were, the readers' own worlds and replace these by the narrated reality.'[35] But that is not all that happens. As we enter the world of Scripture, the biblical stories also penetrate the crusted surface of our lives and enter us, changing the ways we perceive God, our neighbours, our planet and ourselves. In this way, stories expose us (far more than stale routines or weighty rules) to profound opportunities for transformation, as the Spirit of the Word leads us.

The 1984 film *The Neverending Story*[36] amply illustrates what I am getting at. The main protagonist, Bastian, is an adolescent schoolboy (and an unlikely hero) who retreats from the stress and strain of his real life into an imaginative, literary world called Fantasia. (He is, in fact, running from school bullies when he discovers the *Neverending Story*.) Despite the bookstore owner's warning that this book is 'not safe' because you can never go back to being the person you were prior to reading it, Bastian is spellbound by the old tome. He runs off with it and, arriving late at school, decides to skip class and devote the entire day to reading it. As Bastian is drawn into the world of Fantasia, various parallels between the lives of Atreyu (the book's main character) and Bastian (the reader) become evident. Their lives intersect in ways that seem impossible, and as Bastian becomes increasingly absorbed in the book, he actually becomes part of its story. Indeed, there is some ambiguity as to whether he is reading, or being read by, the *Neverending Story*. The film reaches its climax when it dawns on Bastian what a critical role he has to play in determining the future of Fantasia. Flicking forward to find an ending, Bastian finds only blank pages, indicating that his decisions are critical for shaping a future that has not yet been written. He must verbalize his response (in his world) to the request of the Childlike Empress (in the book) in order to prevent her kingdom from being consumed by a destructive evil known as 'the Nothing'.

Narrative theology—talking about God through stories—has much to say about Christian spirituality, since being human means being bound by the narrative quality of experience.[37] We are all characters in a drama, working our way through the complexity of a plot (or more likely, numerous simultaneous plots) toward some form of resolution, and the stories we are immersed in dictate where we have come from, where we are going, and what role we play in the plot's development.[38] This is certainly true for Bastian, who undergoes significant growth as he digests the *Neverending Story*, emerging at the end a renewed and more confident person. At the film's conclusion, the *Neverending Story* fully merges with Bastian's world; Bastian rides Falkor the luck-dragon through the streets of his city, chasing the boys who had bullied him earlier. It is somehow an anticipated conclusion to a story that promises to be continued . . .

The Neverending Story powerfully illustrates the junction between the real world and a literary world of human composi-

tion. An early review of the original novel noted that 'imaginative readers know the story doesn't end when the covers close',[39]
which is precisely what the author intended to communicate. Of
course, the very same thing could be said of the biblical story.
Without the church's active participation in the literary world of
Scripture, 'the Nothing' also threatens the identity and mission of
God's people in the world.

> When biblical narrative falls silent, the people of God have noth-
> ing to remember, and with nothing to remember they soon forget
> who they are. Their untutored imaginations turn to other narra-
> tives and other gods. It is a familiar story.[40]

When Christian preaching fails to remind congregations of the
whole biblical story, our sense of identity falters and alternative
stories that crown idols as gods become increasingly compelling.

We begin our journey through the biblical story, therefore, in
the knowledge that God's good intention for people to enflesh his
image upon the earth (Gen 1.27) is *most* evident in the lives of the
prophets. More than that, the prophets are the focus of our study
because we wish to stand *with* them in the gap between God's
relentless love for the world and the human propensity to sin (see
Eze 22.30). How then may we proceed to learn from the narrative
world of Scripture in order to live our own lives differently?
Reciting ancient stories in today's language or melting complex
tales down into so-called timeless truths may serve a purpose, but
if we wish to experience biblical narratives in some way, we must
be prepared to fill the gaps left by the narrator—both on and off
the page.

Filling the Gaps

Good stories don't say everything. They leave gaps to be filled by
the reader's imagination. Suddenly one character betrays another and it is left to us to figure out why. Or a flashback is inserted
into the temporal order of a narrative and we are expected to
make the necessary connections to make sense of it. Gap-filling is
one of the keys to successful storytelling, scriptwriting, and for

that matter, good preaching. For when a story says *everything*, leaving insufficient opportunities for the audience to connect the dots, boredom sets in. (Incidentally, books about the Bible—including this one—will, of course, offer suggestions about how to make sense of a narrative's gaps, but it is important to keep in mind that alternative readings are often possible.)

Unlike novels and films, however, an appropriate response to Scripture requires more than just a mental response, since 'faith by itself, if it is not accompanied by action, is dead' (Jas 2.17). When the Bible presents us with a question, it is almost always more than a riddle requiring a brainy solution. In fact, the Bible's tough questions and challenges cannot be solved in the pulpit at all. They must be answered by our living, by the decisions we make from Sunday to Saturday. And if a Bible reader gets a sense of how they *should* respond to a text but fails to do anything about it, their very lack of response is already an act of resistance against what was read and said to them. As the bookstore owner in *The Neverending Story* put it, 'This book is not safe!'

So if, when Elijah urges the Israelites to 'choose Yahweh' on Mount Carmel (1 Kgs 18.21), readers also find themselves convicted of 'wavering between two opinions' and are prompted to join Israel in putting false gods aside, then an appropriate response to the text will include an act of repentance (off the page). False gods such as career, body-image, status and money may be put aside in response to a Word that seeks to engage our whole lives. Gap-filling, for Bible readers, is much more than an intellectual exercise, for we seek not only the renewing of our minds, but also fresh opportunities to offer our *selves* as living sacrifices before a God who awaits our answer (1 Kgs 18.39; Rom 12.1–2). The point is not simply that interpretation and transformation are of equal importance, but rather that one's wholistic response to God's Word *is* the most meaningful interpretive act. One result of our endeavours to absorb the implications of biblical narratives in this way is that their plots will remain intertwined with our own stories, even after the Bible is back on the bookshelf or bedside table.

Finally, a few brief words about how to get the most out of this book. Chapters 2 to 17 contain chronological studies in the lives of biblical prophets, twelve from the Old Testament and three from the New. It should be noted from the outset that the Bible chapters listed for each chapter are *essential* reading. Unless you are very familiar with the biblical texts, you will need to read them before or alongside the studies; only select verses from the Bible are quoted in the chapters for emphasis. (I stress this because there is a strange but widespread desire among Christians to understand the Bible without reading it!) At the end of each chapter, the Dig Deeper page offers further opportunities for personal or group study through questions intended for reflection and, where possible, discussion.

Although each chapter examines the life of a particular prophet in relation to a particular aspect of prophetic spirituality, I do not mean to suggest that Moses is the only prophet who exemplifies prayer, or that Nathan is the Bible's only model of prophetic speech. Of course, prayer could just as easily be explored in the lives of Samuel, Jeremiah, or Daniel, and prophetic speech in the lives of Isaiah, Jeremiah, or John the Baptist. The characters and stories in each chapter simply reflect my own choices within the context of my aims and understanding.

Whatever your goals or reasons for picking up this book, I hope the prophets capture your imagination and heart as they have captured mine, and that you find yourself comforted and confronted in these pages. It is my sincere conviction that God's passion to live among his people is fulfilled when the church embodies his nature as the prophets sought to do. And it is my prayer, as you embark on this journey with the prophets, that you will learn lessons from their struggles that are pertinent to your own gifts and character, your own way of being in relation to God and his people. May you be filled with the Spirit of our mighty God, to share his passion as the prophets did so faithfully.

Dig Deeper

- What does God's desire to live among us say about him?

- Why do you think God is reluctant to impinge on human freedom?

- What is your response to the notion that God has entrusted so much into human hands?

- In what ways should all believers be prophetic?

- What opportunities do you have to manifest God's presence in the world?

- How can you become more vigilant in living your responses to biblical texts?

2

Prophetic Prayer: Living In-Between

MOSES

I cannot carry all these people by myself;
the burden is too heavy for me (Num 11.14).

Exodus 32

Shaping the Future

The biblical picture of reality is not one where everything is pre-determined, set out like a blueprint from which we cannot stray. This perspective (more common than one might think) easily defers to a dangerous form of fatalism[1] which breeds laziness and apathy: 'It doesn't matter what I do or say, because in the end God will have his way.' The more difficult reality presented in the Bible is that our speech and actions, in conjunction with other factors outside of our control, supply the bricks and mortar paving our way through life. Decisions quickly become set in stone, never to be undone as time marches on unmercifully, offering no way back. A sobering thought, is it not?

Spielberg's imaginative *Back to the Future* films explore this notion in a memorable way. As Marty McFly travels back in time and then 'back to the future' again, he finds that even seemingly insignificant decisions prove critical in creating a pathway towards a certain and irreversible future—unless, of course, one has access to Doc's DeLorean. All three films toy with this idea, leading up to Doc's final words (ironically spoken from a time machine) to Marty and Jennifer at the end of Part III: 'Your future hasn't been written yet. No one's has. Your future is whatever you make it, so make it a good one!'[2]

The Bible places significant emphasis on the capacity of human beings to influence future events. In the previous chapter we noted that God's desire to live among his people sits in tension with his decision to share power over the future with them. However, the ability to make genuinely free choices is just one factor affecting the future. There is still something else that can be done, since the notion of a personal relationship with God is no façade, no mere ploy to increase one's sense of importance. On the contrary, the things people say through the gift of prayer are of overwhelming significance for shaping a future which is yet undetermined.

The extraordinary intimacy between Yahweh and his prophets is a source not only of inspiration, but also of astonishment, for Christians today. The language of their prayers is often so intimate that readers feel uncomfortable with it, and yet their boldness exposes God's openness to be moved by his human partners. The special significance of prophetic prayer is evident in the following six instances:

- Abraham is referred to as a prophet only once in the Bible, notably in the context of his intercession for others (Gen 20.7).
- Moses changed God's mind through his insistent prayers on Mount Sinai (Exod 32.1–14), as we shall see below.
- Samuel considered prayer so vital to his prophetic office that he called it a sin to neglect praying for God's people (1 Sam 12.23).
- Isaiah was summoned in earnest by King Hezekiah to intercede when no other way forward was apparent (2 Kgs 19.1–4).[3]
- Jeremiah was instructed by God not to pray on three occasions (Jer 7.16; 11.14; 14.11) because God did not want any prophetic interference with his judgement of Israel.[4]
- Jesus' prophetic ministry was grounded in regular, solitary prayer (Mk 1.35; Lk 6.12–16).

Even a brief glimpse at the biblical evidence such as this suggests that the prayers of prophets were especially potent. No doubt this can be attributed, at least in part, to their uncompromising obedience (Prov 15.29; Jas 5.16–18), but something must also be said for the prophets' daring manner of speech before Yahweh. Think, for instance, of the way Jeremiah accused God of deceiving both the nation (Jer 4.10) and himself (Jer 20.7)! Such raw forms of protest expose an audacious honesty before God.

Similarly, Moses' encounter with Yahweh on Mount Sinai offers a window into the dynamics of a divine-human friendship that understands God not as an abstract Being defined by labels ('eternal', 'unchanging', 'omniscient'), but as a personal Being who invites genuine engagement through prayer.

Invitation to Prayer (Exodus 32.1–10)

For all that the Israelites had been slow to understand, one lesson they did learn very quickly was that no one may enter God's presence lightly. As we noted in the previous chapter, Israel's fear of proximity to Yahweh led to the request that Moses approach God on her behalf, that he be the one to hear God's words and pass them on (see 'I Wish You Were All Prophets!' in chapter 1). And so, in Exodus 24, it is Moses alone who enters the cloud upon Mount Sinai to converse with Yahweh and to receive the tablets of stone from him.

Ironically, even as Moses was meeting with God on the mountain, the Hebrews grew so restless and impatient that they resorted to idolatry (granted, he was there for well over a month). They demanded of Aaron, 'Make gods for us!' and he complied without dispute (Exod 32.1). It is quite likely that the Israelites picked up habits of idol worship in Egypt, and perhaps the golden calf was an expression of their desire for a less confronting access to God. But in any case, what was most inexcusable was that God's people credited the newly fashioned golden calf with their deliverance from Pharaoh. The gravity of their sin was comparable to committing adultery on one's wedding night;[5] no sooner had Israel been chosen to establish an exclusive covenant with Yahweh than she was caught in the act of worshipping another god! Understandably, Israel's Husband responded with a burning fury. His immediate inclination was to be rid of his adulterous bride and to start over again.

'I have seen these people,' the LORD said to Moses, 'and they are a stiff-necked people. Now leave me alone so that my anger may burn against them and that I may destroy them. Then I will make you into a great nation' (Exod 32.9–10).

But in making what appears a rather harsh judgement, God says something very interesting: 'Now leave me alone so that my anger may burn against them' (Exod 32.10). Odd, is it not, that God requires Moses to 'leave him alone' in order that he may destroy Israel? Perhaps, in light of the unique relationship between Moses and Yahweh (Num 12.6–8), God's words are to be understood as an invitation for Moses to intercede; I'm furious, Moses! If you leave me alone now, I will destroy these people!

'God himself leaves the door open for intercession. He allows himself to be persuaded . . . God could have shut the door—indeed slammed it—as he did in Deuteronomy 3:26 when Moses requested permission to enter the promised land.'[7] But no doors are slammed here. God remains genuinely open to conversation as One who does not act *upon* the world but *within* it—in close association with his friends (Exod 33.11). And as the certainty of Yahweh's anger is suspended, even for just a moment, the prophet seizes his opportunity.

Moses is brazen in his response to God's verdict, but the narrative condones his courage. His 'bold speech of assault is in fact received at the throne not as disobedience but as a new kind of obedience.'[8] Just as Abraham had done with regards to Sodom and Gomorrah (Gen 18.25), Moses appeals to God on the basis of his character, summoning the courage to say, in effect, Please, Yahweh, don't do this . . . This is not who you are! Through prayer, 'humans (in this case Moses) are given the chance, if they will accept the responsibility, to contribute to a future that will be different from what it would have been, had they remained passive.'[9] And Moses is anything but passive. As a prophet he lives *in-between*, pressed on one side by a genuine love for God's people and on the other by a binding commitment to God's purposes. However the story is interpreted, one thing is certain. Moses plays a critical role in its outcome.

Persuading God (Exodus 32.11–14)

The narrative does not mean to portray God as indecisive or easily persuaded by the right mix of passion and reason. But it does establish that 'human prayer is in some fashion part of the "mechanism", of the "apparatus", of divine activity in the universe.'[10] Patrick Miller has suggested that prayer is one of the primary means through which 'God is pushed and prodded to help in order to preserve [his] own place in the world.'[11] In other words, the realization of God's will on earth requires human participation through prayer. This may seem a radical statement, but the biblical testimony is fairly self-evident. In this particular situation, Moses' refusal to leave God alone (see Lk 11.5–10) leads to a change of the divine mind and to the sustenance of God's plan for Israel. Moses, who knows the will of God and is himself driven by God's passion, offers a prayer that becomes a part of God's decision-making process.

> Moses was not so much arguing *against* God (though it doubtless felt like it), as participating in an argument within God . . . Such prayer, therefore, not only participates in the pain of God in history, but is actually invited to do so for God's sake as well as ours.[12]

The events on Mount Sinai illuminate the nature of prophetic prayer. Moses empathizes with Yahweh's pain as One whose trust has been betrayed, but he also understands Israel's dilemma as a sinful people, mere infants in their faith. Moses thus participates in the 'argument within God', reaching *with* Yahweh for a solution that has everyone's best interests in mind. The whole idea of helping God make decisions may seem rather foreign to us. However, the point is not that God cannot cope without us, but that he *wants* to renew his creation *with* us. We are invited to reflect God's image in the world by adopting his purposes as our own and praying accordingly.

In a comprehensive study of biblical prayers that seek to persuade God, Patrick Miller has shown that they always include a 'motivational clause', a reason why God ought to respond to the plea.[13] Interestingly, though not surprisingly, these clauses often 'point to the *relationship between God and the petitioner(s)* as a basis for God's response.'[14] Biblical prayers appeal to God's relationship with his people using words such as 'hear' (Neh 4.4–5), 'remember' (2 Kgs 20.3), 'forgive' (1 Kgs 8.30), 'heal' (Num 12.13), and 'save' (Gen 32.11). Further to this, *thanksgiving* can draw God's attention to what he has already achieved in a person's life as a means of motivating him to complete the work begun in them (Php 1.3–5).[15]

None of this is to say that God is governed by formulas. He does not respond in our favour just because we have managed to pull the right strings. Rather, in its various forms and contexts, prayer opens up new possibilities for God's future course of action (as well as new possibilities for spiritual growth within the person praying). For Israel's prophets, simplistic 'Thy will be done' prayers were insufficient in situations that threatened Yahweh's reputation or his people's welfare. The prayer of the prophets was instead, 'Thy will be changed'.[16] While we cannot force God's hand, we can be confident that words uttered in prayer actually *do* something. As Karl Barth put it, God 'does not act in the same way whether we pray or not. Prayer exerts an influence upon God's actions, even upon his existence. This is what the word "answer" means.'[17]

On Mount Sinai Moses seeks an answer that is consistent with God's character. More specifically, he offers three reasons why Yahweh ought to spare unfaithful Israel. The first has to do with God being *reasonable*, since he has only just redeemed the very nation he now wishes to destroy (Exod 32.11). The second concerns God's *reputation* within Egypt and the surrounding nations (Exod 32.12), and the third calls God to *remember* previous promises made to Abraham (Exod 32.13). Confident that he has Yahweh's listening ear, Moses suggests why God ought to rethink his initial verdict and act differently. But most astounding of all is the prophet's depth of insight into God's purposes. Moses knows that God's purposes revolve around having a nation on earth that uniquely reflects his nature, so he appeals to this very idea. The destruction of Israel would be a contradiction, at best a heavy setback, to God's grand plan.[18] Without a people to reflect his image on earth, how would God's name ever be proclaimed to the nations?

Moses' prayers are ultimately rewarded with an answer, and a surprising one for those who believe that God never changes his mind. The Hebrew verb used in Exodus 32.14 regarding God's 'change of mind' (NRSV; *niham*) does not denote a moral repentance (turning from sin), but rather, a change or reversal of mind and heart.[19] Exodus 32.7–14 narrates exactly this kind of reversal, where God's course of action is genuinely changed in response to prayer. Moses succeeds in co-shaping a future that would have been otherwise if he had consented to leave God alone.

Significantly, this openness on God's part was etched into Israel's creeds over time, as Yahweh came to be known as One whose mind could even be expected to change due to his compassionate disposition.

> Rend your heart
>   and not your garments.
> Return to the LORD your God,
>   for he is gracious and compassionate,
> slow to anger and abounding in love,
>   and he relents [*niham*] from sending calamity.
> Who knows? He may turn and have pity
>   and leave behind a blessing (Joel 2.13–14a).[20]

The God of Israel gained a reputation for taking his human covenant partner seriously enough that no initial judgement was necessarily final. It was in Yahweh's nature to be merciful, and the prophets always prayed in earnest that his compassion would win the day.

Living In-Between (Exodus 32.15–35)

Even so, the apparent success of Moses' plea for mercy did not guarantee that the nation had escaped judgement, for having placated Yahweh, Moses proceeded to make his way back down the mountain to see for himself what had caused such a stir in Yahweh. Upon seeing the people dancing around a false god, Moses smashed the stone tablets at the foot of the mountain (a dramatic enactment of Israel's broken covenant with Yahweh), made the Israelites ingest their false god (Exod 32.20) and demanded answers from Aaron.

Israel's lack of order had led to a reversal of God's purposes, the *shaming* of his name on earth. Instead of standing out to their neighbours as a holy nation, God's people had 'become a laughing-stock to their enemies' (Exod 32.25) and Yahweh had been humiliated. Therefore, Moses' response to the situation is almost as violent as God's initial thought. Embodying the fierce anger of Yahweh, Moses implements the deaths of about three thousand Israelites by the hands of their own kinsmen. The prophet is not simply 'playing God' in an enacted drama; rather, he becomes a veritable *embodiment* of God (see Exod 7.1). To press this point, the narrator uses exactly the same phrase to describe the 'burning anger' of Yahweh in verses 10–11 and the 'burning anger' of Moses in verses 19 and 22. Moses mirrors Yahweh's emotional response to the broken covenant.

The next day, as the people of Israel come to terms with the tragic consequences of their idolatry, Moses returns to Mount Sinai to plead again for divine mercy on Israel's behalf (Exod 32.30–35). What's going on here? One minute Moses is begging Yahweh for forgiveness, and the next he is dishing out divine judgement. Then he is back on his knees again! Why all the to-ing and fro-ing? Is Moses uncertain about whose side to take? Not at all. For Moses understands, 'both as mouth of God and as advocate of the people',[21] that choosing sides is not an option. As Israel's advocate, he participates in God's decision-making process (Exod 32.14); as the mouth of God he executes God's judgement (Exod 32.27). It is his prophetic responsibility to operate between God and Israel, which is why, in the chapters that follow, Moses goes on to mediate the renewal of Israel's covenant relationship with Yahweh (Exod 34.10).

The prophetic vocation requires a capacity to empathize with the sinful condition of God's people—as Aaron puts it, 'You know how prone these people are to evil' (Exod 32.22)—whilst simultaneously dealing with the magnitude of God's emotional responses (ranging from frustrated anger to merciful compassion). With such powerful attachments on either side, it is no wonder the prophets often felt pressured and sometimes crushed.[22] When Israel's walls were down, i.e. she was deserving of punishment, it was left to them to 'build up the wall and stand before [God] in the gap' (Eze 22.30).[23]

Engaging God

Moses' engagement with God provides us with ample reason to question simplistic notions of God that suggest his will as the final explanation for everything that happens. From the biblical evidence it seems more accurate to say that sometimes God's future actions are contingent upon the choices we make (Jer 18.1–10) and sometimes our prayers move him to act differently by placing alternatives before him. Like Moses on Mount Sinai, we are invited to effect change in the world through words exchanged with God. What a remarkable responsibility! The Bible is clear about God's right to freely choose his response (prayer is not a formula that is guaranteed to 'work' in our favour), but it is equally clear about the impact our prayers can have on God's future activity. So the prophet is never one to say, 'Just leave it in God's hands', precisely because he or she understands just how much God has entrusted into ours.

But where did Moses get the idea that he could challenge God's judgements and perhaps even convince him to alter an intended course of action? Is there not a hint of arrogance in this kind of attitude before God? Evidently not. Actually, it was God who invited the prayer, listened to the prophet's reasoning, and responded with a change of heart and an alternative course of action. And besides, Moses' motives were far from self-seeking; he did not enter Yahweh's presence with a list of personal demands, but so that Yahweh's own purposes would be fulfilled.

The Bible does not present us with a closed view of the future. On the contrary, various biblical narratives support the notion that human beings have been invited to collaborate with God in renewing everything he has made, including the earth itself, social structures, personal relationships and the integrity of each human life. Prayer is one of the greatest gifts God has given his covenant people in order that we may join with him in this awesome undertaking.

Moses' radical speech in Exodus 32 is not an isolated example of insistent prayer that pushes past God's initial judgements. Actually, Moses keeps good company within the pages of the Old Testament.

In Genesis 18.16–33, **Abraham** urged God not to destroy righteous people along with the wicked in the impending judgement
of Sodom and Gomorrah. Like Moses' prayer in Exodus 32,
Abraham's bargaining with God stemmed from his understanding of God's own moral character: 'Far be it from you! Will not *the
Judge of all the earth* do what is right?' (Gen 18.25) Readers fear for
Abraham's life, but the patriarch apparently feared nothing other
than the injustice of an angry God as he insisted (repeatedly) that
Yahweh spare the two wicked cities even for the sake of just ten
righteous inhabitants. Yahweh relented a number of times in
response to Abraham's prayers, and when the cities were ultimately destroyed—such was their depravity—Lot's family (some
of the righteous ones Abraham was concerned about; Gen 19.29;
2 Pet 2.7–8) were given the opportunity to run for their lives.

Jacob was a man who literally wrestled with God in pursuit of
a divine blessing. In one sense he had been fighting all his life for
God's favour, even prior to his birth (Gen 25.22,26). With the passing of time, Jacob's brother (Esau), his father (Isaac) and his uncle
(Laban) all became casualties of Jacob's trickery. But one night, on
the banks of the Jabbok River, even as Jacob resorted to guile once
again in the hope of placating his angry brother, he found himself
alone and vulnerable. It was in that moment that God came, also
in vulnerability, to wrestle with Jacob through the night (Gen
32.24–32). Jacob did not realize he had been wrestling with God
until afterwards[24] (not an uncommon experience) when he stood
humbled and crippled with a new name, the recipient of God's
blessing. And as the sun began to rise on a new day, Jacob—no,
Israel—stepped out in faith, limping in his new dependence on
God. His desperate petition for divine blessing had indeed been
answered, though certainly not in the way he had anticipated.

Another Old Testament character with something important to
add to discussions about prayer is **Job**. As the result of a wager
between God and 'the Accuser'[25] concerning the motives behind
Job's exemplary behaviour, the poor man lost everything and fell
violently ill (Job 1–2). During what was undoubtedly the lowest
point in his life, his so-called 'friends' visited to inform him that
such misfortune could only be the direct result of sin.
Throughout the many chapters that follow, Job insists on his
innocence and continues to protest the injustice of his situation.

As the book draws to a close, God's judgement upon Job's friends seems somewhat surprising: 'My servant Job will pray for you, and I will accept his prayer and not deal with you according to your folly. You have not spoken of me what is right, as my servant Job has' (Job 42.8). At least one of the morals to be drawn from the story is that God prefers *honest engagement* in prayer to the simple formulas and clichés we are tempted to resort to (e.g. 'ill health is a direct consequence of sin').

Finally, when one of Israel's better kings, **Hezekiah**, became sick to the point of death (2 Kgs 20.1–6), the prophet Isaiah was sent to him with these words: 'Put your house in order, because you are going to die; you will not recover.' Ouch! How does one respond to such a prophecy? Well, despite the judgement's irrevocable tone, King Hezekiah did not accept the prophet's first words to be his last. He pleaded with God on the basis of his 'wholehearted devotion', and before Isaiah had even left the building, Yahweh sent him back to the courtroom to grant Hezekiah an extra fifteen years of life.

Returning to where we began in this chapter, the past cannot be changed (without access to Doc's DeLorean). Past events are now set in concrete, whether we are speaking about yesterday or something that occurred thousands of years ago. But this is not to say that history *could* not have taken a different course. At the risk of stating the obvious, the outcomes of various wars in history could have been otherwise if certain political and military leaders had adopted different attitudes or strategies in their moments of decision. Or, to scale things down somewhat, the grades you received for any given test could almost certainly have been better (or worse) if your study habits had been different. While the past is *now* set in stone, we cannot deny that it *could* have been a different past, leading to an alternative present.[26] Having observed God's grief when the world failed to match up to his hopes (Gen 6.6) and his frustration when Israel failed to grasp their critical role in his redemptive plan (Jer 13.11), it is difficult to avoid the implications; these expressions of divine emotion reflect a sense of loss over real (and better) alternatives for Israel and the world.

While prophecy is often associated with the future, the prophets are much more than foretellers of the future. They are people who live between an intimate grasp of God's good intentions and the human propensity to resist those intentions, people who act decisively and pray fervently for the best possible outcome in every situation. And for you, reading this book, the future lies open before you too, starting with *this* present moment.[27] Let Moses' prophetic intervention on Mount Sinai be a reminder that you can never underestimate prayer's potential to turn future possibilities into wonderful moments in history.

Dig Deeper

■ How do you feel about God's decision in Exodus 32.7-9?

■ What strikes you about the way Moses speaks with God in verses 11-13?

■ Does it surprise you that God changed his mind (verse 14) in response to Moses? Why/why not?

■ How would you describe the way you speak with God?

☐ face to face   ☐ distant   ☐ impersonal
☐ friendly   ☐ demanding   ☐ humble
☐ respectful   ☐ intimate   ☐ infrequent

■ How does prayer draw you into the space between God and his people?

3

Prophetic Wisdom: Collaborating with God

DEBORAH

For we are God's fellow-workers;
you are God's field, God's building (1 Cor 3.9).

Judges 4 – 5

Cycles of Sin (Judges 4.1–5)

God's people are called to be different. Our commitment to God's ideals and priorities should cause a stir so that neighbours become increasingly curious (in a positive way!) about the beliefs behind our behaviour. Sounds simple enough, but we don't live in a world where the church is always recognized as a community that reflects God's character. Often what prevents Christians from achieving that end is a mixed appetite, the conflict between a genuine desire to serve God and a pressing hunger for worldly things. Yes, we want others to know God, but at times we also feel compelled to trade a few juicy morsels of gossip for social acceptance. Yes, we love the idea of God's kingdom taking root in the world, but we also want to go on entertaining a few favourite 'private' sins. (After all, we've been fooled into believing that they're not hurting anyone.) And of course we want God's people to renew the world, but we're sometimes reluctant to step up and play our part because, quite frankly, it will cost us. In many respects, things haven't changed much since the time of Deborah.

After the death of Moses, the directives given to Joshua about ridding the promised land of rivals were a necessary step in establishing a holy kingdom in the land of Canaan. The purity of God's people was intended to prove Yahweh's holiness under the watchful eye of surrounding nations, but 'like sheep without a shepherd'[1] Israel had strayed from God's will, settling for a comfortable coexistence with the Canaanites. The command to break down foreign altars had been disregarded, and as a consequence idolatry would haunt Israel for centuries to come. In the opening chapters of Judges, God's angelic messenger makes it abundantly clear that Israel's compromise was to become a thorn in her side.

> The angel of the LORD went up from Gilgal to Bokim and said, 'I brought you up out of Egypt and led you into the land that I swore to give to your forefathers. I said, "I will never break my covenant with you, and you shall not make a covenant with the people of this land, but you shall break down their altars." Yet you have disobeyed me. Why have you done this? Now therefore I tell you that I will not drive them out before you; they will be [thorns] in your sides and their gods will be a snare to you' (Jdg 2.1–3).

Israel's surrounds were a constant source of distraction, generating an unhealthy mix of holy and unholy desires among the people. Like many Christians today, the Israelites had good intentions (see Josh 24.16–24), but compromise was made easier by the immediate presence of other gods and practices. As Israel's neighbours proceeded to make names for themselves, led by rich and powerful kings armed with horses and chariots,[2] Israel began to covet kingship for herself.

God had good reason for not anointing kings in Israel. He himself was their rightful King. Accordingly, whenever the Israelites suffered at the hands of Canaanite oppressors, God faithfully raised up judges to deliver them.

The judges themselves were misfits, but valiant and victorious misfits in Yahweh's service. It is doubtful that any of them would have been permitted to serve as institutional leaders, considering their various shortcomings. (Abimelech would try to assert himself as king in Judges 9, but with disastrous and bloody consequences.) God's line-up of rogue deliverers included a left-handed assassin named Ehud (Jdg 3), a wise prophetess named Deborah (Jdg 4–5), an indecisive sign-seeker named Gideon (Jdg 6–8), a prostitute's son named Jephthah (Jdg 11–12) and a hairy brute named Samson (Jdg 13–16). On first impressions, perhaps none of these seemed worthy of leadership, but each one turned the tide in service of Israel's true King.

So, having condemned Israel's lack of obedience upon entering the land of Canaan, the narrator sets out a cyclical pattern in Judges 2.11–19, which the rest of the book follows.

1. Sin

4. Deliverance
(by judge)

2. Oppression
(by foreign nation)

3. Cry for help

The monotony of this cycle throughout the book of Judges makes it clear that Israel has her feet stuck in a mire. She tirelessly repeats the same mistakes and struggles to stay in line with Yahweh's covenant purposes. Judges 3 establishes this pattern in the lives of Othniel and Ehud (Shamgar barely gets a mention) before chapter 4 opens with some obvious cues to the reader. Verse by verse, we are once again led through the stages of Israel's cycle of sin.

- v. 1 'After Ehud died, the Israelites once again did evil in the eyes of the LORD.'
- v. 2 'So the LORD sold them into the hands of Jabin, a king of Canaan . . .'
- v. 3 'Because he [Sisera] . . . cruelly oppressed the Israelites for twenty years, they cried to the LORD for help.'

Verse 4 is where we can expect to be introduced to a brave warrior whom Yahweh will use to deliver Israel from oppression. But what follows is more than a little surprising:

- v. 4 'Deborah, a prophetess . . . was leading Israel at that time.'

After being led to anticipate the story's proximate man of valour, we are introduced to a woman! To twenty-first-century readers, women in leadership are a part of everyday life and it may not surprise us in the least to read that Deborah is a gifted prophetess,[3] endowed with sufficient wisdom to judge over Israel's disputes. But considering how much has changed in just the last century (only since 1900 have women in Australia, Europe and the USA had the freedom to vote),[4] it is not difficult to imagine that in a patriarchal age over three thousand years ago, the mere suggestion of a woman's active presence anywhere near a battlefield was nothing short of scandalous. Also, from a literary point of view, when expectations established by the narrative are turned back on us like this, we can be sure that a point is being made.

The point, quite simply, is that in an age defined by men and their wars, Deborah's heroism is Israel's disgrace. In her ancient context, Deborah should not have been associated with military action. This is made explicit in Judges 9.50–54, when Abimelech's skull is crushed by a woman who drops a millstone on his head from a tower. With his dying breath, the man of war commands his servant to finish him off with a sword so that no one may ever say of him, 'He was killed by a woman.' In Deborah's time, a similar label of shame is cast over *all* Israelite men, when 'not a shield or spear was seen among forty thousand in Israel' (Jdg 5.8).

Israel's leaders and warriors had grown complacent, and in Judges 5 the songwriter explicitly links Israel's vulnerability with the choosing of 'new gods' (Jdg 5.8). To Israel's shame, 'village life in Israel ceased', at least until Deborah 'arose a mother in Israel' (Jdg 5.7). The distinct emphasis on female heroines in Judges 4–5 makes the point that Yahweh's roaming eyes simply could not find an Israelite *man* sufficient for the task of leading his people in their wars. So, in place of the much-anticipated male warrior to carry on the cycle of deliverance in Judges 4, the narrator surprises us with Deborah, a 'woman of fire'[5] who will give Israel's general (Barak) a push and call men to their battles.

> Deborah, a prophetess, the wife of Lappidoth, was leading Israel at that time. She held court under the Palm of Deborah between Ramah and Bethel in the hill country of Ephraim, and the Israelites came to her to have their disputes decided (Jdg 4.4–5).

Various information is offered in these verses, but Deborah is essentially characterized as a wise prophetess. Many of Israel's prophets exercised a special gift of wisdom (not unlike that of King Solomon) due to their operation in the Spirit, and Deborah is a prophetess whose reputation clearly extends far and wide as Israel's judge, in continuity with Moses before her (see Exod 18). So even if Deborah's presence in the narrative comes somewhat as a surprise, she raises our hopes nonetheless, for the narrator has led us to expect that her wisdom and prophetic gifts will provide the key to breaking Israel's cycles of sin.

Lady Wisdom

A persistent theme throughout Scripture is the way wisdom brings clarity, much as a lighthouse penetrates darkness, to benefit those who are lost. The first chapter of Proverbs personifies wisdom as a figure standing in the streets, crying out to those who have ears to hear. The themes are familiar among Yahweh's prophets, but here they are cast in the mouth of Lady Wisdom.[6]

> Wisdom calls aloud in the street,
>   she raises her voice in the public squares;
> at the head of the noisy streets she cries out,
>   in the gateways of the city she makes her speech (Prov 1.20–21).

God's messenger rebukes fools who ignore correction and remain stuck in destructive cycles of 'calamity', 'disaster' and 'distress' (Prov 1.27). She warns against complacency, since all 'will eat the fruit of their ways and be filled with the fruit of their schemes' (Prov 1.31). In stark contrast to The Seductress (Prov 7.10–27), who also summons men from the streets, dragging them to her 'chambers of death', Lady Wisdom is Yahweh's creative companion, 'rejoicing in his whole world and delighting in mankind' (Prov 8.31). She is able to act as God's agent of change because she understands what God is doing in the world.

Lady Wisdom's role has been identified as that of a preacher, teacher, counsellor, goddess and prophetess. And while numerous elements in her speech are typically prophetic, not least the call to turn (*shuv*), a close analysis of Proverbs 1.20–33 reveals that Lady Wisdom is depicted as *more* than a prophetess. As one scholar has expressed it, she is a divine 'mediatrix', a female mediator whose speech and authority 'move Lady Wisdom into the closest association with Yahweh.'[7] She understands God's big-picture plan and is at the same time a personalized expression of Yahweh's desire to dwell among his people. She was present at the inception of the world (Prov 8.22–31), but is no less at home on the streets, rubbing shoulders with resistant humanity (Prov 8.2–3).

Since God speaks primarily through his prophets, it is not surprising that wisdom and prophecy are fused in Proverbs 1 to give Lady Wisdom her authoritative voice. But where Lady Wisdom exists only as a *literary* persona, Deborah embodies God's intentions in *history* by rallying the Israelites into cooperation with God. Attuned to what God is doing in and through Israel, Deborah takes the spotlight (initially) to summon Israel's military general into action.

Having set the scene and established Deborah's character for the narrative that will follow (Jdg 4.1–5), the chapter divides to tell of the respective victories of Barak (Jdg 4.6–15) and Jael (Jdg 4.17–24). Both are narrated in such a way as to highlight the important role God's human partners play in fulfilling his purposes.

Barak (Judges 4.6–16)

As the nation's divinely appointed judge, Deborah initiates the action by sending for Barak, Israel's military general, and giving him Yahweh's orders.

> Go, take with you ten thousand men of Naphtali and Zebulun and lead the way to Mount Tabor. I will lure Sisera, the commander of Jabin's army, with his chariots and his troops to the Kishon River and give him into your hands (Jdg 4.6b–7).

Barak is not commanded to engage the enemy in battle, but only to rally his troops in order that Yahweh might 'lure Sisera'. This is not to say that Barak will have no significant role to play in the battle, but as a faithful young Israelite would later say, 'the battle is the LORD's' (1 Sam 17.47). As long as Barak makes his presence known to draw the enemy out, Yahweh promises, 'I will . . . give him into your hands.' It sounds like victory is being handed to Barak on a silver platter, but even so, he remains uncertain.

> Barak said to her [Deborah], 'If you go with me, I will go; but if you don't go with me, I won't go' (Jdg 4.8).

What an embarrassing ultimatum from Israel's military commander—and tantamount to confessing that he wishes to hide behind Deborah's skirts! 'Of the two leaders, it is he who plays the woman; and having been summoned to do a man's job, he refuses to act unless the woman who delegated it to him comes along to give him moral courage.'[8] Deborah's response to Barak's cowardice therefore contains a sting of poetic justice.

> 'Very well,' Deborah said, 'I will go with you. But because of the way you are going about this, the honour will not be yours, for the LORD will hand Sisera over to a woman' (Jdg 4.9).

You want a woman to hold your hand in battle? All right, but a woman will also have the glory. In one breath, Deborah chides Barak for his lack of nerve whilst prophesying that the death of Sisera will be at the hands of a woman. (At this point, readers naturally assume that Deborah is referring to herself.) God needs willing human participants to fulfil his purposes, not faint-hearted generals who cannot lead their armies without a security blanket. The narrator goes on to emphasize Barak's weakness by stating twice that Deborah kept him company—even with his army of ten thousand in tow!

> *So Deborah went with Barak* to Kedesh, where he summoned Zebulun and Naphtali. Ten thousand men followed him, *and Deborah also went with him* (Jdg 4.9b–10).

To his credit, Barak successfully leads his army to the mountainside so that in accordance with God's plan, Sisera is lured to the

Kishon River (Jdg 4.13). God's reasons for choosing the Kishon River are not immediately obvious, but the location takes on geo-graphical and theological significance as God's battle plan unfolds.

The Kishon 'River' is probably better translated 'Wadi' (Jdg 4.7,13 NRSV) since its terrestrial features are of significance to the story. Wadis, quite common in the Middle East, are essentially harmless ravines when dry, but with the potential to become dev-astating forces immediately after heavy rain. Judges 5.21 (also Ps 83.9) describes the Kishon Wadi as one of Yahweh's allies in this battle, quite literally sweeping the Canaanite army off their feet as heavy rains flood the valley. We can safely surmise from read-ing the narrative account (Jdg 4) in conjunction with the song (Jdg 5), that God's plan was to bring a flash flood into the Kishon Wadi once Sisera had been lured to that location. Divine intention and human decision, drawn together by prophetic wisdom, would ensure certain victory.

> At Barak's advance, the LORD routed Sisera and all his chariots and army by the sword, and Sisera abandoned his chariot and fled on foot (Jdg 4.15).

At first glance this verse seems to ascribe the victory entirely to Yahweh, although it seems curious to say that 'the LORD routed Sisera and all his chariots and army by the sword'. Was God really brandishing a sword on Israel's behalf? Almost certainly not. And yet, despite the fact that God intervened with a sudden torrent of rain that bogged down 900 iron chariots, verse 15 credits 'the sword' with victory over Sisera and his army. Without the active presence of Israel's swords, would God still have won the battle?

The simple answer is that we cannot know.

Perhaps God would have found another way or, without the collaboration of Barak's army, the event might not have been recorded as a tale of victory in the book of Judges. The pattern emerging, however, is that God needs cooperative human part-ners—not because he is incapable, but because he has *chosen* to bind his life to Israel's in a covenant relationship that he takes very seriously indeed.

It is interesting that in Exodus 15.20–21, where another prophetess (Miriam) also celebrates a military victory in song, the sequence of events is very similar. On that occasion also, Israel's enemies were lured to a specific location (the Red Sea) where they were overcome by an aquatic force under Yahweh's command. Isaiah's poetic reflection on the exodus happens to provide an equally apt description of Barak's victory at the Kishon Wadi:

> This is what the LORD says—
>   he who made a way through the sea,
>   a path through the mighty waters,
> who drew out the chariots and horses,
>   the army and reinforcements together,
> and they lay there, never to rise again,
>   extinguished, snuffed out like a wick (Isa 43.16–17).

The unfolding of events at the Kishon Wadi testifies to the importance of human obedience *in conjunction with* God's almighty power. Even though victory ultimately rests in God's hands (Jdg 4.15; Prov 21.31), the narrator has evidently gone to significant lengths to emphasize the importance of human collaboration.

But the story is not over yet.

Jael (Judges 4.17–24)

With Sisera's 900 iron chariots proving useless in the now-flooded Kishon Wadi, it is not difficult to imagine Sisera scrambling from his chariot to flee on foot until the sounds of battle begin to fade behind him. He seeks refuge among the Kenites, which seems sensible in light of their alliance (Jdg 4.17), but Jael, who also lures Sisera as Barak had done, has no intentions of helping him. We are not privy to her motives, but she offers him milk, lays a blanket on him, and reassures him, 'Come, my lord, come right in. Don't be afraid' (Jdg 4.18–19). These three maternal actions achieve their purpose and the powerful military commander is soon fast asleep—and completely vulnerable. Without so much as a second thought, Jael seizes her opportunity and drives a tent peg through his skull, just moments before Barak arrives in hot pursuit of the already-dead Canaanite general. Stepping into Jael's tent, Barak no doubt hears Deborah's voice ringing in his ears: 'The honour will not be yours, for the LORD will hand Sisera over to a woman.' As the words of the prophetess prove true, the narrator again concludes with a dual recognition of both God and Israel:

> On that day *God subdued Jabin*, the Canaanite king, before the Israelites. And the hand of *the Israelites* grew stronger and stronger against Jabin, the Canaanite king, until they *destroyed him* (Jdg 4.23–24).

'God subdued Jabin', but the Israelites 'destroyed him.' To whom should credit be given for defeating the Canaanite king?

Was it God's victory?

Deborah's, who initiated the action?

Should we credit Barak and his ten thousand Israelite soldiers who braved the battlefield?

Or does the glory belong to Jael, a Kenite, who took down Jabin's military commander?

Obviously, all of these played their parts, and that is precisely the point, for this is a story of divine-human cooperation and its author has deliberately sought to accentuate the collaborative success of God *together with* his people. And while it is true that Deborah exemplifies Yahweh's working relationship with his prophets, hers are not the only actions that matter.[9]

Helping God (Judges 5)

Deborah's prophetic leadership is highlighted in a particular way in the song of Judges 5, which juxtaposes human leadership with a divine Hero. God's partnership with the prophets is critical, for his word never falls, disembodied, from heaven. Rather, it is always delivered *through* his messengers, whether as an expression of God's concern for personal disputes (Jdg 4.5) or for the outcomes of war (Jdg 4.7). The Song of Deborah expresses this truth through the interplay of Yahweh's decisive acts and the willing cooperation of the prophetess. Notice how the songwriter oscillates between the actions of Deborah and the *praise of Yahweh*:[10]

On that day Deborah and Barak son of Abinoam sang this song:

When the princes in Israel take the lead,
    when the people willingly offer themselves—
praise the LORD!

Hear this, you kings! Listen, you rulers!
    I will sing to the LORD, I will sing;
    I will make music to the LORD, the God of Israel.

O LORD, *when you went out from Seir,*
    when you marched from the land of Edom,
the earth shook, the heavens poured,
    the clouds poured down water.
The mountains quaked before the LORD, *the One of Sinai,*
    before the LORD, *the God of Israel.*

In the days of Shamgar son of Anath,
    in the days of Jael, the roads were abandoned;
    travellers took to winding paths.
Village life in Israel ceased,
ceased until I, Deborah, arose,
arose a mother in Israel (Jdg 5.1–7).

And so it goes on, with glory being ascribed both to God as Lord of creation and to Deborah and other human agents who have taken initiatives on the ground. In Judges 5.11, the point is reinforced by placing 'the righteous acts of the LORD' in parallel with 'the righteous acts of his warriors'. But then, having paid tribute to the tribes of Israel that came willingly to Yahweh's aid (Jdg 5.14–15a,18), the songwriter goes on to condemn the reluctance of those tribes that failed to participate in God's initiatives (Jdg 5.15b–17). Perhaps the clearest (and most surprising) expression of God's desire to collaborate with human partners comes in verse 23, where the people of Meroz[11] are cursed for not helping God in his battle against the mighty forces of Canaan.

    'Curse Meroz,' said the angel of the LORD.
    'Curse its people bitterly,

because they did not come to help the LORD,
    to help the LORD against the mighty.'

> One could claim from this verse that, at the least, God demands
> help or desires help. Yet, the verse seems to push us even further,
> namely, God *needs* help, or at least has chosen to be dependent upon
> that which is not God to get certain objectives accomplished.[12]

It is critical that God's people resist having an attitude that abandons God to do 'his work', and that we seek instead to understand the pivotal role he has invited us to play in renewing the world. And if it seems strange (or wrong) to speak of helping God, it is only because of our tendency to think of God as the only One who makes things happen. The point, of course, is not that God is helpless without us. We would be in dire straits if that were so! Rather, God has chosen for it to be this way, for better or worse. Deborah's resounding message is, Get on board with what God is doing! (Actually, this was every prophet's concern within their particular historical context.) Deborah is honoured in this ancient song as Yahweh's prophetic representative because she roused Israel to obedient action. And to really hammer the point home (if you'll excuse the pun), the songwriter juxtaposes a blessing for Jael with a curse on those who refuse to cooperate with God. Even Jael, a non-Israelite, serves as God's instrument of victory because of her swift initiatives in the heat of the moment (Jdg 5.24–27). God may not need human assistance, but it cannot be denied that he *wants* our help and that he happily blesses those who choose to help him.

Complacency is a killer. Monotonous cycles of sin, no matter how small, are an early symptom of the dangerous malaise of indifference, a sign that we have begun to lose sight of the big picture. Deborah's story is a powerful reminder that when we are wise enough to share God's vision for his world and courageous enough to collaborate with him, a spark of initiative can break the cycles of sin that bind and oppress.

It is significant that Deborah turned out not to be Israel's military leader (although the opening verses led us to anticipate that possibility). Nor was she the one who defeated Sisera (though her prophecy in Judges 4.9 led us to expect that, too). She is, at the end of the day, one who *facilitates* God's operations in the world. Rather than seeking her own glory as kings were prone to do, Deborah's chief desire was that God should maintain his rightful place in the hearts of his people. In the final words of the song, she is commemorated as one who loved Yahweh and who rose in strength to shine like the morning sun (Jdg 5.31). The ancient song brings to mind another more familiar tune that begins with the same verbal imperatives:

> Rise and shine
>> and give God the glory, glory!
>
> Rise and shine
>> and give God the glory, glory!
>
> Rise and shine
>> and give God the glory, glory!
>
> Children of the Lord!

Dig Deeper

■ Write your own definition of wisdom.

■ In what specific ways can you cooperate with God?

■ In what contexts are you able to function as a prophetic voice, encouraging others to take action in obedience to God?

■ How can Christians become better equipped to collaborate with God's purposes?

■ Reflect on the 'cycles of sin' in your own life. What suggestions does Judges 4 - 5 make concerning how those cycles may be broken?

4

Prophetic Conflict: Heart Reorientation

SAMUEL

The prophet, along with my God,
is the watchman over Ephraim (Hos 9.8).

1 Samuel 3; 12; 15

Watchmen

Growing up with missionary parents in Africa granted me some interesting childhood memories. My brothers and I attended a boarding school in Nigeria, which housed a lively mix of local and international students. Behind the school was a farm which existed primarily to provide food for the staff and students living there, but which also offered endless hours of entertainment. When classes were finished for the day, or on weekends, I used to love going to the farm with four or five like-minded friends and getting up to all kinds of mischief. Some days we would let small rabbits loose into giant piles of hay and see who could find theirs first while on other occasions we would watch some poor animal being prepared for the dinner menu. But of all the possibilities afforded by the farm, our favourite activity was tormenting the pigs.

On the days we were feeling more adventurous, my friends and I would shinny our way along a pipe that ran above a series of pig-pens until we got to the end, where it was possible to drop down onto a big boulder next to one of the pens. From there we had access to a herd of pigs who awaited our visitation. Slowly, armed with sticks, we would edge our way into the pen and carefully choose one of the fatter, lazier-looking pigs as our target. (By the way, these were huge boars; all bristles and tusks.) Whoever had the stick would begin prodding the selected pig, lightly at first, but enough to get its attention. The pig's first response was usually a loud snort that made it clear our presence wasn't appreciated. But what nine-year-old boy is satisfied with a grunt from a pig? No, the prodding and poking would increase in intensity, urged on by the laughter and cheers of the others, until one of the pigs finally decided that enough was enough. In the split second it took for us to realize that a large boar was about to teach us a lesson, we would turn in unison and make a dash for the big rock. Leaping onto it, we would cram up against each other, laughing hysterically, beyond the reach of the boar's tusks. But with all the adrenaline and excitement, we occasionally forgot to designate a lookout . . .

You see, the pigs were only one cause for concern. If, while we were dashing about madly in the pen, one of the farmers heard the commotion and came to see what was happening, then we were *really* in trouble. (Persecuting pigs was not considered an acceptable pastime!) After being caught a few times, we certainly came to appreciate the wisdom in appointing a lookout.

In the ancient world, the vigilance of a city's watchman was critical for the safety of its inhabitants. Lookouts were responsible not just for recognizing threats before it was too late, but for sounding an alarm so that citizens could prepare for the possibility of attack. So when God told the prophet Ezekiel that he was to function as a 'watchman for the house of Israel', the young prophet-priest came to understand his responsibilities by comparing them to those of a scout, patrolling the city walls.

> Son of man, speak to your countrymen and say to them: 'When I bring the sword against a land, and the people of the land choose one of their men and make him their watchman, and he sees the sword coming against the land and blows the trumpet to warn the people . . . if the watchman sees the sword coming and does not blow the trumpet to warn the people and the sword comes and takes the life of one of them, that man will be taken away

because of his sin, but I will hold the watchman accountable for his blood.'

Son of man, I have made you a watchman for the house of Israel; so hear the word I speak and give them warning from[1] me (Eze 33.2–3,6–7).

A city's lookout would be held accountable if he failed to blow the trumpet at the right time, and so too with Yahweh's messengers. It was incumbent upon them to confront those whose evil ways invited divine judgement. Of course, once the proverbial trumpet had been blown, Israel's choices were ultimately her own and the prophets could not be held directly responsible for the sins of the people. After all, no prophet could *force* a change of heart upon their audience. However, this is not to say that the prophets simply reported sin out of obligation with little or no concern for how Israel would respond. Rather, as we have noted already, they shared Yahweh's acute sensitivity to right and wrong. As Abraham Heschel has expressed it, prophets 'feel fiercely because they hear deeply.'[2] And while the prophetic disposition to confront compromise was a central dynamic in the lives of all God's prophets, it seemed especially strong in Samuel, whose ability to 'feel fiercely' grew out of a childhood experience that taught him to 'hear deeply.'

Prophet vs Priest (1 Samuel 3)

1 Samuel 3 does not begin on a very hopeful note: 'In those days, the word of the LORD was rare . . .' The scarcity of God's word was most likely a consequence of Israel's disobedience. (More than two hundred years later, the prophet Amos would threaten to withdraw Yahweh's word from a people who paid it no heed; Amos 8.11–12.) These were dark times, as indicated by the themes of light and sight in the opening verses:

. . . there were not many visions.

One night Eli, whose eyes were becoming so weak that he could barely see, was lying down in his usual place. [But] the lamp of God had not yet gone out (1 Sam 3.1b–3).

Eli's was not the first priestly family to fall out of divine favour, but the carelessness of Aaron's sons in Leviticus 10 seemed almost trivial compared to the disgraceful actions of Eli's sons (1 Sam 2.12–25). Hophni and Phinehas had treated the sacrifices of the people with contempt, even sleeping with the female servants at the tent of meeting which Moses had established as a place to meet with God! Rather than preserving purity in Israel, these men were perverting the priesthood and leading others into sin. In response to their abhorrent behaviour, an anonymous prophet paid a visit to Shiloh, condemning Eli for being so lenient with them (1 Sam 2.27–36).

Enter Samuel, a boy called by a God he does not yet even know (1 Sam 3.7), despite the fact that he serves in Yahweh's temple. (This is an indictment of Eli, not young Samuel.) The story of Samuel's thrice-repeated 'Here I am' as he confuses Yahweh's voice with Eli's is a familiar one for its portrayal of childhood innocence responding to God's call. But the story doesn't end with Samuel's recognition of the voice of God.[3] Having been introduced to Yahweh during the night, Samuel awakens with the knowledge that he must bring down the man who has brought him up. One might have forgiven him for sleeping in! But at Eli's bidding, the young prophet faithfully delivers a word of severe judgement, a word which Eli appears to accept quite readily, probably because he has already heard it once before (1 Sam 2.30).

Part of the judgement upon Eli's house echoes the wider judgement upon Israel that we noted in the opening verses, i.e. the increasing scarcity of God's word. In 1 Samuel 3.7–10, Samuel had been dependent upon Eli in order to make an appropriate response to God, for 'the word of the LORD had not yet been revealed to him.' But now that Samuel has become attuned to Yahweh's voice, the positions of power between Eli and Samuel are reversed, and Eli becomes dependent upon the young prophet for God's word (1 Sam 3.17).[4]

The chapter concludes with the report of Samuel's reputation spreading like wildfire. This is a prophet of Yahweh whose words never fall to the ground (1 Sam 3.20), which is to say that they never fail to accomplish the purpose for which they are sent (Isa 55.11; see 1 Kgs 2.27). Verbal assaults on compromise continue to characterize Samuel's prophetic ministry throughout his life, from his first confrontation with Eli (as a boy) to his final words to King Saul (as a ghost!), but before Samuel can reckon with Saul, he must challenge the people about their decision to anoint a human king in God's place.

Prophet vs People (1 Samuel 12)

The judges were successful in establishing peace in Israel for periods of time, but none were able to fully curb the nation's resistance to Yahweh. By the end of the book of Judges, Israel's tribes are even at war among themselves (Jdg 19–21), much like the dysfunctional families of Genesis. Israel needed a stronger form of leadership than the judges were able to offer, but they were unwilling to throw their lot in with a King who did not dwell among them in flesh and blood.

The Mosaic Law includes instructions for various forms of leadership—judges, kings, priests, and prophets (Deut 16.18–18.22)—each of which had a particular role in upholding Israel's ethical identity. Judges and kings were to uphold *justice*, priests to ensure *purity*, and prophets to confront compromise within the other spheres of governance, calling Israel to account for her sins.[5] Although the stipulations in Deuteronomy 17.14–20 allow for the possibility of kingship, they do not suggest or recommend a human king, quite simply because Israel's ideal mode of leadership was one of theocracy; God's rule enacted through human regency. So when Israel came to Samuel, asking for a human king 'such as all the other nations have', God perceived their request as a rejection of his rule, and said as much to his prophet (1 Sam 8.5–7). Even so, Yahweh did nothing to diminish Israel's freedom, but rather incorporated their decision into his purposes.

> God does not press the point. He accepts this disobedience. He says to the judge: 'They have not rejected you, but they have rejected me' (1 Samuel 8:7) . . . Israel wants a king? Even at the cost of rejecting God? Even at the cost of being enslaved? Very well then![6]

As God humbly adapts to a situation shaped by human choices, the monarchy itself becomes a significant testament to God's way of relating to humanity. He does, however, inform the people of the gravity of their decision (1 Sam 10.17–18a; 12.12) and in 1 Samuel 12, God's prophet turns 'prosecutor' in a speech that conveys the hostility of a courtroom. Samuel's chief concern is that Israel's insistence on a monarchy undermines her *raison d'être* as Yahweh's counter-community among the nations. His well-constructed legal argument[7] divides into five sections:

1. *Vindication of Israel's human leadership (vv. 1–5).* As Israel's prophet (1 Sam 3.20) and judge (1 Sam 7.15), Samuel has provided excellent leadership, never taking from the people (in contrast to Eli's sons and the future kings of Israel). The Israelites have had no complaints and therefore have no need for a mode of authority other than what they already have in Samuel.
2. *Vindication of Israel's divine leadership (vv. 6–11).* A brief overview of Israel's history is all the evidence needed to prove that Yahweh has always been Israel's true King. Israel is rejecting a King who would have continued to save her, just as he had done so faithfully in the past.
3. *Covenant expectations are unchanged (vv. 12–15).* Here Samuel gets to the heart of the matter: Israel's sin is not so much her desire for a king as it is her longing to become 'like the other nations'; the demand to blend in is shameful because it constitutes an outright denial of her calling to stand apart. Moreover, expectations of the human king will be no different from what they are for other Israelites. Samuel makes it clear that 'the king has no individual role to play but is simply one more member of the covenant community . . . Theologically these verses nullify the institution of kingship!'[8] Covenant expectations still apply—for everyone (see Deut 17.20).
4. *Yahweh and his prophet retain power (vv. 16–19).* Samuel concludes with a miraculous sign (a thunderstorm during the dry season) that leaves Israel with no doubt that her God-King can do anything, be it a matter of agriculture or war. The sign verifies Samuel's message that Israel has sinned as well as his authority as God's messenger.

5. *Reaffirmation of Israel's role in God's purposes (vv. 20–25).*
Immediately following Israel's confession, Samuel assumes a
priestly role and proclaims forgiveness for the people, reaffirming their special place in Yahweh's purposes:

> For the sake of his great name the LORD will not reject his people,
> because the LORD was pleased to make you his own (1 Sam 12.22).

Samuel's legal assault declares Israel faithless in her request for a
human king, reinforces God's covenantal expectations, demonstrates God's power as true King, and even graciously reaffirms
Israel's place in God's purposes. Israel's watchman has keen
vision and a voice that demands a hearing, but even so, he cannot force obedience. He can do no more than identify the failure
of his people and call them to account; now the blood is off his
hands and the consequences theirs (1 Sam 12.25; see Eze 33.4).

1 Samuel 12 marks a turning point in Israel's history of particular pertinence for Yahweh's prophets. With the establishment of
Israel's monarchy, the prophetic vocation becomes the primary
vehicle for mediating any discord between Israel's true King and
her representative human kings. Although the institution of
kingship brings greater consistency to Israel's religious life, there
is still 'an aspect of spirituality which cannot be poured into permanent forms, cannot be institutionalized.'[9] From this point
onward, confrontations with Israel's kings would become the
bread and butter of prophetic activity,[10] beginning almost immediately for Samuel with the newly appointed King Saul (1 Sam
13,15).

Prophet vs King (1 Samuel 15)

1 Samuel 15 opens with a conversation between prophet and king
in which it soon becomes apparent which of them wields the
greater authority. I anointed you, says Samuel, so listen up! The
Hebrew verb for 'listen' (*shama'*) appears eight times in the chapter, making it a central theme and ultimately the reason for Saul's
rejection as king. On first impressions, the expectation upon Saul
to 'attack the Amalekites and totally destroy everything that

belongs to them' (1 Sam 15.3) seems unreasonable, but there were grounds for the command to 'totally destroy' Amalek.

Many years earlier, following the exodus, as the Israelites were making their way through the desert, the Amalekites had pursued them and cut them down, taking advantage of their exhaustion—and without reason, since Israel had no land to give up at that point in time (Exod 17.8–16). Later, during the period of the judges, the Amalekites had joined the Midianites to oppress God's people again, going beyond military victory to ruthless oppression just as they had done previously. They forced the Israelites to live in mountain caves, destroyed their crops and invaded the land for no other reason than 'to ravage it' (Jdg 6.3–5). It was because of such inhuman brutality that Israel was to also go *beyond* victory and wipe the Amalekites off the face of the earth once peace in the land had been established (Deut 25.17–19). Since Saul had achieved this peace (1 Sam 14.47–48), it was incumbent upon him as Israel's king to remember, obey, and 'blot out the memory of Amalek from under heaven' (Exod 17.14).

In Samuel's speech to the people, he stressed that rigid covenant obedience was to be the foundation for kingship in Israel (see above). But the stark contrast between 'Do not spare them' (1 Sam 15.3) and 'He took Agag . . . alive' (1 Sam 15.8) exposes the arrogance of a king who alters Yahweh's instructions to suit himself. To make matters worse, Saul's disobedience in a prior matter (1 Sam 13) had already suggested his ineptitude for kingship.

Regardless of his failures, however, Saul gives the impression that any sins he may have committed have been swept under the royal carpet, for he greets Samuel the very next morning with some exuberance. 'The LORD bless you! I have carried out the LORD's instructions' (1 Sam 15.13).

Really, Saul?

Samuel begins by asking Saul some questions that require no answer (a use of rhetoric that will be explored further in the next chapter).

> What then is this bleating of sheep in my ears? What is this lowing of cattle that I hear? (1 Sam 15.14)

It is unclear at first whether Saul understands the rhetorical nature of the prophet's enquiry, for his response seems genuine enough. 'The soldiers brought them from the Amalekites; they spared the best of the sheep and cattle to sacrifice to the LORD your God . . .' But then Saul betrays his guilt with a veiled confession; he knows exactly what he *should* have done: '. . . but we totally destroyed the rest' (1 Sam 15.15).

Like a child who has stolen from the cookie jar, Saul's best defence is, 'But I didn't take all of them!' As the dialogue unfolds, the narrator interjects with his own perspective (1 Sam 15.9) and Saul's lies begin to stick out like sore thumbs as he becomes increasingly defensive (1 Sam 15.15,20). It is time for Samuel to change tack and confront Saul's compromise directly.

> Stop! . . . Let me tell you what the LORD said to me last night (1 Sam 15.16).

Samuel proceeds to reiterate the command given to Saul, before asking him plainly:

> Why did you not obey [*shama'*] the LORD? Why did you pounce on the plunder and do evil in the eyes of the LORD? (1 Sam 15.19)

'But . . . but . . .' Saul begins (1 Sam 15.20).

No buts! Samuel cuts in. God doesn't want your sacrifices; he wants your obedience! Arrogance amounts to self-idolization, and because you've rejected God's word, he has rejected your kingship.

Many of Israel's prophets after Samuel would also speak about the tension between obedience and sacrifice, but the verdict never changed: God prefers allegiance over acts of religious sacrifice.[11]

'I may not represent you well from Monday to Saturday, but I give you a tenth of all I earn at church . . .'

Stop!

'But, God, I sacrifice precious time with my own family to serve you . . .'

Stop!

Efforts to dupe God with religious sacrifice lead to prophetic conflict every time: 'Stop! . . . Let me tell you what the LORD said . . .' (1 Sam 15.16)

In his refusal to accept God's judgement, Saul pulls in desperation at Samuel's robe when the prophet turns to leave. But the tearing of Samuel's robe only reinforces God's verdict:

> Samuel said to him, 'The LORD has torn the kingdom of Israel from you today and has given it to one of your neighbours—to one better than you' (1 Sam 15.28).

Yahweh's decision is final; Saul will not get a third chance.[12] In his place, God will appoint a man with a heart like God's own, one who will function as a *prince* under Yahweh's *King*ship.[13]

Finally, the chapter concludes by referring back to Yahweh's command to 'totally destroy'. Taking up a sword in his own hand, Samuel hacks the Amalekite king to pieces.[14] 'As your sword has made women childless, so will your mother be childless among women!' (1 Sam 15.33) It is a horrific scene wherein Yahweh's prophet does what Israel's king had refused to do.

Samuel's confrontation with Saul concludes with parallel expressions of grief from God and his prophet (see 'Living In-Between' in chapter 2), though surprisingly, God appears to be the first to recover (1 Sam 15.35–16.1). And while the narrator's closing comment, that 'until the day Samuel died, he did not go to see Saul again' (1 Sam 15.35) is perfectly true, it hints at the fact that many years later Saul would seek Samuel out again, even *after* the prophet's death.

For many years (1 Sam 15–28), Saul continued to resist God's verdict upon his kingship until finally one day, fearing for his life at the hand of the Philistines and failing to hear from God 'by dreams or Urim[15] or prophets' (1 Sam 28.6), he attempted to forcefully extract a prophetic word from Samuel by dragging his ghost up from the grave. Saul's action broke God's Law (Lev 20.27), disregarded Samuel's rebuke (1 Sam 15.23) and even went directly against his own ban (1 Sam 28.3), reinforcing his contradictory nature as a man who makes and breaks rules to suit himself.

When Samuel's ghost did in fact make an appearance (a surprise in itself to many readers), he simply reiterated Yahweh's previous judgement:

The LORD has done what he predicted through me. The LORD has
torn the kingdom out of your hands and given it to one of your
neighbours—to David. Because you did not obey the LORD or
carry out his fierce wrath against the Amalekites, the LORD has
done this to you today (1 Sam 28.17–18; (see also 1 Chr 10.13–14).

Whatever Saul had been hoping to hear in this final exchange
with Samuel's ghost, he could only have been disappointed. But
as well as confirming God's previous words to Saul, Samuel went
on to offer one last, devastating prophecy: 'The LORD will hand
over both Israel and you to the Philistines, and tomorrow you
and your sons will be with me' (1 Sam 28.19). Even beyond the
grave, Samuel continued to confront compromise and, as ever,
his words proved true (1 Sam 31.6).

Heart Reorientation

Samuel's experiences of prophetic conflict exposed deep problems within Israel and the nation's leadership. In each case, however, the sinful behaviour addressed was only the symptom of a
deeper 'heart problem'.

Eli was punished because 'his sons were blaspheming God,
and he did not restrain them' (1 Sam 3.13 NRSV). Blasphemy, the
profaning of God's name, is something more than just saying the
wrong kinds of words when you feel frustrated. Rather, it refers
to the misrepresentation of God's character that ends up giving
him a bad name; in other words, saying you represent God ('taking God's name . . .') but not behaving like it ('. . . in vain'). It is
one of the most common themes in the preaching of the prophets.

To the people, Samuel pointed out that their sin lay in their
request to be 'like all the other nations' (1 Sam 8.20). The very
purpose of Israel's distinct identity was to make God known by
being *unlike* the surrounding nations, so the request for a human
king was not just a matter of Israel coveting what others had, but
one of trading in her divine calling.

Saul clearly failed to recognize that Israel's human king must
remain subservient to her true King. He bent rules and commands to suit his royal self, and as a result the crown passed to

David, whose heart was a more accurate reflection of Yahweh's (1 Sam 13.14).

Do you see the pattern? Eli's sons misrepresented God by doing awful things in his name; Israel misrepresented God by wanting to be like everybody else; and Saul misrepresented God by making up his own rules as Yahweh's representative. In each case, beneath the distinct acts of disobedience and rebellion was a wayward heart needing reorientation so that God's covenant people might properly present his character to the nations.

And if we find ourselves tut-tutting at the blasphemous acts of Hophni and Phinehas or the misguided wants of Israel or King Saul's flagrant rule-bending because our *obedience* is so much better, we should pause to consider that even obedience falls short of the mark! When being good (abstaining from sin) becomes life's goal so that week after week we listen to sermon after sermon in the hope that little by little we might become better Christians, we short-change ourselves for a limited vision of life's purpose. The goal of Christian ethics is not simply to 'be good' so that we are less plagued by guilt on our journey through life. The problem with that kind of tunnel vision is that we become obsessed with our own personal war against sin, which then becomes the primary means of measuring success or failure. Samuel's prophetic ministry suggests a helpful corrective.

The prophets longed to see God's people reflecting his likeness while the rest of the world looked on. Therefore, their confrontational ethic sought to establish not just obedience, but *obedience as a means of speaking for God*. The intended purpose of Israel's obedience is expressed quite simply in Leviticus 19.2:[16] 'Be holy because I, the LORD your God, am holy.' Not because he says so or because it makes life easier on everyone, but 'because I, the LORD your God, am holy.' The same directive applies to the church today. In light of our (prophetic) calling to make God known, obedience—being holy—fulfils God's passion by enhancing his reputation in the world so that others may also be drawn into a life-giving relationship with their Maker.

The implications may seem obvious, but are worth stating for the sake of clarity: (a) *God has a moral character* and (b) *he wants his image-bearers to reflect it on earth*. God doesn't want people to be good for goodness' sake. He wants us to live lives characterized by obedience and forgiveness for the sake of *his name*. Indeed, being a *Christ*-ian is all about making Christ visible to our neighbours.

So as it turns out, the watchmen who relentlessly patrol the walls of God's kingdom are at the end of the day keeping watch over God's reputation in the world. When Abraham prayed fervently that God would do what is right (Gen 18.25), and when Moses begged God to reconsider an action that would almost certainly make him appear capricious to onlooking nations (Exod 32.12), these men were acting out of their concern for the world's perception of God. By all means, let us continue to confess our faults and do what is good, but let us also go beyond 'behaving ourselves' to keeping a watchful eye on God's reputation.

Dig Deeper

■ What does 1 Samuel 3.1-10 suggest about the importance of recognizing God's voice? (Also see Ezekiel 33.7)

■ What does Hosea 9.8 say about the life of a prophet/watchman?

■ In what ways has your Christian faith led to moments of confrontation? How have you dealt with those situations?

■ Why is obedience not enough?

■ What difference can you make to God's reputation in the coming week?

5

Prophetic Speech: Say It Sideways

NATHAN

*Son of man, set forth an allegory
and tell the house of Israel a parable (Eze 17.2).*

2 Samuel 7; 11 – 12; 1 Kings 1

Shooting the Messenger (2 Samuel 7)

On 16 April 2008, an incident in the Gaza Strip drew international attention when Fadel Shana'a, a 23-year-old Palestinian cameraman working for the UK news service Reuters, was fired upon and killed along with three other innocent civilians (each younger than Shana'a). The Al Mezan Centre for Human Rights denounced the killings as a deliberate war crime (media professionals are to be treated as neutral civilians when passing through war zones), but only four months after the death of Fadel Shana'a the investigation was shut down without any action taken against the soldiers responsible. The international news network Al Jazeera followed up on the tragic event with an award-winning six-part television series entitled *Shooting the Messenger*.

All of Yahweh's messengers quite regularly found themselves between a rock and a hard place, and a number of them were imprisoned for speaking God's word.[1] (Evidently, the tongue is not always mightier than the sword!) Samuel's experiences of conflict explored in the last chapter were by no means unique to him, but some prophets appear to have been better practised in rhetorical strategies that encouraged their audiences to swallow that which was unsavoury. In this regard, Nathan appears to have had a peculiar talent.

Each narrative about Nathan presents him as one who moves and speaks freely in the king's chambers and no doubt he owes this privilege, at least in part, to his skill as a wordsmith.[2] He makes three appearances in the Old Testament, using a different form of speech on each occasion to bring the word of God to King David.

Nathan is first introduced in 2 Samuel 7, where he is engaged in casual conversation with the king. There is no mention of God sending him with a particular message. He is simply there in the royal palace, expressing his unreserved support for David, who has risen from shepherd boy, the youngest of eight brothers, to bold and faithful king. As conversation turns to their surroundings, David expresses his desire to build a more permanent and elaborate dwelling place for Yahweh, and Nathan responds with what seems sensible to him. However, it soon becomes clear that Nathan's initial words—'Whatever you have in mind, go ahead and do it, for the LORD is with you' (2 Sam 7.3)—do *not* constitute prophetic speech. Already the narrative has distinguished between Word of God and word of man.

Later that night, however, Nathan receives a message from Yahweh for the king. Through his prophet God explains that he has not yet commanded any of Israel's 'shepherds' to build him a permanent residence because he has been quite content to move from place to place with his 'flock'. But to counter any doubts King David may have,[3] God assures him, 'I will provide a place for my people Israel and will plant them so that they can have a home of their own and no longer be disturbed' (2 Sam 7.10a). The wordplay that follows turns David's offer to build a house for Yahweh on its head (*bayit* means both 'house' and 'dynasty' in Hebrew). If anyone is going to build a *bayit*, it will be Yahweh building an eternal *dynasty* for David. A plethora of promises follow ('I will' statements), but they are not set into cedar and stone; rather, they must be held in faith:

Now *I will* make your name great, like the names of the greatest men of the earth. And *I will* provide a place for my people Israel and *will* plant them so that they can have a home of their own . . . *I will* also give you rest from all your enemies.

The LORD declares to you that *the LORD himself will* establish a house for you: When your days are over and you rest with your fathers, *I will* raise up your offspring to succeed you, who will come from your own body, and *I will* establish his kingdom. He is the one who will build a house for my Name, and *I will* establish the throne of his kingdom for ever. *I will* be his father, and he shall be my son. When he does wrong, *I will* punish him with the rod of men, with floggings inflicted by men. But *my love will* never be taken away from him, as I took it away from Saul, whom I removed from before you. Your house and your kingdom *will* endure for ever before me; your throne shall be established for ever (2 Sam 7.9b–16).

Through Nathan's prophetic speech, God affirms the legitimacy of David's appointment as 'prince' over the people (2 Sam 7.8 NRSV) and makes a number of unconditional promises to him.[4] For Nathan, it has been no difficult task. Good news is easily given and readily received.

David's Story (2 Samuel 11)

It is not long, however, before Israel's best king stumbles and falls. When David sees Bathsheba bathing on a rooftop nearby and decides to let his lust hold sway, his life story takes a turn for the worse.

The story of David and Bathsheba is a familiar one: the king's desire for his beautiful neighbour, their affair leading to her pregnancy, and the king's efforts to sweep things under the proverbial rug. Even King David, the measuring stick for all who would wear the crown after him, is not immune to temptation. Like Saul, he makes an autonomous decision that flies in the face of Yahweh's stringent demands, breaking three of the Ten Commandments in quick succession: coveting, adultery, murder. At the sordid tale's conclusion, David has married the pregnant

Bathsheba and successfully disposed of Uriah. But David's ensuing course of action, marked by deception and abuse of power, is arguably even more disturbing than his blatant disregard for God's Law. His attempts to save face by rewriting history reveal the self-deception of a man whose power has well and truly gone to his head. David's alternative version of events was to go something like this:

> *During the siege against Ammon a soldier named Uriah returned to Jerusalem to give the king a report on the war's progress. During that time, Uriah's wife fell pregnant. Nine months later, Uriah and Bathsheba became the proud parents of a son. Nothing out of the ordinary; nothing scandalous.*

But the king soon realizes that Uriah's moral integrity is going to render this particular story unwriteable (2 Sam 11.11). So, without further ado, David proceeds to concoct a second version which, with great irony, is delivered to the army general by Uriah's own hand:

> *In a battle between Israel and Ammon a valiant soldier named Uriah was killed in the frontline when he drew too close to the enemy's city walls. His bereaved widow, Bathsheba, was taken in by King David and, nine months later, the king's (legitimate) wife gave birth to a child. Nothing out of the ordinary; nothing scandalous.*

Since history is written by the victors, and the victors are generally those who wield the most power or the best strategic forethought, it is to be expected that David will succeed one way or another in putting a new spin on events. And sure enough, Uriah is killed and Bathsheba becomes David's wife, just as planned (2 Sam 11.14–27).

Before the chapter ends, however, the narrator interjects to affirm the reader's suspicions. David is playing God, and God does not take kindly to pretenders (yet another broken commandment; Exod 20.3). Not only is David assuming a kind of lordship over history through his words and actions, but he is effectively rewriting God's Law by presuming to tell Joab what is evil and what is not. Although it is not evident in most English translations, the repetition of a Hebrew phrase contrasts David's compromised point of view with Yahweh's perspective:[6]

And David told the messenger, 'Say this to Joab, *"Do not consider this thing to be evil in your eyes,* for the sword devours this one and that"' (2 Sam 11.25a)	But *the thing David had done was considered evil in the eyes of the* LORD (2 Sam 11.27b; see also 2 Sam 12.9).

The repeated phrase highlights David's moral blindness, a consequence of deliberately averting his eyes (and Joab's) from sin. As Joab unquestioningly follows the king's orders by tying up loose ends (namely Uriah), it seems more and more likely that David's version of events will prevail. But in his desperate attempt to salvage his good repute, David forgets that he is not the only one capable of invention.

Nathan's Story (2 Samuel 12)

Following the successful termination of Uriah, tension mounts as 2 Samuel 12 begins with the words, 'The LORD sent Nathan to David . . .' First-time readers imagine the worst as Yahweh's messenger is sent to address a king who considers himself to be above the Law. What is to stop David from treating Nathan as he treated Uriah?

Had Nathan stormed the palace like a bull in a china shop, demanding an explanation for the king's outrageous actions, then perhaps he would not have lived to tell the tale. But Nathan's manner is quite unlike the punishing anger of Moses or the harsh confrontations of Samuel. Recognizing the sensitivity of his situation, Nathan avoids frontal assault by 'saying it sideways' by way of a story. And since kings were often expected to make judgements for their people (e.g. 1 Kgs 3.16f.), it is quite possible that David assumed this to be the purpose of the prophet's visit as he sat back in his throne to listen.

Upon hearing Nathan's parable, readers immediately understand its relevance to the king, though David is not so quick to join the dots. By rewriting history to suit his own moral agenda,

David has conveniently blinded himself to the error of his ways. However, Nathan's counter-word also takes the form of a story, a parable designed to kindle the king's anger . . . against himself.[7] David's lie is countered by Nathan's truth-telling, which seeks to draw the disoriented king back into the all-important story of God and Israel.

Parables are not typical stories. They have a beginning and a middle, but lack a definitive conclusion. Like good sermons, they are left open-ended so that the audience (not the speaker) can take responsibility for the outcome. That is why Nathan's story stops short of any justice being done for the poor man whose lamb has been taken from him. In fact, it stops precisely at the point where justice *should* be done so that King David has to resolve the matter himself. It is an excellent rhetorical strategy with which David complies most forcefully!

> David burned with anger against the man and said to Nathan, 'As surely as the LORD lives, *the man* who did this deserves to die! He must pay for that lamb four times over, because he did such a thing and had no pity' (2 Sam 12.5–6).

Suddenly David is on his feet in a rage, emotions bubbling to the surface as he demands the identity of *the man* responsible.

In that moment the prophet swaps indirect for direct speech: 'You are *the man!*' (2 Sam 12.7a)

As the truth strikes home, King David collapses back into his throne. In light of God's desire for all people to be drawn to him via Israel, David's reckless morals have caused a disaster of the worst kind: the shaming of God's name (2 Sam 12.14). David has not simply broken some arbitrary rules; he has disturbed the forward momentum of God's story by turning Yahweh's holy nation into a 'laughing-stock' (see Exod 32.25). Therefore, Nathan's prophetic speech pushes past the king's Law-breaking (coveting, adultery, murder, self-idolization) to the paramount importance of Israel's moral witness as Yahweh's counter-community. Like Samuel in the previous chapter, Nathan wants *more* than obedience from the king; he hopes to (re)turn David's heart Godward (see 'Heart Reorientation' in chapter 4), and the events that follow achieve just that.

David can count his lucky stars that God does not force his kingly judgement back upon him: 'The man who did this deserves to die!' In fact, Nathan assures David almost immediately, 'The LORD has taken away your sin. You are not going to die' (2 Sam 12.13). This is not to say, however, that the punishment of death is avoided entirely. Nathan is, on this occasion, the bearer of bad tidings: 'The son born to you will die' (2 Sam 12.14b).

God's verdict seems so final that we are compelled to ask why there is such a long hiatus between the giving of God's word and its fulfilment. It seems cruel that David should go on fasting for seven days before the baby's final breath. However, as we have seen, God's initial judgements are not always final (see 'Persuading God' in chapter 2), and it is possible that David's prayers will lead to the baby's life being spared. Another possibility is that the delayed death of the child is precisely what sustains David's state of fasting and prayer so that God may bring about a transformation in him. David does not get what he asks for, but he is answered in accordance with God's wisdom like other biblical pray-ers (see 'Engaging God' in chapter 2). 'The "answer" to David's prayer is his rehabilitation into a person capable of humble prayer before God.'[8] This, after all, is what God desires from us when we rebel against him; 'a broken and contrite heart' (Ps 51.17).

David fully acknowledges and confesses his sin (2 Sam 12.13; Ps 51.7–14). He prays for mercy and accepts the consequences God has decided upon (2 Sam 12.22–23). There is no tugging at Nathan's robes, no lingering or self-pity. To his credit, David moves beyond the construction of stories that excuse his poor decisions and gets on with *living* a story that is consistent with what God is doing in the world. Strangely but surely, it is often failure that redirects us most powerfully towards what is true and right.

A final prophetic word of mercy, however, is still available to the grieving king. Through Nathan, God places a special call upon the next son born to David and Bathsheba:

> Then David comforted his wife Bathsheba, and he went to her and lay with her. She gave birth to a son, and they named him Solomon. The LORD loved him; and because the LORD loved him,

he sent word through Nathan the prophet to name him Jedidiah [Loved-by-the-LORD] (2 Sam 12.24–25).

Only at this point does the narrator stop referring to Bathsheba as 'the wife of Uriah' (2 Sam 11.3,26; 12.10,15; also Mt 1.6) and for the first time calls her the wife of David. No reason is given for Yahweh's special favour upon this child, but Nathan is sent to rename him and presumably to inform Solomon's parents of God's special purposes for the boy. The narrator's comment concerning Yahweh's love for the child 'simply maintains space in which Solomon can become a prince and then a king. Taken as dynastic theology, which it surely is, this affirms Yahweh's commitment to the dynasty and leads directly to I Kings 1:20.'[9] If we are left pondering the significance of the name Jedidiah (Loved-by-the-LORD), we need only turn to 1 Kings 1, where the same four characters come together again, and the significance of Solomon's renaming becomes evident.

Leading (with) Questions (1 Kings 1)

The books of Kings open with two brief characterizations: an aged King David and a resourceful Adonijah. Iain Provan has articulated the sense of the opening verses well:

> Here is a very beautiful girl. The David of old has not shown himself to be impervious to such women's charms . . . [Abigail in 1 Sam 25.3; Bathsheba in 2 Sam 11.2] he had been known to take great trouble to possess a woman he desired. Yet now, with Abishag in bed beside him and fully available to him, we are told that **the king had no intimate relations with her**. The king is, to coin a phrase, 'past it'; he is impotent, and Adonijah sees his chance to gain power. That is the significance of the immediate juxtaposition in verses 4 and 5 of **the king had no intimate relations with her** and **Now Adonijah . . . said, 'I will be king.'** The one event (or non-event) leads to the other.[10]

David's fourth-born son, Adonijah, wants the throne for himself and David has done nothing (so far) to prevent it. And this is not the first time King David has demonstrated weakness in managing his family. Years after his affair with Bathsheba, David failed to manage his sons when Absalom killed Amnon for raping his half-sister, Tamar. Absalom then tried to take his father's throne, only to end up dead at the hands of Joab. Now it is Adonijah who wishes to usurp the throne (and who will also end up dead at his brother's command). King David's family tree is riddled with dysfunctional strife, and it is a tree with many branches.[11]

1 Kings 1.5–10 highlights the power already in Adonijah's hands as he reaches for his father's crown:

- Adonijah is determined: 'I will be king' (v. 5).
- Adonijah has 'chariots and horses'[12] and a personal guard (v. 5).
- Adonijah has not been challenged by his father about his behaviour (v. 6).
- Adonijah is handsome and was born after Absalom (v. 6). These details invite comparison between these two good-looking, wayward sons of David who both sought their father's throne.
- Adonijah's order of birth ('after Absalom') suggests his right as successor to the throne.[13]
- Adonijah has a powerful military alliance in Joab, Israel's army general (v. 7).

The details may seem rather disjointed, but they all serve to make one thing clear; the odds are stacked in Adonijah's favour. David is on his way out and Adonijah seems full of kingly potential. Indeed, why shouldn't he be king? The story revolves around this question, and it is one to which we will return in due course. But for now we must take our cues from the narrator, who proceeds to introduce Nathan as the mover-and-shaker in this story. David may be senile and Adonijah ambitious, but the arrogant would-be king's biggest mistake is that he 'did not invite Nathan the prophet' to his mutinous get-together (1 Kgs 1.10). Both factions include a priest and a military leader, but military power (the pride of kings) will not be enough for Adonijah's coup to succeed, for it is Yahweh's prophets who turn the tables, and the only prophet mentioned is on David's side.

So, with the scene set, the action (almost entirely verbal action in this chapter) commences in 1 Kings 1.11. Nathan has a double-edged message for the king. He wishes to draw David's attention to Adonijah's coup while at the same time prompting the king to publicly identify Solomon as his heir. As before, Nathan does not burst into the throne room with a barrage of caustic accusations, condemning King David's carelessness or ignorance. But neither does he come equipped with a parable. On this occasion Nathan plans to ask a series of leading questions in a sort of dramatic presentation before the king.[14]

Nathan's strongest potential ally is Solomon's mother, Bathsheba, so he begins by raising her stakes in the family feud.

> Then Nathan asked Bathsheba, Solomon's mother, 'Have you not heard that Adonijah, the son of Haggith, has become king without our lord David's knowing it?' (1 Kgs 1.11)

A straightforward question? Well, not really.

First, Nathan implies that Adonijah's coronation has already occurred, increasing the urgency of the matter. Second, he mentions Adonijah's mother Haggith by name (another of David's many wives) since that is likely to provoke a response from Bathsheba, who is, as the narrator makes explicit, 'Solomon's mother'. And third, Nathan does not wait for an answer to his question, but proceeds to warn Bathsheba of the imminent danger of her situation, for which he (of course) has a solution. 'Now then, let me advise you how you can save your own life and the life of your son Solomon' (1 Kgs 1.12).

This is a man skilled in using words to his advantage, and it is hardly surprising that Nathan's plan to save Bathsheba and Solomon consists almost entirely of more timely and suggestive words. The plan is that Bathsheba will speak for Nathan, at least until the prophet can make his own timely entrance to 'fill up'[15] her words (1 Kgs 1.14). Bathsheba's twofold task consists of reminding the king of his oath[16] and alerting him of his rival. Therefore, these are the questions Bathsheba is instructed to put to King David:

> My lord the king, did you not swear to me your servant: 'Surely Solomon your son shall be king after me, and he will sit on my throne'?

Why then has Adonijah become king? (1 Kgs 1.13)

Whether Bathsheba lacks Nathan's tact or whether she chooses to
speak more directly as the queen, both of Nathan's questions are
turned to *statements* in her mouth (1 Kgs 1.17–18). To her credit,
though, Bathsheba adds some spice of her own, reminding David
that 'the eyes of all Israel' are watching and that Solomon and his
mother will be treated as outcasts (literally 'sinners') if Adonijah
gets his way (1 Kgs 1.20–21). As they are speaking, Nathan
arrives on cue to expand on Bathsheba's intimations with two
further questions of his own, which are notably more direct. (He
evidently feels safer chiding the king now that Bathsheba has
broken the ice.)

> Nathan said, 'Have you, my lord the king, declared that Adonijah
> shall be king after you, and that he will sit on your throne?' (1 Kgs
> 1.24)

> Is this something my lord the king has done without letting his
> servants know who should sit on the throne of my lord the king
> after him? (1 Kgs 1.27)

Obviously, the real reason David hasn't notified his advisors of
any changes is because he is completely *unaware* of Adonijah's
coup. Or at least, he was unaware. But now, speaking for the first
time in the story, David-the-man-of-action takes the reins again,
reiterating his oath to Bathsheba and ordering Solomon's coronation (1 Kgs 1.28–35). Once again, Nathan's persuasive rhetoric
has won the day.[18]

Poets of Persuasion

Through the clever orchestration of his prophets, God's will is
done on earth as it is in heaven. Nathan's prophetic modes of
speech summon artists, actors, preachers and poets the world
over to recognize their potential for destabilizing oppressive
power through the 'art of indirection.'[19] Each of Nathan's interactions with the king *raises awareness* by various means: in 2 Samuel

7, direct speech is sufficient; in 2 Samuel 12, the unmasking of David's idolatry requires a subversive story; and in 1 Kings 1 the old king's state of oblivion calls for acute and timely rhetorical questions. For those who feel compelled (called) to open ears to the whisperings of God's Spirit, a few lessons may be drawn from Nathan's prophetic speech.

First, Nathan's creative use of a parable to 'say it sideways' suggests that propositional statements are not always an appropriate or effective mode of communication. By the same token, reading biblical stories with the goal of extracting their 'main points' can be a valuable exercise, but it is at great cost that rich, storied ideas are melted down into snappy statements so that we may moralize from them. Narratives are powerful precisely because 'the story is the meaning',[20] and when so-called timeless truths are extracted from the vibrant contexts that supply their potency, too much dies in the process.

Second, questions should be permitted to linger unresolved. While it is generally good practice to open a sermon/drama/lecture/song with a question that hooks the audience and draws them into a shared experience of discovery,[21] preachers/actors/teachers/musicians must resist the temptation to then answer such questions too quickly—if at all. Questions remain potent only until they are shut down with an answer. Resolving the tension of *ignorance* is one thing (i.e. filling gaps with knowledge), but the tension of *obedience* is not something a preacher can ever resolve for a congregation. So when addressing the rift between belief and behaviour, create an itch but don't scratch it. Those with ears to hear must do that for themselves.

In our contemporary context, preaching is arguably the task most like that of the prophets. A preacher's role must never be taken lightly, for when she stands with Bible open, whether before a handful or stadium-full of people, she does not speak *about* God's word; she speaks God's word. Moreover, she speaks God's word in a particular moment of history to a particular group of people, and heaven help any preacher who hasn't asked God what *he* would like to say in that moment! While we are on the subject, two creative explorations of the preaching task I heartily recommend are Frederick Buechner's *Telling the Truth: The Gospel as Tragedy, Comedy and Fairy Tale* and Walter

Brueggemann's *Finally Comes the Poet: Daring Speech for Proclamation.*

Musicians, painters, sculptors, dramatists, and authors need encouragement if they are to become God's faithful poets of persuasion, communicating through poetry and parable, rhythm and rhyme, story and song. For *God's* sake, creativity must find its feet in the church, for 'it is the vocation of the prophet to keep alive the ministry of imagination, to keep on conjuring and proposing futures'.[22]

> Tell all the Truth but tell it slant—
> Success in Circuit lies
> Too bright for our infirm Delight
> The Truth's superb surprise
> As Lightning to the Children eased
> With explanation kind
> The Truth must dazzle gradually
> Or every man be blind—[23]

Dig Deeper

■ When have you been treated with hostility as the bearer of bad news?

■ In your opinion, which is worse: David's adultery or his attempts to cover it up? Why?

■ What makes a parable such a powerful mode of communication?

■ What does Proverbs 18.17 suggest about the power of a good question?

■ How might your speech be adjusted so as to be more glorifying to God?

6

Prophetic Judgement: Give and Take

AHIJAH

See, today I appoint you over nations and kingdoms
to uproot and tear down,
to destroy and overthrow,
to build and to plant (Jer. 1.10).

```
1 Kings 11 – 14
```

Torn Robes and Tarnished Crowns (1 Kings 11.1–28)

Measured by worldly standards (sex, power and wealth), Solomon was an impressive success story. Under his governance Israel well and truly satiated her desire to become 'like the other nations', but the shine and gleam of Solomon's kingdom was borne on the backs of slaves. 1 Kings 9.15–21 describes how Solomon used Amorites, Hittites, Perizzites, Hivites and Jebusites as the forced labour for his various building projects. His oppression of other nations was reminiscent of Israel's own oppression under Pharaoh, even in spite of God's clear command, 'Do not oppress an alien; you yourselves know how it feels to be aliens, because you were aliens in Egypt' (Exod 23.9).

Solomon sought to build Israel's wealth and power in gold and chariots, as Sisera and other non-Israelite rulers had done (1 Kgs 10.26).[1] But as Israel's mission became gradually subverted by the lures of royal power, the nation grew up into the bully she had once been mercifully delivered from.[2] Worse still, Solomon defiled the purity of God's covenant people by building places of worship for the gods of his foreign wives (1 Kgs 11.7–8). The wayward king was fast realizing Samuel's ominous prophecies (see 1 Sam 8.11–18) and it was only a matter of time before the kingship would be torn away from Solomon—an inevitably messy business, the business of prophets.

During the period of the judges, Israel's true King had destabilized his people when they became insubordinate, and Solomon's insolence was treated in much the same way. In keeping with the promises of 2 Samuel 7.12–14, Yahweh raised up three adversaries ('the rod of men') to discipline Solomon ('my son'): Hadad the Edomite, Rezon of Zobah, and Jeroboam, one of Solomon's own officials (1 Kgs 11.14–27). God's intentions are scripted by the narrator before they are played out 'on the stage' so that even before a prophet arrives on the scene we are already privy to God's verdict.

> So the LORD said to Solomon, 'Since this is your attitude and you have not kept my covenant and my decrees, which I commanded you, I will most certainly *tear* the kingdom away from you and give it to one of your subordinates. Nevertheless, for the sake of David your father, I will not do it during your lifetime. I will *tear* it out of the hand of your son. Yet I will not *tear* the whole kingdom from him, but will give him one tribe for the sake of David my servant and for the sake of Jerusalem, which I have chosen' (1 Kgs 11.11–13).

The mention of 'tearing' in relation to kingship is deliberately reminiscent of Saul's unhappy encounter with Samuel (see 'Prophet vs King' in chapter 4). But even after Samuel's torn robe had provided an apt image for the ruined kingship, Saul had tried desperately to retain the crown. Years later, as Saul was pursuing David in the Desert of En Gedi, an interesting turn of events took place near the Crags of the Wild Goats (1 Sam 24).

As fortune would have it, King Saul had decided to relieve himself inside the very same cave where David and his men were hiding, providing an opportunity for David that his companions saw as an obvious gift from God. But despite their encouragement to take advantage of Saul's vulnerability and to 'deal' with him (1 Sam 24.4), the young fugitive secretly cut a corner from Saul's royal robe instead. In light of the parallel already established between the kingdom and a robe, David's action was significant.

Almost immediately, however, stricken by guilt, David followed Saul out of the cave and confessed in broad daylight what he had done. Impressed and humbled by David's mercy, Saul acknowledged that David was indeed destined to be crowned Israel's king, and as they parted ways he asked only that David would not also 'cut off' (the same word used in 1 Sam 24.4–5) Saul's family line when he did take the throne. Even Saul was eventually able to accept that the robe/kingdom was in David's hands because Yahweh had ordained it.

So, with the image of tearing fresh in our minds, let us turn our attention to a prophet named Ahijah, as he sets out to meet Jeroboam with a new cloak[3] on his back.

Giving (1 Kings 11.29–43)

It was not unusual for prophets to act before they spoke. Enacted parables were a powerful means of communication (to be explored more fully in chapter 10) that generally used a prop of some kind to reinforce a prophet's verbal message. The analogy between the twelve pieces of Ahijah's torn cloak and the twelve tribes of Israel speaks largely for itself as Jeroboam is handed ten pieces of the cloak and told that he will rule over most of Israel (1 Kgs 11.29–32).[4] God's judgement on Solomon is then articulated by Ahijah, whose speech plays on the verbs 'give' and 'take'.

> **Take** [*laqach*] ten pieces for yourself, for this is what the LORD, the God of Israel, says: 'See, I am going to tear the kingdom out of Solomon's hand and **give** [*natan*] you ten tribes . . .
>
> But I will not **take** [*laqach*] the whole kingdom out of Solomon's hand; I have made him ruler all the days of his life for the sake of David my servant, whom I chose and who observed my commands and statutes. I will **take** [*laqach*] the kingdom from his son's hands and **give** [*natan*] you ten tribes. I will **give** [*natan*] one tribe to his son so that David my servant may always have a lamp before me in

Jerusalem, the city where I chose to put my Name. However, as for you, I will **take** [*laqach*] you, and you will rule over all that your heart desires; you will be king over Israel' (1 Kgs 11.31,34–37).

The numerous references to David in 1 Kings 11 (fifteen in total) signal the extraordinary generosity of God's offer to Jeroboam,[5] but Yahweh's taking from Solomon should not be understood as an unconditional giving to Jeroboam.

> **If** you do whatever I command you and walk in my ways and do what is right in my eyes by keeping my statutes and commands, as David my servant did, **[then]** I will be with you. **[Then]** I will build you a dynasty as enduring as the one I built for David and will give Israel to you (1 Kgs 11.38).

The offer of God's presence, a dynasty like David's and the governance of Israel renders Jeroboam speechless (Ahijah does all the talking during their encounter), but the grandeur of these magnificent promises all rests on the little word 'if' (or the equally small Hebrew word '*im*). Without rigorous obedience to God's commands, the offer would be retracted, just as it had been from Saul and Solomon.

In light of such divine generosity, we are compelled to ask, what makes this Jeroboam fellow worthy of such extravagant promises? When the kingship passed from Saul to David we were informed of David's worth through a number of stories that characterized him in a positive light. David was a talented musician who ministered to Saul in his torment (1 Sam 16.23); he slew the champion Goliath (1 Sam 17); and he led Saul's armies to victory again and again with Yahweh's blessing (1 Sam 18). But of Jeroboam we know very little. He was an Ephraimite whose father had passed away, leaving his mother a widow (1 Kgs 11.26). We have been informed that 'Jeroboam was a man of standing, and when Solomon saw how well the young man did his work, he put him in charge of the whole labour force of the house of Joseph' (1 Kgs 11.28), but that's it. No impressive tales of heroism precede God's generous offer.

It may come as a surprise, but many of those entrusted with great responsibility in the Bible were not required to prove themselves first. Indeed, these chapters about Jeroboam's rule and Ahijah's prophetic judgements demonstrate that nothing is certain; God *trusts* and *hopes* in the decisions of his human partners. There are no guarantees that those who try on the kingly crown will not leave it tarnished. Solomon was trusted and he failed; now Jeroboam will have his chance. But before we can discover how Jeroboam will respond to the prophet's generous oracle, the narrative diverts our attention to Solomon's son, Rehoboam (1 Kgs 11.43).

Fools for Kings (1 Kings 12)

In Shechem, where Rehoboam was to be anointed king, 'all the Israelites' had gathered to plead that he would not treat the nation as harshly as his father had done. It was no secret that Solomon's grand achievements had come at great cost (1 Kgs 5.13), and if the tribes of Israel were going to maintain fidelity to his heir, they wanted assurance that Solomon's taxes and forced labour would become things of the past. Rehoboam requested three days to seek counsel before responding, during which time he consulted two groups of people, one old and one young.

The advice of the elders (who had previously offered counsel to Solomon) was sound; Serve them today and they will serve you forever (1 Kgs 12.7). But Rehoboam lacked his father's wisdom. Disregarding the voice of experience, he decided instead to commence his rule with menacing threats, according to the foolish counsel of youth.

> My little finger is thicker than my father's waist.[6] My father laid on you a heavy yoke; I will make it even heavier. My father scourged you with whips; I will scourge you with scorpions (1 Kgs 12.10b–11).

Rehoboam is a fool. One commentator has gone so far as to call him 'harsh, despotic, and autocratic . . . stupid and incompetent . . . a weak and fragile personality . . . cowardly and indecisive',[7] and his subjects were inclined to agree! In fact, upon hearing Rehoboam's threats, they immediately revolted against the house of David by making Jeroboam king—in accordance with the will and word of God.

Having been ousted, Rehoboam immediately mustered 180,000 fighting men from the two tribes at his disposal in order to regain a hold on the other ten. But since his intentions were inconsistent with God's expressed will (1 Kgs 12.16–20), prophetic intervention was to be expected. Sure enough, Shemaiah the man of God arrived soon afterwards to defer the war between north and south and to inform Israel of God's purposes: 'Do not go up to fight against your brothers, the Israelites. Go home, every one of you, for this is my doing' (1 Kgs 12.24). According to 2 Chronicles 12.15b, 'There was continual warfare between Rehoboam and Jeroboam', but in this instance at least, civil war was delayed by Shemaiah's intervention.

Having characterized Rehoboam as a fool, the narrative
returns to Israel's newly
appointed King Jeroboam, who
is already feeling anxious about
losing subjects to Rehoboam.
Despite his appointment as
king over ten of Israel's tribes,
Jeroboam had been cut off from
Jerusalem (in Judah) where the
nation's temple-worship was
based, and this had set him
thinking.

Jeroboam thought to him-
self,[8] 'The kingdom will now
likely revert to the house of
David. If these people go up
to offer sacrifices at the temple of the LORD in Jerusalem,
they will again give their
allegiance to their lord, Rehoboam king of Judah. They will kill me and return to King Rehoboam.'

After seeking advice, the king made two golden calves. He said to the people, 'It is too much for you to go up to Jerusalem. Here are your gods, O Israel, who brought you up out of Egypt.' One he set up in Bethel, and the other in Dan (1 Kgs 12.26–29).

Like Rehoboam, Jeroboam received foolish advice, and like Rehoboam, he followed it. Jeroboam's golden calves, reminiscent of Israel's first act of idolatry (Exod 32),[8] were set up in strategic positions in the far north of Israel (Dan) and in the south near Judah's border (Shiloh) so that Israelites heading south to worship in Jerusalem would be tempted to cut their journey short and go only as far as Shiloh.

'It is too much for you to go up to Jerusalem,' says the king, 'Here are your gods . . .' (1 Kgs 12.28). His intention was to keep people away from the Jerusalem temple where he feared their allegiance would return to Rehoboam, but his priority was clearly something other than the glory of God.

In this way Israel's newly appointed king commenced his rule by establishing his own religion. Jeroboam cut himself off from the Mosaic covenant (which Yahweh commanded him to follow in 1 Kgs 11.38) by setting up two images of golden calves and appointing as priests anyone who wanted the job, completely disregarding God's appointment of a Levitical priesthood. Twice the narrator states that Jeroboam instituted a religious festival day on 15 August, a time 'of his own choosing', and that he himself made sacrifices to the golden calves (1 Kgs 12.32–33). Jeroboam's cultus would be long remembered for enticing Israel away from following the LORD (2 Kgs 17.21). The number of contradictions between the Deuteronomic Law and Jeroboam's actions speaks largely for itself.[10]

By the end of 1 Kings 12, it is clear that *both* the newly divided kingdoms rested on shaky foundations. Rehoboam had provoked rebellion from the outset with talk of 'scourging the people with scorpions', and Jeroboam had turned his back on the Law, the very heart of Israel's national identity. But whatever questions we may have about the fate of Jeroboam must be postponed until after the dramatic interlude of 1 Kings 13.

Torah commands (Deuteronomy)	Jeroboam's actions (1 Kings 12)
Isralites must keep the Torah in their heart (6.5–6)	Jeroboam decides in his heart to break the Torah (v. 26)[11]
Israel's king must obey the law to 'reign a long time over his kingdom' (17.18–20)	Jeroboam breaks the law in order to extend his reign (v. 38)
Yahweh alone is God, who brought Israel out of Egypt (5.6–8)	Jeroboam credits false gods with Israel's salvation from Egypt (v. 28)
Go (only) to Jerusalem to celebrate your festivals (16.5–6,11,15	Jeroboam establishes new sanctuaries in Bethel and Dan (vv. 29–30,33)
Only Levites were to serve as priests (18.5)	Jeroboam 'appointed priests from all sorts of people, even though they were not Levites' (v. 31)
Israel was to follow Yahweh's specific times and dates for festivals (16.1–17)	Jeroboam creates his own festival 'like the festival held in Judah' during 'a month of his choosing' (vv. 32–33)

A Tale of Two Prophets (1 Kings 13)

As the curtain rises on the next act, Jeroboam is standing by an altar of his own creation. He is about to make an unlawful sacrifice when a spotlight singles out a prophet who has appeared uninvited on the other side of the stage. The man of God does not address the king, but rather prophesies against the *altar*, the false system of worship Jeroboam has invented. The judgement is verified by the splitting (literally 'tearing') of the altar and the anonymous prophet goes on to prophesy about a future king named Josiah, an

oracle which will also be verified in due course by the destruction
of similar altars (2 Kgs 23.5,12–14). In contrast to Jeroboam, who
has managed to bury the Law and guaranteed Israel's fall, Josiah
will resurrect the Law and rid the nation of Jeroboam's false priests
by sacrificing *them* on these illegitimate altars!

The words are an affront to Jeroboam's royal power, with
which he attempts to seize the unwelcome intruder. But the out-
stretched hand of the king immediately coils back useless, evidence that the prophet represents an even greater power. Even so,
Jeroboam shows no sign of repentance. Instead, he asks the
prophet to intercede for his withered hand and invites him to the
royal palace for lunch. (No doubt, he would like to have this kind
of power onside.) But the unnamed prophet will have none of the
king's hospitality. He resists the invitation outright and reveals
for the first time that he is subject to a threefold commandment
from God: 'You must not eat bread or drink water or return by
the way you came' (1 Kgs 13.9).

For our purposes, the unusual details of the command are less
important than the fact that rigid obedience is expected of the
man of God from Judah. And so far, so good; he has faithfully
delivered God's word and resisted the king's invitation to wine
and dine. As the lights dim and the prophet vanishes from sight,
we catch a parting glimpse of the bewildered king, flexing his
revitalized fingers and staring blankly at the mess of stone and
ash on the floor.

Scene two opens with the anonymous prophet making his way
back to Judah by a different route, in accordance with Yahweh's
command. But as he travels (slowly across the rear of the stage), the
plot begins to thicken as an older prophet from Bethel takes the
spotlight. Having received news of the king's encounter from his
sons, the intrigued prophet saddles his donkey and sets off in
search of the man of God until he finds him sitting under a tree (not
having his lunch). The narrator does not say why, but the older
prophet has his heart set on testing the man of God from Judah.

Just as the king had done, the prophet from Bethel invites the
man of God home for lunch, but again he holds fast to God's
commandment. However, when the older prophet goes a step
further, claiming to be the herald of a contradictory word from
God, then comes the downfall of the man of God from Judah.

So the prophet said to him, 'Come home with me and **eat**.'

The man of God said, 'I cannot **turn back** and go with you, nor can **I eat bread** or **drink water** with you in this place. I have been told by the word of the LORD: "You must not **eat bread** or **drink water** there or **return** by the way you came."'

The old prophet answered, 'I too am a prophet, as you are. And an angel said to me by the word of the LORD: "**Bring him back** with you to your house so that he may **eat bread** and **drink water**."' (But he was lying to him.) So the man of God **returned** with him and **ate** and **drank** in his house (1 Kgs 13.15–19).

Note the monotonous repetition of the threefold commandment, which is fully broken as the younger prophet returns, eats, and drinks with the elder prophet. It is ironic that the man of God from Judah repeats the command verbatim in verse 16 and yet proceeds to violate every part of it in verse 19. Mind you, the only reason the audience knows of the elder prophet's ruse is because the narrator has cupped his hand toward us and whispered, 'But he was lying to him.'

As the man of God turns (*shuv*), thereby breaking God's commandment, the story also reaches its turning point. 'While they were sitting at the table, the word of the LORD came to the old prophet who had brought him back' (1 Kgs 13.20). This time with a genuine word of prophecy, the older prophet pronounces judgement on the man of God for being so easily duped. The Judean prophet saddles up to leave (no doubt, there was some awkwardness between them) and is promptly met by a lion who kills him, throws his body onto the road and then casually stands by as if to draw attention to the scene. As reports of a lion and donkey standing side by side over a dead prophet quickly become the talk of the town, the prophet from Bethel forms his own conclusions.

It is the man of God who defied the word of the LORD. The LORD has given him over to the lion, which has mauled him and killed him, as the word of the LORD had warned him (1 Kgs 13.26).

To the old prophet at least, the bizarre sequence of events makes some sense. But they have a wider significance as well. Within Israel's overarching narrative, 'the story assumes that there is a special seriousness about this failure at such a crucial moment in the [bigger] story, a moment where black and white have to be seen as such and when the man of God has let them become muddied.'[12] Prophets do not get off scot-free just because they are God's harbingers of judgement.

However, the moral of the story appears to have been directed at Jeroboam. Before the final curtain falls, the narrator makes one last comment about how the whole strange ordeal, somehow intended for the king's benefit, has made no impact whatsoever on him. 'Even after this, Jeroboam did not change [*shuv*] his evil ways' (1 Kgs 13.33). Both Jeroboam and the anonymous prophet failed to uphold God's commands, and as a consequence they would share the same fate; neither of them would be buried with dignity in the tombs of their fathers (1 Kgs 13.22; 14.13).

Taking (1 Kings 14)

Many years after Ahijah's initial encounter with Jeroboam, the prophet again received a word from God for Jeroboam. In his old age Ahijah had lost his sight, and Jeroboam knew (well and truly by now) that he held favour with neither Yahweh nor his prophet. Unwilling to face Ahijah himself, Jeroboam had sent his wife in disguise to ask about the fate of their ill son, whose name—to keep readers alert—was Abijah. Jeroboam hoped to harness Ahijah's foreknowledge through deception, but as things turned out, Jeroboam's wife was unable to get a word in edgeways. The blind prophet saw through her falsehood before she was even at the door, and to really rub it in, he began by stating that he was the one who had been sent!

> When Ahijah heard the sound of her footsteps at the door, he said, 'Come in, wife of Jeroboam. Why this pretence? I have been sent to you with bad news' (1 Kgs 14.6).

The queen most likely assumed that Ahijah was referring to 'bad news' about her son, but it soon became apparent that God wished to address more than just the health of Jeroboam's heir. In the prophecy that followed, the queen got much more than she bargained for. God evidently had a number of things to say.

- I gave Jeroboam a unique and wonderful opportunity, and he ruined it (vv. 7–9).
- Jeroboam has done so much evil during his reign that I will treat him and his family like excrement (vv. 10–11).[13] I am taking back what was offered because he is completely unworthy.
- As for your sick son, he will also die (vv. 12–13).
- What's more, Israel's future is also ruined because of the sins Jeroboam has caused her to commit. In time she will lose her promised land and be exiled to Assyria ('beyond the Euphrates'; vv. 15–16 NRSV).

Yahweh judged Jeroboam by *taking* everything from him: his son, his crown, his family line and even the future security of the nation. But it was not a judgement that came without warning, for both of Ahijah's prophecies identified the fulcrum upon which Jeroboam's future rested.

> If you do whatever I command you and walk in my ways and do what is right in my eyes by keeping my statutes and **commands** [*mitzvoth*], as David my servant did, I will be with you. I will build you a dynasty as enduring as the one I built for David and will give Israel to you (1 Kgs 11.38).

> I tore the kingdom away from the house of David and gave it to you, but you have not been like my servant David, who kept my **commands** [*mitzvoth*] and followed me with all his heart, doing only what was right in my eyes (1 Kgs 14.8).

Obedience (like that of David) was the means by which Jeroboam could either receive or dismiss the opportunity offered him. Throughout the rest of the books of Kings, 'the sins of Jeroboam . . . which he caused Israel to commit' is cited again and again (more than twenty times) as a measure of idolatry.[14] 'No other king is so strenuously distanced from the principles of the prophetic tradition, the theological standards of Israelite covenantal identity, or the inherent grace of the Davidic house . . . Solomon made mistakes, but Jeroboam turned them into catastrophes.'[15]

1 Kings 11–14 is not about a bad king having his falsehood brought to light and getting his just desserts. It is about a king who had a real chance at something—and blew it. The opportunity to rule as David had done was a completely genuine offer on God's behalf, but a series of bad choices cut Jeroboam off from what his future might have entailed. The same was true for the man of God from Judah. He was not a false prophet to begin with, but one who *became* false through disobedience.

In a related discussion, Walter Moberly cites Jacob as a prime example of the biblical pattern whereby 'God chooses a people, and calls particular persons, irrespective of their moral quality at the time of God's initiative.'[16] Both Saul and David were chosen by God to be kings. Their selection in itself did not guarantee success but meant only that God was willing to trust them with great responsibility. Similarly, the extraordinary gift placed in Jeroboam's hands reveals the extent to which God puts his faith in human partners. He offers everything (as a gracious gift) and expects everything in return (in grateful obedience). It is precisely because God has pinned his hopes on us that he insists on our full cooperation (see Lk 12.42–48). These chapters, therefore, recall a devastating moment in Israel's history, when Jeroboam's choices had a critical impact on God's design.

Moreover, at the heart of this story of give and take is a solemn warning to those who would take it upon themselves to proclaim God's judgement on his behalf. 1 Kings 13 begins with King Jeroboam and the man of God from Judah standing in opposition to one another, but ends with the 'downfall' and 'destruction' of them both (1 Kgs 13.34).[17] Deviation from the word of God has disastrous consequences not just for kings, but for prophets too, and in the telling of such tales, for Israel, for the church, for you and for me.

Dig Deeper

- Why do you think Yahweh delivers judgement through his prophets?

- Why might the verb 'to turn' be a keyword in these chapters about prophetic judgement?

- How does the story of the two prophets (1 Kings 13) fit within the wider literary context of 1 Kings 11 - 14?

- Why do you think God's judgement on Jeroboam was so harsh? (1 Kings 14.7-16)

- Why did God entrust his kingdom into the hands of men like Saul and Jeroboam, as well as to good kings like David?

7

Prophetic Faith: Making Space for God

ELIJAH

Trust in the Lord with all your heart
and lean not on your own understanding (Prov 3.5).

---
1 Kings 18 – 19

There Is No Other

Which god? Whose god? Your god or our God?

As a monotheistic nation living in a polytheistic world, Israel was often tempted to honour other gods, such as Baal-Zebub of Ekron (2 Kgs 1) or the Queen of Heaven (Jer 44), to cite two examples. And yet, the most common response to the notion of other gods in the prophetic books of the Bible is an outright denial of their legitimacy. The Bible is emphatic. There is one true God (Deut 6.4); all others are impostors, mere fabrications of human minds.

However, this is not to say that false gods may be dismissed with a wave of the hand. Whether people put their hope in wealth, a carved statue, karma, technology, Asherah poles, sexual gratification, intellect, superstitious beliefs or golden calves, such things are not ultimately classed as 'gods' because they are powerful to act or capable of love, but because they pose a genuine threat to God's rightful place in our lives. False gods are powerless to release us from the guilt that eats at our souls, powerless to help us overcome cycles of destructive behaviour, and powerless to shape us into what we were created to become, but they have put up a solid battle for human allegiance for thousands of years, and are not about to lay down their arms. That is why the Bible treats them with utmost seriousness even whilst ridiculing their claims. The psalmist Asaph, for instance, paradoxically affirms the uniqueness of Israel's God even as One who takes his place 'in the midst of the gods' (Ps 82.1 NRSV).

> God presides in the great assembly;
>> he gives judgement among the 'gods':[1]
>
> 'How long will you defend the unjust
>> and show partiality to the wicked?
>>> *Selah*
> Defend the cause of the weak and fatherless;
>> maintain the rights of the poor and oppressed.
> Rescue the weak and needy;
>> deliver them from the hand of the wicked' (Ps 82.1–4).

The psalm implies a context where the earth has been crying out against 'the gods' because the oppressed get no justice or relief. Yahweh's presence in such an assembly is not surprising in itself,[2] but on this particular occasion 'God has stood up to judge the assembled.'[3] The cries of humanity have reached Yahweh's ears, and in response he turns in judgement on those who have been trusted to uphold justice. Yahweh 'stands up'[4] as plaintiff to challenge these other gods who are giving divinity a bad name, for gods who cannot maintain equality and justice are no gods at all. Yahweh's verdict is that these so-called gods 'will die like mere men' and 'fall like every other ruler' (Ps 82.6–7); the psalmist's verdict (or plea) is that God must arise to preserve justice on earth, since he alone is worthy of the task (Ps 82.8).

By speaking of an assembly of gods, the psalmist is not suggesting that Yahweh is on par with other contenders for the thrones of human hearts. Nor is he saying that Yahweh should be seen as the most powerful in a pantheon of gods, like Zeus to the Greeks or Jupiter to the Romans. Rather, Asaph emphasizes Yahweh's unique, divine status by comparing him with unjust and incompetent alternatives.

A similar scene is depicted in Isaiah 41.21–24, where Yahweh's prophet takes the stand in an imaginary courtroom to speak against false idols that vie for Israel's devotion. Where's your proof? God's representative shouts at the defendant (an idol) before an Israelite jury, Present us with some sort of evidence to support your claim to be a god. Tell us about the past! Or tell us about the future! Do *anything* to persuade us that you are real!

But there is only silence. The idol does not—*cannot*—answer.

In response to the idol's empty gaze, the prophet-lawyer turns in disgust, throwing his hands in the air. I knew it! he cries. You are *nothing*! And those who put faith in you are equally false. Yahweh's prophet returns to his seat, even as his words continue to ring in the ears of the jury, the ones whose verdict ultimately matters.

From Egypt to Canaan, Israel failed to honour Yahweh as the one true God. In Gideon's day they adopted the practices of the Canaanites, erecting Asherah[5] poles and constructing altars to Baal[6] (Jdg 6.25–28), and with the institution of the monarchy Israel's kings continued to lead the nation astray. But if we thought, after Jeroboam's shenanigans in the previous chapter, that Israel's kings could not get any worse, Ahab proves us wrong.

> Ahab son of Omri did more evil in the eyes of the LORD than any of those before him. He not only considered it trivial to commit the sins of Jeroboam son of Nebat, but he also married Jezebel daughter of Ethbaal king of the Sidonians, and began to serve Baal and worship him. He set up an altar for Baal in the temple of Baal that he built in Samaria. Ahab also made an Asherah pole and did more to provoke the LORD, the God of Israel, to anger than did all the kings of Israel before him (1 Kgs 16.30–33).

Under the rule of Ahab, Israel's mission was traded in for a pick-and-mix belief system, comparable to today's New Age movement. Exclusive faith in Yahweh should have made Israel shine among the nations, but there were very few in Israel who trusted in him *alone*. Times like this called for faith-full prophets, men who embodied Yahweh's jealous love for Israel (see Deut 4.24). Elijah, whose name bespeaks his mission (Yahweh-is-my-God), is one such beacon on a hill. In 1 Kings 18, Elijah finds himself pitted against 400 misguided prophets and a weak king before a nation that wants to have it both ways.

You Are What You Worship

The first two commandments given to Israel prohibited the worship of false gods and the creation of idols (Exod 20.3–6). Although these commands are distinct from one another (for Protestant Christians at least), they are essentially two ways of looking at the same reality.

The worship of anything other than God is a misplacement of trust that distorts God's intentions for human life. But false worship is not just wrong because God says so. A principle undergirding the prohibition against false worship is that humans come to resemble that which they worship. Since Yahweh is the only God who genuinely sees, hears, speaks and feels, the worship of any other god diminishes these relational abilities in a person.

The second commandment is closely related to this because 'the human being, with all of its capacities for relationships, is believed to be the only appropriate image of God in the life of the world.'[7] Idolatry is abhorrent to the Creator because it distorts the images of God (human beings) that he created to populate the earth.[8] So, for instance, when Israel worships idols made of iron and bronze, the nation develops an iron neck (stubbornness) and a bronze forehead (dull mind) as direct consequences (Isa 48.4). Similarly, Jeremiah warns his people with the words, 'Do not follow other gods *to your own harm*' (Jer 7.6), because he understands that their idolatry dehumanizes them. Since human beings were made to reflect God's image, the worship of anything else desecrates what God has entrusted to us, whether that damage be psychological, emotional, or even physical (see below).

The first two commandments, therefore, affirm the reality that there is one true God and one appropriate image for God on earth. Again, Israel's psalmists prove themselves most adept at expressing theological truth in poetic language.

> But their idols are silver and gold,
>   made by the hands of men.
> They have mouths, but *cannot speak*,
>   eyes, but they *cannot see*;
> they have ears, but *cannot hear*,
>   noses, but they *cannot smell*;
> they have hands, but *cannot feel*,
>   feet, but they *cannot walk*;
>   nor can they utter a sound with their throats.
> *Those who make them will be like them,*
>   *and so will all who trust in them* (Ps 115.4–8).

It is perhaps understandable, in a world of such swift and uncertain change as ours, why people grope optimistically at false idols that promise security through wealth, popularity, sex or power. But sadly, if the psalmists (and the prophets) are right, trusting in impersonal, sense-less things only makes people less *personal* and less sensible, in other words, less like the God whose image we were created to reflect.

In keeping with this, idolatrous actions are presented in 1 Kings 18 as having dangerous consequences. Ahab, for instance, fails to grasp the fact that Elijah's three-year weather forecast reflects the nation's dried-up spiritual condition (1 Kgs 17.1). And even more vivid is the demonstration on Mount Carmel by the prophets of Baal, who prove idolatry to be a life-threatening form of *self-harm*.

Gods at Odds (1 Kings 18)

Chapter 18 begins by juxtaposing the charismatic and bold Elijah with the devout but fearful Obadiah. Their paths cross while Obadiah is looking for fertile land because of the drought. Elijah cuts to the chase, 'Go tell your master, "Elijah is here"' (1 Kgs 18.8), but Obadiah objects. If he passes on the message and Ahab cannot find Elijah, Obadiah will pay with his life. With many words, Obadiah goes on to explain that he doesn't deserve such a sorry fate, considering how good he has been to Yahweh's prophets over the past few years. So Elijah promises, 'As the

L ORD Almighty lives, whom I serve, I will surely present myself to Ahab today' (1 Kgs 18.15).

Later that day, Ahab initiates the conversation with an insult, 'Is that you, you troubler of Israel?' (1 Kgs 18.17) Without missing a beat, Yahweh's prophet responds in kind, for he knows full well that the drought is only a symptom of the corrupt king's idolatry. In the conversation that follows, a challenge is laid out, pitting one god against the Other; Baal vs Yahweh; Ahab's 400 prophets of Baal and Jezebel's 450 prophets of Asherah vs Elijah.

At the king's command, the people gather on Mount Carmel and Elijah begins proceedings by rebuking Israel for having mixed loyalties.

> Elijah went before the people and said, 'How long will you waver [limp] between two opinions? If the L ORD is God, follow him; but if Baal is God, follow him.'
> *But the people said nothing* (1 Kgs 18.21).

In the style of Nathan's prophetic speech, Elijah asks a rhetorical question: 'How long will you limp between two opinions?' The word translated 'waver' in the NIV may also be translated 'limp' (see NRSV). The wording of Elijah's question makes it clear that Israel's idolatry has already crippled her spiritual condition. The critical issue now is 'How long?'

But Israel's silence is deafening.

Perhaps it is understandable that Israel struggled to make a firm choice, since the claims of Yahweh and Baal were in many ways quite similar.[9] But in any case, a pep talk followed by a command to choose was obviously not going to suffice. The Israelites were up to their necks in idol worship and obviously needed something more. They needed evidence, a contest with only one victor, and it was evidence they would get.

The rules of the contest were straightforward. Two altars were to be set up, bearing sacrifices that could only be set alight by a deity in response to the pleas of representative prophets. A demonstration of genuine power (fire from heaven) would prove one god's superiority over the other. And so the contest began, with the prophets of Baal[10] going first and Elijah taunting them from morning until evening.

To press his theological point, the narrator uses the same word from Elijah's challenge in verse 21 to describe Baal's prophets as they 'limp' around their altar—with no response from their god. Yahweh's people limp because they are uncommitted just as the prophets of Baal limp because they are misguided. And as the prophets of Baal begin slashing themselves with swords and spears in desperation, the story reinforces the observation of the psalmist: *idolatry* equates to *self-harm* (also see Jer 7.18–19).[11]

There is only one true God, shouts the prophet. If it is Yahweh, follow him! If Baal, then seek him! Just stop limping along with a foot in both camps! A similar mandate was given centuries later to the Christian church in Laodicea.

> I know your deeds, that you are neither cold nor hot. I wish you were either one or the other! So, because you are lukewarm—neither hot nor cold—I am about to spit you out of my mouth (Rev 3.15–16).

Israel's covenant stipulated wholeheartedness. Anything less was an insult to Yahweh's redemptive activity and continual provision for his beloved people. If the language of the prophets is strong, it is only because Israel (and the church) cannot reflect God's character while their worship is focused elsewhere. Trying to have it both ways does more harm than good.

And so the entire day passed with Baal's prophets shouting and screaming, praying and prophesying, and cutting themselves to shreds. Elijah taunts his rivals all day by stressing Baal's absence, until finally the narrator affirms the same reality.[12]

> But there was no response, no-one answered, no-one paid attention (1 Kgs 18.29b).

Silence. Nothing. No one.

In accordance with Isaiah's preaching (Isa 41.21–24; see above), false gods are deaf, mute and powerless. Baal is evidently as harmless as 'a scarecrow in a melon patch' (Jer 10.5), although it is not just Baal who is lost in deathly silence. The people of Israel offering him (half) their allegiance are equally silent and King Ahab is also conspicuously absent from the whole affair. The silence of Baal is reflected in the muteness of his subjects. You are what you worship.

And then it was Elijah's turn.

Two significant actions pave the way for Elijah's intercession. First, he reinstates Israel as God's chosen people by rebuilding the altar in their presence to remind them of their national identity and vocation; 'Your name shall be Israel' (1 Kgs 18.31). This is not a showdown *to* the nations or *for* the nations. It is for God's own people who have strayed from him.

Elijah's second action makes the altar impossible to burn. More than 15 litres of water are poured over the sacrifice and the altar before Elijah begins to pray.

> O LORD, God of Abraham, Isaac and Israel, *let it be known today that you are God in Israel* and that I am your servant and have done all these things at your command. Answer me, O LORD, answer me, *so these people will know that you, O LORD, are God*, and that you are turning their hearts back again (1 Kgs 18.36b–37).

The point of the whole saga—that Israel may know that *Yahweh is God*—is as clear as Yahweh's response.

> Then the fire of the LORD fell and burned up the sacrifice, the wood, the stones and the soil, and also licked up the water in the trench (1 Kgs 18.38).

As Yahweh's indisputable response to Elijah's faith demonstrates his Lordship, the people return to their senses.

> When all the people saw this, they fell prostrate and cried, 'The LORD—he is God! The LORD—he is God!' (1 Kgs 18.39)

They were right, and the truth of their proclamation would have serious repercussions. The false prophets were slaughtered in the Kishon Wadi (where Deborah's enemies also fell) and Ahab was sent on his way before the incoming storm could catch up with him. Elijah's bold faith had made space for Yahweh to demonstrate that he, and not Baal, was the real 'Storm God' of lightning and rain (1 Kgs 18.38,45).[13] Moreover, the arrival of rain signified the end of Israel's spiritual drought as God began to draw the hearts of his people back to him (1 Kgs 18.37). Like Isaiah's courtroom drama, where the final verdict lies with the jury, 'dénouement comes not when Baal fails, or even when Yahweh succeeds, but when the people who have been limping on two opinions worship and confess, "Yahweh, he is God! Yahweh, he is God!"'[14]

What Are You Doing Here? (1 Kings 19)

In 1 Kings 17–18, Elijah presents an exemplary model of genuine faith in action. When Yahweh says go, Elijah goes (1 Kgs 17.1–5,8–10; 18.1–2); and when the prophet speaks, he speaks in Yahweh's name (1 Kgs 18.15,36). Elijah's prayer on Mount Carmel is guided by typically prophetic concerns—that Yahweh be made known to Israel and that their hearts be turned back to him (1 Kgs 18.37)—and his tremendous faith (against 400 opponents!) makes space for God to display his glory to Israel.[15]

Immediately after the stand-off on Mount Carmel, however, Elijah's bravado falters when his life comes under threat. Queen Jezebel, who never made an appearance on Mount Carmel,[16] has heard a full report of the extraordinary events and has sworn vengeance on Elijah. The prophet's response to Jezebel's threat is narrated in 1 Kings 19.3 with three Hebrew verbs in rapid succession: he was afraid; he got up; he fled.

A closer look at these chapters reveals that the events of chapters 17 and 19, either side of Mount Carmel, are introduced in a similar fashion so that the incongruity of Elijah's actions stands out. In 1 Kings 17.2–3, Elijah responds to the *word of Yahweh* and hides in *faith*, but in 1 Kings 19.2–3, Elijah responds to the menacing *word of Jezebel* and hides in *fear*. (In both instances, God sustains the prophet and provides for his needs; 1 Kgs 17.6,15; 19.6.) The disparity between Elijah's responses in chapters 17 and 19 is clear enough, but what exactly has happened to our bold role-model of prophetic faith? Why the sudden shift from faith to fear, from caring so deeply for the hearts of his people to fleeing in order to save his own skin?

The change in Elijah catches the attention of Yahweh too, who has a question for his runaway messenger. Twice he asks Elijah,

'What are you doing here?' (1 Kgs 19.9,13) and both times, before and after God's Self-revelation, Elijah's response is exactly the same.

> I have been very zealous [literally 'jealous'] for the LORD God Almighty. The Israelites have rejected your covenant, broken down your altars, and put your prophets to death with the sword. I am the only one left, and now they are trying to kill me too (1 Kgs 19.10,14).

The prophet's response is marked by self-defence and self-pity, and there is very little truth in what he says. Everything is articulated in reverse as if Elijah's mind has become jumbled, and from his report one might be led to believe that nothing ever happened on Mount Carmel!

(a) Elijah speaks of the Israelites rejecting the covenant, when in fact they have only recently fallen on their faces in worship before Yahweh; (b) he speaks of the breaking down of Yahweh's altars but says nothing of the more recent rebuilding of the altar atop Mount Carmel; (c) he reports that *Yahweh's* prophets have been put to death by the sword but neglects to mention the 400 prophets of Baal who have just suffered that very fate; (d) he claims to be the only one left, despite Obadiah's report that there are many other prophets of Yahweh hidden in caves; and (e) he tells God that *the Israelites* are trying to kill him, when in fact that is Queen Jezebel's intention! Elijah's answer to God's question reveals a man who is disillusioned and disoriented, probably because he has invested too much faith in himself.

Ironically, the very prophet who rebuked and reoriented the nation now 'limps' all the way from Carmel to Horeb. Elijah's crippled faith must be restored if he is ever again going to make space for God to do things God's way. And so, what follows is a second dramatic display of power on a mountaintop, this time for the benefit of Yahweh's own prophet.

> The LORD said, 'Go out and stand on the mountain in the presence of the LORD, for the LORD is about to pass by' (1 Kgs 19.11).

It is safe to assume that the reason Elijah fled to Horeb/Sinai, 'the mountain of God' (1 Kgs 19.8), was to meet with God. But now, as three manifestations of great power pass him by—a great wind, a fire and an earthquake—God is not present in any of them. (Especially significant in the aftermath of Mount Carmel is God's absence from the fire.) Yahweh's presence in a 'gentle whisper' suggests that his plan to revive the nation and cleanse it of idolatry will not necessarily be implemented via spectacular showdowns on mountaintops. In short, Elijah is being told to look beyond himself for a solution.

> The LORD said to him, 'Go back the way you came, and go to the Desert of Damascus. When you get there, anoint Hazael king over Aram. Also, anoint Jehu son of Nimshi king over Israel, and anoint Elisha son of Shaphat from Abel Meholah to succeed you as prophet' (1 Kgs 19.15–16).

Elijah is to anoint two kings to purge and reduce Israel (one from within and one from without) as well as a prophetic successor who will make an impact within and beyond the borders of Israel. Jehu, as king over Israel, will purge the nation of its idolatry (2 Kgs 9.22; 10.28); Hazael, as king of Aram, will reduce Israel's numbers (2 Kgs 10.32); and Elisha will succeed Elijah as Yahweh's prophet. The way forward will be subtle and political, and 'Elijah must be content with being *part* of the plan and not *the plan itself.*'[17]

Making Space for God

These narratives about Elijah can teach us a great deal about faith. Elijah takes up the prophetic tasks of confronting and reorienting[18] Israel so that the nation may make space in their consciousness for God, or in the jargon of the church, 'have faith'. He rebukes their waywardness with the command to *choose* (1 Kgs 18.21) and then reorients them: 'Your name shall be Israel' (1 Kgs 18.31). Prophetic conflict seeks to turn hearts in a Godward direction so that his people may properly represent him (see 'Heart Reorientation' in chapter 4), and Elijah's actions on Mount Carmel are typical in this regard. But in 1 Kings 19 it is Elijah who becomes the subject of the same pattern and God who takes up the twin tasks of confrontation: 'What are you doing here?' and reorientation: 'Go back the way you came'. In the same way that Israel must avoid idolatry in order to properly represent the God she worships, so Elijah must resist leaning on his own under-standing of God's purposes (which place him at the centre).

These back-to-back stories about Elijah juxtapose an open faith that invites God's life-giving power (1 Kgs 18.38–39) with a claus-trophobic view of God and self that is life-diminishing (1 Kgs 19.4). There is a world of difference between the prophet in 1 Kings 18.8 who announces with such certainty, 'Elijah is here!' and the one who stammers his way through a muddle of excus-es in answer to God's question, 'What are you doing here?' (1 Kgs 19.9,13) Even Elijah proves susceptible to misplacing his trust and leaning too heavily on his own sense of importance. Moreover, it is hardly coincidental that Elijah's excessive self-interest follows hard on the heels of a flashy, mountaintop show-down from which he emerged the victor (Prov 16.18).

Genuine faith broadens our horizons by making space for God to display his faithfulness and assure us that nothing is impossi-ble (Mt 17.20). It is easy, without our being aware of it, to put boundaries and limits on ourselves by allowing God *some* space in our living, but not too much. Jesus' acts of healing in the gospels suggest that genuine faith releases God to act in ways that he appears not to without our trusting consent: 'And [Jesus] did not do many miracles there because of their lack of faith' (Mt 13.58). A lack of genuine faith is crippling primarily because it limits divine intervention in our lives. If we would prefer to lean on God only now and then, when it suits us, then we may expect to find ourselves limping along between divided loyalties.

> Now to him who is able to do immeasurably more than all we ask or imagine, according to his power that is at work within us, to him be glory in the church and in Christ Jesus throughout all gen-erations, for ever and ever! Amen (Eph 3.20–21).

Dig Deeper

- How would you define idolatry to a new Christian?

- Why is idolatry harmful to human beings?

- Have you ever noticed yourself becoming like something you idolized?

- Take a moment to consider your present 'location'. What would be your answer to God's question: 'What are you doing here?' (1 Kings 19.9)

- What spiritual disciplines can help you become more attuned to God's gentle whisper?

8

Prophetic Insight: Discerning God's Ways

MICAIAH

*Surely the Sovereign Lord does nothing without revealing
his plan to his servants the prophets (Amos 3.7).*

---

1 Kings 22.1–40

Narrators and Insight

Reading biblical narratives can be a tricky business. Christians
approach the Bible expecting to receive moral guidance, and yet
biblical characters (with one obvious exception) are not perfect.
We have already seen in previous chapters that a national hero
such as King David can quickly lose his way (2 Sam 10–11); that
even a bold prophet like Elijah can faithfully honour God one
moment only to flee shamelessly the next (1 Kgs 18–19). Making
judgements about a character's right or wrong behaviour in any
given story is part of the difficulty (and the thrill) of reading
Scripture, a challenge that is particularly pertinent to preachers,
whose task it is to draw out the ethical implications of biblical
texts. Readers of biblical narrative need guidance in determining
which characters are trustworthy and which are worthy of suspicion, but where are such clues to be found?

Fortunately, one of the most reliable sources for assessing the
moral integrity of biblical characters is already *within* the text,
namely, the voice of the narrator. While it is quite common in Old

Testament stories for the narrator to take a back seat, on occasion it becomes necessary to reveal a motive or private thought, even of God, for the purposes of the tale. We have already come across a few of these interjections from the narrator in previous chapters:

> The LORD was grieved that he had made man on the earth, and his heart was filled with pain. So the LORD said, 'I will wipe mankind, whom I have created, from the face of the earth' (Gen 6.6–7a).

> Jeroboam thought to himself, 'The kingdom is now likely to revert to the house of David' (1 Kgs 12.26).

We may not know precisely *how* the narrator comes to know these things, but readers may trust the narrator's insight as the authoritative voice telling the story. Generally speaking, Christian faith in the inspiration of Scripture (at least with regards to narrative texts) amounts to trusting the narrator's god-like omniscience and point of view. 'He is all-knowing and also perfectly reliable: at times he may choose to make us wonder but he never misleads us.'[1]

When it comes to discerning God's ways so as to report from a divine perspective, Israel's prophets and the biblical narrators stand on common ground.[2] Consider, for example, the 'omniscient and prophetic qualities'[3] of the narrator's voice as it subtly intrudes on the narrative in 1 Samuel 9.9 to clarify something for the reader.

> (Formerly in Israel, if a man went to inquire of God, he would say, *'Come, let us go to the seer,'* because the prophet of today used to be called a seer.)
> 'Good,' Saul said to his servant. *'Come, let's go.'* So they set out for the town where the man of God was (1 Sam 9.9–10).

Immediately following the narrator's expository comment in verse 9, Saul fulfils the words spoken by the narrator in verse 10. The repetition of 'Come, let us go' directs the reader's attention to the parallel, reaffirming the authority of the narrator not just as storyteller, but as another prophetic voice.[4] Prophets and narrators share the task of making God's ways known, although their roles differ somewhat; the prophet takes the spotlight as a discoverable personality within the text while the narrator functions as an omniscient voice from behind the curtain, so to speak, revealing selected details along the way to grant the reader a meaningful experience. The narrator's 'godlike comprehensiveness of knowledge'[5] permits the reader to understand why certain things come to pass—e.g. 'for the LORD had determined to frustrate the good advice of Ahithophel in order to bring disaster on Absalom' (2 Sam 17.14). Prophets, on the other hand (perhaps with the exception of Nathan), do not care for such subtleties. They personify God's direct and dangerous speech.

> Therefore I cut you in pieces with my prophets,
> I killed you with the words of my mouth;
> my judgements flashed like lightning upon you (Hos 6.5).

In 1 Kings 22, the subtlety of the narrator combines with the direct speech of the prophet to illuminate the otherwise hidden ways of God.

One Question, Three Answers (1 Kings 22.1–25)

The story of Naboth's vineyard in 1 Kings 21 characterizes Ahab as a king who sulks like a moody teenager, heeds bad advice and misuses his royal power to get what he wants (1 Kgs 21.4–16). That scenario prepares readers for 1 Kings 22, where the stakes are raised from vineyard to city and from innocent neighbour to international war. So when Ahab asks Jehoshaphat, 'Will you go with me?' and the king of Judah responds with great enthusiasm, 'I am as you are, my people as your people, my horses as your horses', it seems likely that Ahab will simply take what he wants . . . again.

But then Jehoshaphat introduces some caution, slowing down the narrative with a plea to 'first seek the counsel of the LORD' (1 Kgs 22.5). The two kings from north and south are promptly surrounded by 400 prophets who gather in response to Jehoshaphat's request. But although these prophets claim to speak for Yahweh (not Baal or any other deity), their unanimous response—'Go!'—arouses suspicion in Jehoshaphat, who insists on a second opinion (1 Kgs 22.7).

Given Ahab's characterization in 1 Kings 21, it is not surprising that the 400 Israelite prophets have been conditioned to foretell only that which pleases their king. And yet 'there is still one man' who resists the king's duress: Micaiah ben Imlah. Needless to say, Micaiah is not popular with the king, who unashamedly declares, 'I hate him because he never prophesies anything good about me, but always bad' (1 Kgs 22.8). Again, Ahab comes across as being rather childish; he does not care for 'right' prophecies so long as they are 'pleasant' (Isa 30.10).

The scene is described in greater detail with the introduction of Micaiah (22.10–12) who makes his entrance even while Zedekiah, the only other prophet named, is adding weight to his prophecy with a visual aid (see 'Enacted Parables' in chapter 10).[6] Holding up a set of iron horns (which we can only assume he prepared earlier), he cries, 'With these you will gore the Arameans until they are destroyed!' (1 Kgs 22.11) Zedekiah's colleagues corroborate his prophecy before the two kings, and Micaiah is urged to join the throng. The stage is set for another lone prophet's stand against a prophetic horde, but Micaiah appears to lack the charisma of Elijah. Instead of making preparations for a showdown, Micaiah cryptically offers three distinct responses to the question he has been summoned to answer. First, to the man at the door who urges him not to be a stick-in-the-mud, Micaiah replies much as we expected him to:

> As surely as the LORD lives, I can tell him only what the LORD tells me (1 Kgs 22.14).

But then Micaiah's advice for the king takes us by surprise.

> When he arrived, the king asked him, 'Micaiah, shall we go to war against Ramoth Gilead, or shall I refrain?'
> 'Attack and be victorious,' he answered, 'for the LORD will give it into the king's hand' (1 Kgs 22.15).

At this point (with the information given) we can only furrow our brows and read verse 14 again. Yes, there it is, an apparent contradiction: Micaiah swears to be truthful but then proceeds to give the same false prophecy as everyone else.

Or are we missing something?

If we read carefully, we will notice that Micaiah does not actually swear to tell the truth at all. Perhaps we have jumped too soon to the conclusion that telling the king 'only what the LORD tells me' equates to telling the truth.

But then, whether Ahab wishes to look sincere in front of Jehoshaphat, or he assumes the prophet's words to be loaded with sarcasm, or he is perhaps even genuinely interested in what else Micaiah has to say, the king of Israel balks.

> How many times must I make you swear to tell me nothing but the truth in the name of the LORD? (1 Kgs 22.16)

Having been commanded to speak the truth, the whole truth, and 'nothing but the truth', Micaiah now comes clean with a disturbing word-picture for the king:[7]

> I saw all Israel scattered on the hills like sheep without a shepherd, and the LORD said, 'These people have no master. Let each one go home in peace' (1 Kgs 22.17).

Israel scattered like sheep means only one thing for Ahab, the current shepherd of Israel. He turns in his throne to face Jehoshaphat. See? Didn't I tell you! This prophet never has anything good to say . . .

But Micaiah interrupts, for he has not yet told the whole truth.

> Micaiah continued, 'Therefore hear the word of the LORD: I saw the LORD sitting on his throne with all the host of heaven standing around him on his right and on his left. And the LORD said, "Who will entice Ahab into attacking Ramoth Gilead and going to his death there?"
>
> 'One suggested this, and another that. Finally, a spirit came forward, stood before the LORD and said, "I will entice him."
>
> '"By what means?" the LORD asked.
>
> '"I will go out and be a lying spirit in the mouths of all his prophets," he said.

'"You will succeed in enticing him," said the LORD. "Go and do it."

'So now the LORD has put a lying spirit in the mouths of all these prophets of yours. The LORD has decreed disaster for you' (1 Kgs 22.19–23).

In light of the vision, Micaiah's three distinct responses begin to make perfect sense. Initially, when asked to speak favourably with the rest of the prophets who were of one accord, Micaiah had said, 'I can tell him only what the LORD tells me' (1 Kgs 22.14)—which was *not* the same as swearing to tell the truth. Then, because 'the LORD has put a lying spirit in the mouths of all these prophets' and because, as we now know, Micaiah is in on the scheme, his prophecy concurs with the decision of the heavenly council: 'Attack and be victorious, for the LORD will give it into the king's hand' (1 Kgs 22.15). Finally, when Micaiah is asked to speak 'nothing but the truth in the name of the LORD', he explains what has been going on behind the scenes so that readers discover (along with the rest of Micaiah's audience) that *this* prophet has stood in the council of Yahweh and been given critical insight into the bigger picture.

Not that anything Micaiah says will make the least bit of difference to the king. One gets the distinct impression that whether the prophet says, 'Go!' or 'The LORD has decreed disaster for you', Ahab will go to war because he *wants* to go to war. The irony is, having heard about the vision, readers realize that Yahweh also wants Ahab to go to war. If Ahab's desire to take Ramoth Gilead was not strong enough already, a lying spirit in the mouths of his prophets will only strengthen the king's selfish resolve. God wants Ahab to follow his heart where it takes him; in this instance, to his own death at the hands of the Arameans.

It is not surprising that Zedekiah proceeds to initiate a more personal confrontation by punching Micaiah in the face.[8] His decision to strike Micaiah is quite possibly another symbolic action by which he means to clarify which of them has the upper hand, so to speak. Violence is often perceived as a means to resolve power-struggles, especially where an honest minority stands up to a compromised majority. But 'contrary to the cynical theory that violent force is the secret basis of authority, it is in fact always the sign that authority has dissolved.'[9] Perturbed by the genuine insight of Yahweh's prophet,

Zedekiah resorts to clenched fists before attempting to unsteady Micaiah further with a question: 'Which way did the Spirit of the LORD go when he went from me to speak to you?' (1 Kgs 22.24) In other words, Are you not inspired by the same so-called lying spirit?

Despite Micaiah's attempt to hold his ground—'You will find out on the day you go to hide in an inner room[10] [when your king is dead and you are fleeing from your enemies]' (1 Kgs 22.25)— Zedekiah's question is an important one. In essence, 'What makes you any different from the rest of us?' *From* the narrative comes the question we have been led to ask *of* the narrative: how does one discern between true and false prophecy?

True or False?

We began this chapter with a discussion about how to distinguish between exemplary and non-exemplary characters in biblical narratives. A related question may also be asked of prophets: by what criteria can we assess the claims of those who crown their speech with 'Thus says the LORD'?[11]

Just prior to Israel's exile, when self-appointed prophets were increasing in number and the nation was in desperate need of hopeful words, Jeremiah had some important things to say about discerning between true and false prophecies. At the heart of his theology of discernment was the requirement that a true prophet be sent from the divine council.

> *But which of them has stood in the council of the LORD*
>   *to see or to hear his word?*
> Who has listened and heard his word?
>
> . . . I did not send these prophets,
>   yet they have run with their message;
> I did not speak to them,
>   yet they have prophesied.
> *But if they had stood in my council,*
>   *they would have proclaimed my words to my people*
> and would have turned them from their evil ways
>   and from their evil deeds (Jer 23.18,21–22).

The 'council of the LORD' Jeremiah speaks of plays an important role in Micaiah's story. Between the voices of the narrator and Micaiah, a neat parallel is drawn between two councils, one earthly and one heavenly, as twin dimensions in the government of human affairs.

Dressed in their royal robes, the king of Israel and Jehoshaphat king of Judah were sitting on their thrones . . . with all the prophets prophesying before them (1 Kgs 22.10).	Micaiah continued, ' . . . I saw the LORD sitting on his throne with all the host of heaven standing round him on his right and on his left' (1 Kgs 22.19).

In one council 400 advisors quickly affirm the king's selfish want. According to the other, the same 400 prophets unknowingly serve Yahweh by bringing down a king who has consistently behaved badly. But the significance of the two councils runs deeper than simply to remind us of life's spiritual dimension. Vision reports were a common means of authenticating a prophetic message, and Micaiah's report in 1 Kings 22 serves such a purpose in his context. By offering details of his visionary experience in Yahweh's council, Micaiah declares his unique perspective to be truthful.

However, a prophet's claim to have attended the heavenly council is not very helpful for discerning truth in the heat of the moment, as Zedekiah's vehement challenge makes all too clear. For who can tell, without the aid of a lie detector, which prophets have vivid imaginations and a grandiose vocabulary, and which have *actually* stood in Yahweh's council? Does it not boil down to your word against mine? Perhaps the only real criterion is that of hindsight, as expressed in the words of Moses:

> You may say to yourselves, 'How can we know when a message has not been spoken by the LORD?'
> If what a prophet proclaims in the name of the LORD does not take place or come true, that is a message the LORD has not spoken. That prophet has spoken presumptuously. Do not be afraid of him (Deut 18.21–22).

According to this text, the proof of the pudding is in the eating, but that is only helpful for those in the privileged position to look back and assess prophetic oracles in light of how events have unfolded. It appears that neither Jeremiah's criterion (heavenly council) nor that of Moses (hindsight) is able to verify Micaiah's prophetic word in *the present moment* of dispute and decision. Perhaps all that can be done is to let Micaiah die for speaking God's words and to look back later and say, 'You know what? Micaiah was probably right after all . . .'

Actually, neither Jeremiah nor Deuteronomy need take priority over the innate capacity of 1 Kings 22 to answer ethical quandaries on its own terms. Nuanced stories have a greater semblance to the shape of human experience and they are no less forceful in their implications than the theological reflections of Jeremiah or the formulaic summations of Deuteronomy. For a verdict regarding Micaiah's claims, we need look no further than the story itself, where *the narrator's prophetic voice* is what ultimately permits the reader to discern between true and false claims to speak for God.

We noted earlier that Micaiah was asked upon entering the earthly council to ignore his convictions and 'speak favourably' (1 Kgs 22.13). By including this detail, the narrator subtly makes the point that whereas Micaiah must put aside his integrity in order to go with the flow, the other 400 prophets have a history of saying whatever the king wants to hear (1 Kgs 22.8). The narrator's clue suggests that we may *trust* this prophet over and against the others, not because his words will come true (since we don't know that yet), nor because he has stood in Yahweh's council (again, we can't be sure), but *on the basis of his moral character*. The divide between truthful Micaiah and the falsehood of his rivals continues to widen when Zedekiah's violent outburst aligns him with the will of Ahab and not Yahweh. The prophetic insight of the narrator thereby affirms something many readers already suspect to be true: that the truth-claims of those who speak for God should be assessed not merely via simple formulas ('if the shoe fits . . .'), but in light of their moral character which is 'open to scrutiny in the present'.[12] Learning to pick up on the narrator's cues has at least one thing in common with judging the claims (and character) of self-proclaimed prophets: the devil is in the details.

The Final Word (1 Kings 22.26–40)

As the falsehood of the *vox populi* is trumped by Micaiah's gift of insight, Ahab reacts by throwing the prophet in a cell. Of course, the king misunderstands. God's uncontainable word will accomplish the purpose for which it was sent (see Isa 55.11) even if his prophet is fettered. But in any case, with Micaiah locked away on a diet of bread and water, readers are now dependent on the narrator for the final word.

Sure enough, as the kings head to Ramoth Gilead, we are made privy to two pieces of information, one from the king of Israel and the other from the king of Aram. (The narrator's omniscience again proves most helpful!)

> The king of Israel said to Jehoshaphat, 'I will enter the battle in disguise, but you wear your royal robes.' So the king of Israel disguised himself and went into battle.
>
> Now the king of Aram had ordered his thirty-two chariot commanders, 'Do not fight with anyone, small or great, except the king of Israel' (1 Kgs 22.30–31).

The incompatibility of these two statements introduces a tension that builds toward the story's climax. Aram's king wishes only for Ahab's death, but Ahab has entered the battle in disguise. It seems likely that Jehoshaphat will be mistaken for Ahab and die quickly in his stead. (It also seems reasonable to question Jehoshaphat's intelligence for complying with Ahab's strategy!) But the narrator has a different motive for including these details. Whatever Ahab may do to increase his chances of survival (and the disguise reveals his suspicion that there may be some truth to Micaiah's prophecy), it is he and not Jehoshaphat who will die in this battle.

Initially it seems likely that Jehoshaphat will die at the hand of the Arameans because of his royal robes, but when the enemy realize that they are pursuing the wrong man they fall back, leaving Jehoshaphat to fight another day (1 Kgs 22.45). And then something completely unforeseeable happens.

> Someone drew his bow at random and hit the king of Israel between the sections of his armour (1 Kgs 22.34a).

The archer is anonymous, a man of no apparent consequence who has drawn his bow without even choosing a target. Nonetheless, his arrow finds precisely the most vulnerable part of the armour worn by the king, who has entered the battle incognito! The narrator, whose perspective is governed by a profound insight into the ways of God, makes it known that even apparent random events are sometimes the work of a sovereign God whose freedom and power are impervious to deceptive kings and false prophets. The battle continues with King Ahab bleeding to death and watching from the sidelines until finally, with the setting of the sun, a cry goes out across the battlefield: 'Every man to his town; everyone to his land!' (1 Kgs 22.36) The shepherd has fallen and, as foretold,[13] the sheep scatter.

God's Ways

Narratives like this are rarely addressed from the pulpit because the underlying questions, for those who dare to give them voice, are troubling: if God has used 'a lying spirit' to effect a certain outcome in this instance,[14] what else might we expect from him?[15] Or, to put a finer point on it, can God be trusted? If the question seems improper, it is worth noting that the Bible's sanctity does not exempt it from tough scrutiny, lest we fall into the trap of settling for answers like, 'Well, if the Bible says so . . .' which of course is no real answer at all. Worse still is the practice of reading what we already believe back *into* the Bible in order to excuse God from being responsible for his own actions. We need only read the final chapters of Job (38–41) to see that God can stand up for himself! But what categories might we employ to understand God's use of deception in 1 Kings 22?

During the exile, Ezekiel was confronted with a situation that tested his resolve as Israel's watchman (see 'Watchmen' in chapter 4). Some of Israel's elders had come seeking a word from God even whilst their primary devotion was to idols. In a private conversation, Yahweh told Ezekiel of his plot to undo the hypocrisy of such men: 'I the LORD will answer him myself in keeping with his great idolatry' (Eze 14.4), by which God meant that the deception of the hypocritical worshipper would be countered by God's own deception. But the target of Yahweh's poetic judgement was not just the person making the false petition, but also, as per 1 Kings 22, the false prophet who invented oracles of peace and reassurance:

> And if the prophet is enticed[17] to utter a prophecy, I the LORD have enticed that prophet, and I will stretch out my hand against him and destroy him from among my people Israel. They will bear their guilt—the prophet will be as guilty as the one who consults him (Eze 14.9–10).

The principle explained here to Ezekiel seems also to apply to Micaiah's situation, where Ahab's 400 false prophets were subjected to a similar brand of poetic justice. Zedekiah and his throng had become so practised in falsehood that a lying spirit in their midst went unnoticed and the lies upon which Ahab had come to depend so heavily became the very means by which he (and they) met their downfall (1 Kgs 22.25,28). Yahweh quite simply used their deceit against them (see Eze 13). At the risk of oversimplifying, then, we may surmise that people get what their hearts long for (e.g. Num. 14.2,28); false prophets are led astray by lying spirits just as idolaters take on the image of their false gods. David says something similar in his theology-in-song that recognizes God's apt modes of Self-revelation:

> To the faithful you show yourself faithful,
>   to the blameless you show yourself blameless,
> to the pure you show yourself pure,
>   *but to the crooked you show yourself shrewd* (2 Sam 22.26–27; Ps 18.25–26)

Addressing false prophecy in the New Testament, Paul also has some tough things to say about 'those who are perishing . . . because they refused to love the truth and so be saved' (2 Thess 2.10):

> For this reason God sends them a powerful delusion so that they will believe the lie and so that all will be condemned who have not believed the truth but have delighted in wickedness (2 Thess 2.11–12; see Rom 1.21–18).

In answer to questions about God's justice, the Bible makes it clear that God permits us to make our own choices—which have consequences. As the story is told in 1 Kings 22, Ahab was given a second chance to choose differently in light of new revelation, and since we already have it on record that he had previously repented in the face of judgement (1 Kgs 21.27–28), there was a possibility that he would do so again. True, God seemed confident that the plan would meet with success (1 Kgs 22.22b), but that was surely because Ahab had a history of consulting false prophets as a cover for doing whatever he wanted. All things considered, it is difficult to see Ahab's death as the consequence of anything other than the free decisions of a man who resisted God's warnings to his dying breath. Just as God waited upon the decisions of Saul, David, Solomon and Jeroboam, Ahab was equally free to choose his own way forward.

Micaiah's vision and the narrator's story both reveal prophetic insight into the ways of God. 'Indeed the story shows a depth of insight comparable to that of Micaiah himself, for the dynamics of Micaiah's engagement with the king could not have been thus portrayed by someone who did not grasp what is going on.'[18] The implications of this for Bible readers today is that we can trust narrators to guide us just as the prophets guided Israel.

It is evident from Micaiah's story that God neither forces his will upon people nor is limited by human action. Ahab's desire to go to war proved to be the catalyst for his own destruction, but the random arrow that hit its target is also an apt image for Yahweh's propensity to move in mysterious ways. We may be uncertain about *how* God will exercise his sovereignty within time and space, but we can be certain that he *will* maintain Lordship, whether through human collaboration, so-called coincidence, or by the whisper of a lying spirit.

Dig Deeper

- What do biblical narrators have in common with biblical prophets?

- Why did the prophets need to know God's ways? (See Exod 33.13; Amos 3.7)

- How does the heavenly council's plot to use a lying spirit affect your understanding of God's character? (Compare Job 1.6-12)

- How is Micaiah's moral integrity related to his prophetic authenticity?

- How do you understand the tension between divine sovereignty and human freedom?

9

Prophetic Mercy: Digesting God's Word

JONAH

When your words came, I ate them;
they were my joy and my heart's delight,
for I bear your name,
O Lord God Almighty (Jer 15.16).

Jonah 1 – 4

Jonah in Context (Jonah 1)

Among the so-called 'minor'[1] prophets, Jonah is a bit of a misfit. Each of the others is a collection of oracles and sermons whereas Jonah's (mis)adventure feels more at home among the stories of Elijah and Micaiah studied in the previous chapters.[2] Actually, although the book was most likely written in the fifth century BC, Jonah's historical context was closer to that of Elijah, too (the ninth century BC).

Questions of authorship and genre have heralded much debate, and while it is certainly very important to identify the type of literature one is reading in order to properly understand it, it doesn't seem necessary (to me at least) to reduce the book of Jonah to a *single* function: sermon or satire, allegory *or* parable, fiction *or* history. It is the mixed bag of literary forms that makes the book of Jonah so ingenious. Besides, many literary works, biblical or otherwise, simultaneously fulfil more than one purpose. (Think of

John's gospel, a creatively structured historical account that uses symbolic language to engage readers on various levels.) One thing everyone can agree on is that the book of Jonah excels with regards to literary artistry. The author's creative use of irony and other rhetorical devices make Jonah a fascinating and enjoyable read.

In fact, the book is so filled with embellishments and quirks that some have classified it as a made-up story (about Jonah) containing a message of truth (about Israel). While this is quite possible and would not necessarily undermine the authority of Scripture,[3] it does betray a rather selective approach if we dismiss the historicity of the book of Jonah on the basis of the likelihood of its events. If a man being held captive for three days in the belly of a massive sea creature is too much for our minds to accept as a viable act of God, then what about the earth swallowing up rebels in the Israelite camp (Num 16.32), or a deliverer whose superhuman strength matched the length of his hair (Jdg 16.17), not to mention a carpenter-cum-prophet who turned out to be God living among us! If we explain away wondrous events just because they seem unlikely, we effectively turn a blind eye to God's miraculous intervention in human history.

Having said that, Jonah is narrated with plenty of exaggeration and the story of his escapades in Assyria was most likely told with the nation of Israel in mind. In any case, it is not my intention to convince readers one way or another regarding the book's historical credibility. Our aim here is to learn about the spiritual character of biblical prophets through a literary approach to their stories. 'From an ethical perspective at least it makes little difference whether the book of Jonah is historical or fictional: in either case the author delights in mocking Jonah's folly at believing he could run away from God and in challenging his narrow-mindedness in supposing God cares only about the salvation of Israel.'[4]

One thing of which we can be certain is that the author did not want readers to emulate Jonah's attitudes and behaviour! The character of Jonah is instructive through his negative modelling. If the book is an anomaly, the man himself is stranger still. Indeed, it is difficult to understand how one of Yahweh's prophets managed to get so much wrong!

With that much said about literary concerns, let us turn to Jonah's historical setting:[5]

> [Jeroboam II] was the one who restored the boundaries of Israel from Lebo Hamath to the Sea of the Arabah, in accordance with the word of the LORD, the God of Israel, spoken through his servant Jonah son of Amittai, the prophet from Gath Hepher (2 Kgs 14.25).

If we take this verse to provide Jonah's historical context, he followed hard on the heels of Amos and Hosea, who were also active during the reign of Jehu's great-grandson, Jeroboam II (792–753 BC; not to be confused with Jeroboam son of Nebat, whom Ahijah confronted in the tenth century; see chapter 6). While Hosea and Amos were busy proclaiming severe judgement on Israel and Judah for their faithlessness, Jonah was summoned to cross the northern borders of Israel and preach in the enemy territory of Assyria.[6]

In response to Israel's cries of distress, Yahweh had come to her aid yet again and raised up Jeroboam II to restore the boundaries of Israel. (The cycle of *sin, oppression, cry for help,* and *deliverance* introduced in the book of Judges was not exclusive to that period.[7]) Having been the one to proclaim such good news of restoration in Israel (2 Kgs 14.25), Jonah was also instructed to go and address the ominous power of Assyria in the north.

> The word of the LORD came to Jonah son of Amittai: 'Go to the great city of Nineveh and preach against it, because its wickedness has come up before me' (Jnh 1.1–2).

The command to 'preach against' Nineveh would have seemed like the perfect complement to his prophecy of victory for Israel, but Jonah had a niggling feeling about how this short-term mission to the north was going to end. Other prophets had felt somewhat incompetent (Exod 4.10), unprepared (1 Sam 3.7) and young (Jer 1.6), but none responded quite like Jonah.

> But Jonah ran away from the LORD and headed for Tarshish. He went down to Joppa, where he found a ship bound for that port.

> After paying the fare, he went aboard and sailed for Tarshish to flee from the LORD (Jnh 1.3).

His motive is not immediately disclosed, but Jonah clearly has no interest in the task God has given him. If we were to hazard a guess at this point, we might assume that he wants to live a little longer and would prefer not to wander into a powerful city proclaiming judgement on behalf of a foreign deity. But whatever his reasons for running (the narrator withholds that information until later), this prophet of Yahweh is obviously unfamiliar with the rhetorical question of Psalm 139.7, 'Where can I flee from your presence?' and its implicit answer.

It is not long before Jonah and his sailing companions suddenly find themselves in the midst of a violent storm. No one doubts it is an act of God; the only question on their minds is how to appease such an irate and powerful deity—and *soon*! Whether as a self-sacrificial act or simply because he would rather die than contend with Yahweh, Jonah offers a quick-fix solution: 'Pick me up and throw me into the sea . . . and it will become calm' (Jnh 1.12). The men are reluctant but without an alternative, so Jonah is promptly hurled into the tempest.

> . . . and the raging sea grew calm (Jnh 1.15).

The immediate change in weather conditions is astounding, but even more so is the change that comes over the Gentile sailors. Initially, when the storm hit, the men had called upon their own gods to deliver them (Jnh 1.5). But later, after Jonah had eventually woken up and explained that Yahweh was 'the God of heaven, who made the sea and the land' (Jnh 1.9), they had turned to Jonah's God, asking forgiveness for what they were about to do (Jnh 1.14). And as the chapter concludes with Jonah in the belly of a fish, the Gentiles on the boat have already begun making sacrifices and vows to Yahweh, the God of Israel. Ironically, Jonah's incredibly brief testimony managed to turn the hearts of the sailors Godward!

Digesting God's Word (Jonah 2)

Prophets were required to ingest God's mandate fully into their own lives before proclaiming it to others. A vivid image for this in the Bible is the consumption of a scroll before speaking God's word.

> And he said to me, 'Son of man, eat what is before you, eat this scroll; then go and speak to the house of Israel' (Eze 3.1; also 3.2–4; Jer 15.16).

> I took the little scroll from the angel's hand and ate it. It tasted as sweet as honey in my mouth, but when I had eaten it, my stomach turned sour. Then I was told, 'You must prophesy again about many peoples, nations, languages and kings' (Rev 10.10–11).

The pattern is relatively simple—eat the scroll and deliver God's word—but the action suggests not just a command to practise what is preached, but something far more profound: God's word taking on flesh. Sadly, in Jonah's case, the notion of digesting God's word is turned on its head (or tail) when the *messenger* rather than the message becomes the thing swallowed. But fortunately for Jonah, the great fish (let's call it a whale) finds him as unpalatable as he finds God's merciful word.

Since Jonah's attempt to flee from God takes him straight into the belly of a whale, one might have expected the prayer of Jonah to take the form of an extended plea for God's forgiveness and deliverance, but it does not. Instead, Jonah's words, spoken from the belly of the whale, constitute a prayer of thanks to God for rescuing him. In other words, the whale is not perceived as punishment, but as a means of *salvation*. As Jonah sees it, his life was forfeit when he found himself sinking to 'the belly of Sheol'[8] (Jnh 2.2 NRSV) and to 'the roots of the mountains' (Jnh 2.6), so his prayer from inside the fish is one of immense gratitude. If we take the words of Jonah's psalm in chapter 2 at face value, Jonah considers himself very fortunate indeed.

> . . . he answered me.
> . . . you listened to my cry.

> . . . yet I will look again
>   towards your holy temple.
> . . . you brought my life up from the pit,
>   O LORD my God.

> . . . But I, with a song of thanksgiving,
>   will sacrifice to you.
> What I have vowed I will make good.
>   Salvation comes from the LORD (Jnh 2.2,4b,6b,9).

The critical question at this point is whether Jonah has yet digest-
ed the message God wants him to deliver. Has Jonah genuinely
repented of his rebellious attitude or are the words of his prayer,
well, just words? That question cannot be answered fully until
we see how Jonah will behave in Nineveh, but perhaps the language of the psalm contains some indication of the condition of
Jonah's heart.

Jonah 2 has commonly been identified as a pastiche of borrowed phrases from the Psalter. Almost every verse uses seg-
ments or whole lines from various psalms so that Jonah's prayer
comes across as being rather unoriginal in one sense.[9] Given the
fact that many psalms create word-pictures about falling, sinking
and being overcome by flood waters as metaphors for loneliness
and spiritual abandonment, these phrases are ideally suited to
Jonah's situation, where they take on a more literal meaning (e.g.
verses 3,5). But what might the author be hinting at through such
flagrant borrowing?

One possibility is that the author wants to pre-empt Jonah's
lack of sincerity and suggest that his psalm of worship is merely a
concoction of clichés from Israel's songbook, designed to turn the
heart of God and save his own hide. (In light of Jonah's response
to Yahweh once his feet are back on dry land, this interpretation
should not be dismissed too quickly.) Another related possibility
is that Jonah's exaggerated hymn of praise encourages the reader
to compare Jonah's delight in God's salvation when it applies to
himself—'Salvation comes from the LORD!'—with his reaction to
any mercy God might wish to show others later in the story.

In any case, the narrator offers no evaluation of the prayer; he
simply reports what happens next:

And the LORD commanded the fish, and it vomited Jonah onto dry land (Jnh 2.10).

Second Chances (Jonah 3)

Then the word of the LORD came to Jonah a second time: 'Go to the great city of Nineveh and proclaim to it the message I give you' (Jnh 3.1–2).

The parallel between Jonah 3.1–2 and Jonah 1.1–2 is obvious enough; Jonah is being given a second chance. This time, however, his response is more suited to his prophetic status: 'Jonah obeyed the word of the LORD and went to Nineveh' (Jnh 3.3). What is surprising, even shocking, is the way Jonah's *very* short sermon (just five words in Hebrew) has such an enormous impact on the 'exceedingly large city' (NRSV) of Nineveh. The remarkable success of Jonah's single-sentence sermon suggests two things: Jonah's unwilling disposition and Nineveh's readiness for change. 'Forty more days and Nineveh will be overturned,' Jonah proclaims (Jnh 3.4), and suddenly 'the Ninevites believed God' (Jnh 3.5). The king not only calls for city-wide repentance, but leads by example, removing his royal robes and repenting in sackcloth and ashes, as was the custom. Quoting part of a well-known creed concerning the God of Israel, the Ninevite king ponders aloud, 'Who knows? God may yet relent and with compassion turn from his fierce anger so that we will not perish' (Jnh 3.9).

It is remarkable for a foreign king to speak about Yahweh with such clarity. What's more, his words prove to be exactly right, for God responds to Nineveh with the same mercy shown to his own people in the past. The use of a quote from Exodus 32 makes this clear.

And the LORD changed his mind [*niham*] about the disaster [*ra'ah*] that he planned to bring on his people (Exod 32.14 NRSV).	God changed his mind [*niham*] about the calamity [*ra'ah*] that he had said he would bring upon them (Jnh 3.10b NRSV).

In Exodus 32, Yahweh relented concerning Israel in response to Moses' prayer; in Jonah 3, God relents concerning Nineveh in response to Jonah's reluctant preaching. As it turns out, Jonah's few words have indeed 'overturned' Nineveh, but God's merciful response to a citywide repentance is not quite what this prophet was hoping for.

A Right to Be Angry? (Jonah 4)

To say that God's mercy was 'displeasing' to Jonah (as the NIV and NRSV do) is not putting it quite strongly enough. A more literal translation of Jonah 4.1 is: 'But this was evil to Jonah—a great evil [*ra'ah*]—and he burned with anger!' The use of the same word here [*ra'ah*] as that used in the previous verse (Jnh 3.10) makes the point that God's mercy (*not* bringing disaster) is disastrous in the eyes of Jonah. The wordplay in these verses is pivotal to the whole story's meaning; Jonah is so far from sharing God's passion that the characteristic mercy of God is something he considers evil. Now, for the first time in the story, Jonah lets fly with his reasons for fleeing in the first place:

> O LORD, is this not what I said when I was still at home? That is why I was so quick to flee to Tarshish. I knew that you are a gracious and compassionate God, slow to anger and abounding in love, a God who relents from sending calamity (Jnh 4.2).

To this defiant prophet, God's mercy is displeasing because it is far too accessible, reaching even to the *Assyrians*. But in the same breath Jonah reveals that he also knows the creed concerning Yahweh's character. His comment, combined with the Ninevite king's statement, makes up the words found in Joel 2.13–14:[10]

I knew that you are a gracious and compassionate God, slow to anger and abounding in love, a God who relents from sending calamity (Jnh 4.2b; Jonah).	Return to the LORD your God, for he is gracious and compassionate, slow to anger and abounding in love, and he relents from sending calamity.

Who knows? God may yet relent [*shuv*] and with compassion turn [*niham*] from his fierce anger so that we will not perish (Jnh 3.9; the king of Nineveh).	Who knows? He may turn [*shuv*] and have pity [*niham*] and leave behind a blessing (Joel 2.13–14).

By referring to the classic statement about Yahweh's nature from Exodus 34.6 (see 'Persuading God' in chapter 2), the narrative suggests a comparison between Jonah and Moses. Moses prayed to remind Yahweh of his divine purpose; Jonah shamelessly declares that God's actions are not lining up with the wayward prophet's hopes (for the Ninevites to get what they deserve). Moses offered to die on behalf of the people (Exod 32.32); Jonah wishes himself dead because of their salvation (Jnh 4.3). Moses cites the above-mentioned creed to invoke the mercy of God; Jonah uses it to justify his anger with God. Of course, Jonah is bound to come off second best in comparison to Israel's paradigmatic prophet,[11] but the narrative also brings to mind another disoriented prophet who lost his way.

When Elijah fled from Jezebel after the fireworks on Mount Carmel, he too sat under a tree in the desert feeling sorry for himself and wishing he were dead. On that occasion God had posed the question, 'What are you doing here?' (1 Kgs 19.9,13) God's question for Jonah (also asked twice) is different—'Do you have a right to be angry?' (Jnh 4.4,9)—but it goes to the heart of Jonah's burnout in a similar way.[12]

As the dust settles from Jonah's tantrum, God again exercises his power over creation to teach Jonah a lesson. A vine provides Jonah with shade to ease his 'discomfort' (Jnh 4.6). (Again the word *ra'ah* is used to suggest that Jonah's discomfort has been caused by God's mercy.) But no sooner does Jonah begin to cheer up than a worm is sent to kill the vine. Without its shade, Jonah is burnt by the sun and scorched by a wind from the desert. Again comes God's question, 'Do you have a right to be angry?' to which Jonah responds, 'I am angry enough to die' (Jnh 4.9).

To help Jonah understand things from a divine perspective, God gives him a plant to shade him—something the prophet takes great pleasure in—and then takes it away again. Jonah is set up to feel a sense of loss over the vine so that he may (even *slightly*) begin to identify with God's concern for 120,000 spiritually disoriented Ninevites 'who cannot tell their right hand from their left'. But Jonah still cannot bring himself to accept that Yahweh may wish to extend his mercy beyond Israel's borders. So, rather than coming to any neat conclusions, his story ends with a question:

> What's this? How is it that you can change your feelings from pleasure to anger overnight about a mere shade tree that you did nothing to get? You neither planted nor watered it. It grew up one night and died the next night. So, why can't I likewise change what I feel about Nineveh from anger to pleasure, this big city of more than 120,000 childlike people who don't yet know right from wrong, to say nothing of all the innocent animals? (Jnh 4.10–11 MSG)

Of course, if Jonah were worth his salt as a prophet such a question would not need to be asked at all. But since God's first question made no impact on Jonah's stubbornness, these final words may be understood as God's last-ditch attempt to restore his defective messenger.

Biblical narratives invite readers in so that we may live *out* our responses to the text (see 'Storied Spirituality' in chapter 1). So although the book of Jonah ends with a question, and we cannot know whether Jonah repented or ran, readers are able to give the story closure by making their own response to it.

Mercy at Any Cost

As Nineveh bows her head in repentance and ashes, a result most preachers would be delighted with, Jonah sits outside the city walls, seething with rage. One of the book's great ironies is the way in which non-Israelites (the Gentiles on the boat and the Ninevites) rejoice in their salvation even while Jonah holds fast to his narrow-minded view of justice and correctness. God's offer of forgiveness is obviously far more inclusive than the one in

Jonah's purview. The wayward prophet's own agenda, perhaps fuelled by prophecies concerning Israel's geographic expansion in Nineveh's direction (2 Kgs 14.25), seem to have clouded his vision of God's immeasurable grace. It is a tragic scene of course, but before we judge Jonah too quickly for his shortcomings, let us consider what lies beneath his rage, since each of us shares his human condition.

Jonah declares that 'Salvation comes from the LORD' (Jnh 2.9), but he also believes (without shouting it aloud) that salvation is for Israel alone. Therefore, Jonah flees in an attempt to prevent God from forgiving the Assyrians, since their salvation would taint his national identity as an Israelite. (It is, of course, wonderfully ironic that he brings a boatload of Gentiles to faith on the way!) Attitudes of exclusion often grow out of a notion of purity that sees anything *different* or 'other' to be dangerous, a potential threat to our (imagined) purity.[13] 'Others strike us like objects that are "out of place", like "dirt" that needs to be removed in order to restore the sense of propriety to our world.'[14] At their worst, perverse notions of purity like this lead to heinous crimes against humanity, acts of exclusion as horrific as the Holocaust or the Rwandan genocide of 1994.

World events like these perhaps seem far removed from our own spheres of responsibility, but the seeds for such acts of exclusion are much closer to home. Even deeds of apparent righteousness, designed to separate us from 'the world', become exclusionary if we end up distancing ourselves from the very people Jesus came to love, to heal and to save (see Mk 2.17). In Matthew 9.10–13, when his disciples were asked why Jesus regularly dined with reputable sinners, Jesus cut to the heart of the matter by quoting Hosea 6.6: 'Go and learn what this means: "I desire *mercy*, not sacrifice."'

The book of Jonah is about mercy; God's abundance and Jonah's deficiency. The capacity to show mercy to others is a fruit that grows in proportion to one's acceptance of God's mercy; the two are inseparable (Mt 6.14–15). But Jonah simply couldn't stomach the bittersweet message of mercy that finds expression in forgiven-ness and forgiveness.

Putting it like this, however, sounds almost formulaic, and I do not mean to underplay the costliness of forgiveness for the person who has been hurt. To be sure, genuine forgiveness can be extremely painful for the forgiver since he or she must bear the sin of the offender, part of what it means to bear one's cross with Christ.[15] To be sinned against without making things even in any way is to *absorb* that wrongdoing,[16] and if this all sounds just too difficult, let us be reminded that we are not just trying to imitate Jesus. Our acts of forgiveness are *re-enactments* of what God has done in Christ for us (2 Cor 5.18–20) and it is God's own Spirit within us who enables such extraordinary acts of mercy.

> Christ is not just outside us, modeling forgiveness and urging us to forgive. Christ lives in us . . . From Christ, we receive the power and the willingness to forgive. Christ forgives through us, and that is why we can forgive.[17]

Looking back over Jonah's story, it is clear that the deep unrest he felt at the beginning of the story is still there at the end. At no point (unless the prayer of chapter 2 is taken to be more sincere than I have suggested) does Jonah experience any real transformation. He does not properly come to terms with his calling nor with the merciful nature of his God, so we are left with the image of a lonely and bitter man, smouldering away in his 'justified' anger. But then, Jonah's story has been recorded for our benefit so that we might not be so stubborn when we too are asked, 'Do you have a right to be angry?' Rather than fleeing from forgiveness, stomping our feet in anger, or challenging God about his wrongheaded notions of justice, perhaps we will pause to consider the fact that we are already the recipients of a *massive* mercy.

Dig Deeper

■ What is mercy?

■ How can Christians take greater care to digest God's Word?

■ Think of the last time you felt angry. What events triggered that emotion?

■ Do you ever think of certain others as 'pollutants' to your 'purity'? If so, how do you treat them?

■ Read Matthew 18.23-35. How does this parable challenge you?

10

Prophetic Signs: Enacted Parables

HOSEA

Say to them, 'I am a sign to you' (Eze 12.11a).

Hosea 1 – 3; 11

Enacted Parables

The so-called sexual revolution of the 1960s left numerous changes in its wake, not least the attitude that sexuality is no longer a private matter. In fifty years we have gone from repressing sex to obsessing about it. Sex doesn't just sell films and music; it sells ice cream, toothbrushes, furniture and a host of other grocery items and household goods. What's more, it is now near impossible to travel through any major city in Europe, the Americas or Australia without being bombarded by images that are at least suggestive, if not overtly sexual.

Even so, if a local man of the cloth were to leave home one morning in search of a prostitute to marry, we would be rather shocked by the report on the evening news. And if such a thing would cause alarm today, what kind of stir would it have caused almost three thousand years ago? For not only did Hosea marry a prostitute, but he went on to have three children with her and to give each of them rather awful names that had apparent significance for the onlooking nation. Perhaps most disturbing of all was his claim to have done all of this 'because the land is guilty of the vilest adultery in departing from the LORD' (Hos 1.2). Wasn't it rather contradictory for someone representing God to go to such extremes just to make a point about the moral failure of his nation? What are we to make of a sexual scandal like this, involving a prophet of Yahweh?

It will be helpful to step back and ask a few contextual questions. First, is there any precedent for a prophet of Yahweh 'acting out' like this? And second, is there anything peculiar about Hosea's cultural context that might explain his bizarre behaviour?

In answer to the first question, other enacted parables may be recalled from preceding chapters. Generally speaking, an enacted parable uses a prop of some description to add symbolic potency to a spoken message. In 1 Kings 11, for instance, Ahijah tore his cloak into twelve pieces to symbolize the twelve tribes of Israel and then entrusted ten of them to Jeroboam son of Nebat. (Samuel's robe served a similar purpose in his altercation with Saul, although in Samuel's case it was rather more spontaneous.) Similarly, during Micaiah's confrontation with the false prophets in 1 Kings 22, Zedekiah had used a pair of iron horns to reinforce his oracle of victory, 'With these you will gore the Arameans!'

At the outset, then, we can acknowledge that Hosea is not the first prophet to put on a performance, and nor is he the last. As well as Hosea's marriage to a notorious whore from the local fertility cult, a range of other prophetic signs are recorded in Scripture as well, including drawing pictures (Eze 4.1; Jn 8.6–8), shaving in public (Eze 5.1–4) and smashing a pot (Jer 19.10–11) to name but a few. The unique element in Hosea's case, however, is the absence of any external prop; Hosea *himself* provides the substance for the prophetic sign.

In answer to our second question (concerning cultural context), the mixed metaphor of sexual promiscuity with religious devotion was not simply Hosea's clever invention in order to achieve a more emotionally charged message. Even before Hosea took a cult prostitute to be his wife, he was already surrounded by a perverse concoction of sex and religion. His context was not so different from that of Elijah's, in which Israel had struggled to remain pure in a land still heavily involved with Canaanite religious practices. And so, against the backdrop of other enacted parables and his distinct cultural setting, Hosea's sex scandal turns out to be a prophetic sign chosen by God to convey a rather poignant message where 'metaphor and reality are almost synonymous.'[1]

Direct, tell-it-like-it-is approaches are ineffective on audiences who are as deaf as the false idols they worship. So as Israel became increasingly idolatrous and unwilling to heed the warnings of Yahweh's watchmen, many of her prophets resorted to more symbolic means of communication via spoken and enacted parables.[2] But some may wish to ask, why make God's word more cryptic through parables and symbolic actions when Israel was already failing to hear and understand? Wouldn't it have served the nation better to dumb things down and get back to basics? This is an important question that will be addressed head-on in the next chapter; for now it will suffice to understand that God's word was dressed up in riddles and street theatre to distinguish genuine believers from hypocrites. Only those with minds unclogged by idolatry could understand prophetic signs.

Love Triangle (Hosea 1; 3)

Hosea began his ministry under the reign of Jeroboam II (the king Jonah prophesied about in 2 Kgs 14.25) and was active for almost thirty years (750–722 BC). There is no record of him being trained to understand the word of God (see Jer 1) or of his response to a theophany or voice (see Exod 3; 1 Sam 3). We are simply told that 'When the LORD began to speak through Hosea, the LORD said—' and we are projected straight into a drama exposing the inner life of God through the prophet's marriage to a woman of questionable character. As one commentator has expressed it, Hosea crashed onto Israel's public scene waving a banner that read, 'God has a wife!'[3]

Israel's idolatry was akin to an illicit affair. She had betrayed the love and trust of her legitimate Husband, Yahweh, and sought refuge in the arms of Baal.[4] Hosea therefore adopted God's perspective by wedding himself to a harlot, which is precisely what Israel had become in God's eyes (Jer 3.1). It is quite possible, however, that Gomer was not simply a prostitute, but 'one whose sexual promiscuity was a matter of the very harlotry of Israel in the cult of Baal.'[5]

The Hebrew term used to describe Gomer, translated 'adulterous wife' (NIV) or 'wife of whoredom' (NRSV), may suggest that her class was one of promiscuity in relation to the fertility cult.[6] If this was indeed the case, then Gomer's unfaithfulness to Hosea and her role in leading the nation astray are inextricably linked.

In the mythology of Baalism, the Canaanite god Baal died annually and descended into the underworld for the winter period. There he would find his mate, Anat, and enter into sexual union with her, bringing spring's rain and summer's harvest. Since cultic practices aimed to imitate the beliefs inherent in their mythology, Baal worshippers would visit local shrines ('high places'; Hos 10.8) to engage in fertility rites with cult prostitutes and thereby participate in the restoration of fertility to the earth.[7] In Elijah's day, Ahab had already begun to mix Israel's worship of Yahweh with the cultic practices of Baalism (1 Kgs 16.30–33), so by Hosea's time, a hundred years later, the disease of idolatry ran deep in Israel's veins.

Israel's adultery was not so much an outright denial of God as it was a desire to combine Yahwism with other 'options.'[8] The issue was whether fullness of life came from Yahweh *alone* or from Yahweh *plus* . . . This is why God expressed such anger with Israel's habit of giving the Baals credit for *his* gifts (Hos 2.5,8–9). The covenant established between God and Israel was intended to be exclusive, and the true Lord of agricultural and sexual fertility does not share his glory with another (see Isa 42.8; Deut 23.17–18).

Central to Hosea's message was this enacted love triangle between a prophet, a prostitute and the Baal cultus, a complex affair which mirrored the relationships between Yahweh, Israel and the Canaanite gods.

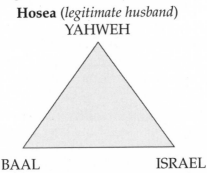

Hosea (*legitimate husband*)
YAHWEH

BAAL   ISRAEL
Baal cult (*illegitimate husband*)   **Gomer** (*cult prostitute* → *wife*)

The names of Gomer's children were expressions of the growing divide between God and his people, but they were not all bad news. While the three names initially signify judgement in Hosea 1.4–9, they are cleverly reversed to become prophecies of hope in Hosea 1.10–2.1. We will consider them here briefly.

The third child, Lo-Ammi (Not-my-people), embodied the rather offensive message that the Israelites had no exclusive claims on Yahweh, a point that was also made by Hosea's contemporary, Amos (Amos 9.7).

Hosea's daughter, Lo-Ruhamah (Not-pitied), was a warning to Israel that God would eventually turn his back on her, even if only for a moment (see Isa 54.8). Later in Hosea's lifetime, when the Assyrians attacked from the north, God would not deliver his people as he had done previously. Both these names are easily reversed by removing *Lo*, meaning 'not,' which is precisely what happens in Hosea 2.1, meaning that Israel would again be shown compassion (*ruhamah*) as God's people (*ammi*) in the future.

The first child's name, Jezreel, also contained messages of both judgement and hope. Because Jehu had taken things into his own hands with an unsolicited bloodbath in Elisha's day (2 Kgs 10), God proclaimed through Hosea that he intended to punish Jehu's family line by 'scattering' (*zara'*) them. In the future, however, God promised once again to 'sow' (*zara'*)[9] Israel in her own land. The verb *zara'*, contained in the name Jezreel, can mean either 'to scatter' (signifying judgement) or 'to sow' (stressing Yahweh's Lordship over fertility). 'Jezreel' therefore turns from a word of judgement ('God will scatter') in Hosea 1.4–5 to a word of hope ('God will sow') in Hosea 1.11. The promise to restore Israel meant that Yahweh was not only the Lord of harvest and fertility, but also of salvation.[10]

Hosea 3 builds on Hosea 1, although it is apparent that much has transpired between the two chapters. Gomer has left Hosea and committed adultery, making Yahweh's next command a tough one:

> The LORD said to me, 'Go, show your love to your wife again, though she is loved by another and is an adulteress. Love her as the LORD loves the Israelites, though they turn to other gods and love the sacred raisin cakes' (Hos 3.1).

Hosea buys Gomer back for 'many days' (Hos 3.3), a period during which she is to cease her promiscuity. By staying away from other lovers, she enacts Israel's coming exile, a time when the nation will be forced to live 'without king or prince, without sacrifice or sacred stones, without ephod or idol' (Hos 3.4). But the immediate burden falls upon Hosea, who is commanded to love her relentlessly even 'as the LORD loves the Israelites'. The prophet's tenacious love for Gomer aims to pierce her numb condition, drawing her back to him just as 'the Israelites will return and seek the LORD their God . . . [and] his blessings in the last days' (Hos 3.5). Although 'she is loved by another' and would prefer to be somewhere else, Hosea is commanded to love her nonetheless, just as Yahweh persists in loving a people who 'turn to other gods and love the sacred raisin cakes.' Yes, that's right, the object of their affection was *raisin cakes:*

> The abrupt mention of raisin cakes seems odd. And that is the point. Her love *is* oddly misplaced . . . the last clause of verse 1 makes the telling point that what attracts Israel to her false lover is a trivial and earthly pleasure.[11]

Before we laugh and shake our heads in disdain, let us pause to consider our own misplaced affections for things equally trivial: a certain item of clothing or pair of shoes, a particular mobile phone or flat-screen TV . . . Fill in the blank yourself and be reminded that we are not so different from the Israelites of Hosea's day.

So the stage is set and the script written. The audience take their seats and the stage-director begins to call the shots. Gomer plays the adulterous wife and Hosea the jealous husband in a relatively simple tale:

> *The main character (Yahweh) pledges his undying commitment to a woman (Israel) in the hope of redeeming her from a sordid past. But romance quickly turns to tragedy as Israel abandons her Husband for the arms of previous lovers (see Eze 16). Although the betrayal creates a massive rift between them, Yahweh cannot bring himself to fully turn his back on Israel. One day, he swears, they will be reunited.*

It is not my intention, in simplifying the story like this, to belittle Hosea's enfleshment of God's emotional life, which surely affected him deeply. By digesting God's word and sharing his passion, Hosea's life became a visible sign of God's longing to be reconciled with his people. But the question still remained, would Israel recognize the unfolding of her own tragic story in the family dynamics of this local prophet?

Idolatry is Adultery (Hosea 2)

Hosea's words and actions had a profound influence on prophets after him, who also sought to address Israel's 'spirit of prostitution' (Hos 5.4). Jeremiah spoke of God giving 'faithless Israel her certificate of divorce . . . because of all her adulteries' (Jer 3.8), and Ezekiel recounted the tragic love story of God and Israel using very sexually explicit language (Eze 16; 23). But whatever metaphors or analogies were used, the heart of the message remained the same: idolatry equates to spiritual adultery.

As an aside, while I cannot know how it feels to read texts like Hosea 1–3 as a woman, I can imagine that some female readers may find this particular metaphor problematic. God is the faithful, loving man and Israel the cheating, promiscuous woman. Is the parable inherently degrading to women? Would a female prophet have used the same language? The short answer (which is all we have space for here) is that prophets like Hosea, Jeremiah and Ezekiel did not use such images to deliberately offend women. Actually, they offended *everyone* with their preaching, regardless of gender, and Hosea explicitly blamed *men* for Israel's whoredom (Hos 4.14). What's more, being inspired as God's messengers did not mean that prophets could rise above their patriarchal, historical contexts to use imagery that would not offend readers some three thousand years later. Some degree of culture clash is inevitable when drawing contemporary meaning from ancient texts.[12]

Thousands of years after these oracles were spoken and written down, we may wonder why the Israelites chose lifeless objects made of wood (Hos 4.12) as alternatives to Yahweh, who had demonstrated real power and love in so many tangible ways. (The sarcastic tone of Isaiah 44.12–20 makes this very point.) But the spirit of prostitution is still alive and kicking today, even if our affairs are with the more sophisticated gods of technology, career, financial security, knowledge, personal appearance and the like. Many Christians today still find themselves caught up in spiritual love triangles which threaten to undermine God's rightful place in our lives.

Hosea 2 is for the most part a message condemning Israel for getting caught up in an adulterous/idolatrous relationship, but Hosea's sermon is more than just a lengthy rebuke. Through the use of a rhetorical device that highlights the crux of a message by placing it at the centre, our attention is drawn to a message of love and restoration.

A. Hos 2.2–5: Israel is no longer my people; she worships other gods.

   B. Hos 2.6–7: Israel will cease breaking covenant and return (*shuv*) to her Husband.

      C. Hos 2.8–13: Israel's lips speak Baal's name in response to my generosity.

         D. Hos 2.14–15: I will woo her (in the desert again) and restore our relationship.

      C'. Hos 2.16–17: Israel's lips will speak my name ('Husband') instead of 'Baal'.

   B'. Hos 2.18–20: Israel will renew her covenant vows and remarry her Husband.

A'. Hos 2.21–23: Israel will again be my people and acknowledge the one true God.

Hosea's sermon spells out the consequences of infidelity for both Israel and Gomer: her children will be rejected since they were conceived in shame (Hos 2.4,5a); her access to rivals will be restricted so that she might learn to appreciate what she has 'at home' (Hos 2.6–7); she will no longer be provided for but rather stripped naked as an act of public humiliation (Hos 2.8–10); the 'gifts' from her lovers will be ruined (Hos 2.12); and she will be punished for dressing up to attract strangers (Hos 2.13). Of course, these statements could refer either to Gomer in particular or, more figuratively, to all of Israel. It is only after a dozen verses that Hosea for the first time utters the phrase, 'declares the

LORD.' Without it, we might have assumed he was still speaking
of his own marriage, and that is precisely the point. God has
drawn Hosea into a place where he 'carries within himself the
awareness of what is happening to God.'[13]

It is just at the point of giving away the identity of the Speaker
that Hosea's harsh language of condemnation turns to pity and a
longing for reconciliation. The Valley of Achor (meaning 'trouble') will be transformed into a Door of Hope (Hos 2.15) as God
and his people are (re)united in marriage 'for ever'. God's
renewed covenant with Israel is described in creational terms and
a continuous line is drawn from God to the skies, to the earth, to
the harvest, and to his people (Hos 2.21–22). In conclusion, Hosea
reiterates the wordplays introduced earlier, stressing their more
hopeful tones.

> And I will sow [*zara'*] him for myself in the land.
> And I will have pity on Lo-ruhamah,
>   and I will say to Lo-ammi, 'You are my people';
>   and he shall say, 'You are my God' (Hos 2.23 NRSV).

Hosea's message powerfully sets this word of hope against one
of the harshest metaphors for betrayal. Even in spite of Israel's
repeated, flagrant adultery, Yahweh chooses to sow seeds of love
yet again. This redemptive turn in Hosea's preaching is developed in a different way in Hosea 11, which has been called 'a
panorama of Hosea's whole message.'[14]

The Prodigal Father (Hosea 11)

Hosea 11.1–11 is a stunning poem within which the metaphor
shifts from a Husband's anguish over his unfaithful wife (Hos
1–3) to the grief of a rejected Father longing for the return of his
prodigal son. The much-used but rarely defined word 'prodigal' can mean one of two things: 'an extravagant generosity' or
'a wasteful and reckless spending of resources', so that what
we have in Hosea 11.1–11 and Luke 15.11–32 are stories of a
Father who is prodigal in affection for his prodigal (reckless)
son.

Hosea 11 follows a similar progression (or regression) to that of Hosea 2. God has loved and rescued his son from Egypt, but the more he calls after him, the more he resists (Hos 11.2). Ephraim was the second-born son of Joseph who was blessed in preference to Manasseh by Jacob (Gen 48.13–20) and it would seem that Hosea speaks of 'Ephraim' in this poem to differentiate between 'Israel' of the exodus and the nation at the time of Hosea's preaching.[15]

Even though God feeds Ephraim and teaches him to walk, the boy resists his every act of lovingkindness. Needless to say, this is not what God had anticipated! Verses 5–7 go on to express the painful sentiment that if Ephraim is so determined to turn from his Father (Hos 11.7), then he may 'return to Egypt' (Hos 11.5) where he was first adopted. As Hosea preaches, his audience is invited to feel God's angst and perhaps even to acknowledge the deservedness of Ephraim's punishment. But just when it seems that divine judgement is an irreversible certainty, something very strange happens.

God hesitates . . . and questions himself.[16]

> How can I give you up, Ephraim?
>> How can I hand you over, Israel?
> How can I treat you like Admah?
>> How can I make you like Zeboiim?
> My heart is changed within me;
>> all my compassion is aroused (Hos 11.8).

God's internal questions compare the ruin of his beloved son, Ephraim, to the complete destruction of Sodom and Gomorrah in Genesis 18 (Admah and Zeboiim refer to Sodom and Gomorrah; see Deut 29.23). As Yahweh reflects on the pain of losing Ephraim, he does not become more bent on anger and justice, but rather less so. The memory of Abraham's persistent prayers and the utter destruction of those cities causes a change of heart so that God's compassion is warmed to an alternative resolution:

> I will not carry out my fierce anger,
>> nor will I turn and devastate Ephraim.

> For I am God, and not man—
> the Holy One among you.
> I will not come in wrath (Hos 11.9).

Hosea has spoken of God as Husband (Hos 1–3) and Father (Hos 11), but these images can take God's Self-expression no further.[17] Analogies and metaphors have reached their limits; 'For I am God, and not man.' God will not respond to his bride/son as a human being would do. Rather, he will remain 'in character' with the way Hosea has presented him: merciful and forgiving.

Incarnate Word

We have considered how Hosea's experiences turned him into 'a double of God';[18] God's word to Israel wrapped in human form in such a profound manner that it becomes more appropriate to speak of *incarnation* than imitation. 'The prophet, in effect, is called to function as an ongoing theophany.'[19] On the subject of God in human form, one scholar has gone so far as to suggest that

> certain special individuals are so decisively seized by God that their lives become a simile, a reflection, of God. In limited, imperfect, and partial form, the lives of these extraordinary servants of God are molded into veritable parables of YHWH so that, on rare but significant occasions, they can even be called 'gods' who are singled out to stand for the divine in the midst of the mundane.[20]

If this sounds too bold or overstated, consider how God's Self-revelation is fully expressed in the life of Christ, and how, after Jesus' resurrection and ascension, the church inhales the divine breath[21] so that his life may continue to be revealed in and through committed believers: 'I am in my Father, and you are in me, and I am in you' (Jn 14.20). The fusion of the prophetic with the divine is expressed in a number of ways in Hosea. As well as the obvious correlation in experience (see 'Love Triangle' above), there is also a merging of voices in Hosea 2. The chapter begins with the cry of a broken and rejected man whose only way of communicating with his ex-wife is by putting words into the mouths of their children:

> Rebuke your mother, rebuke her,
>> for she is not my wife,
>> and I am not her husband (Hos 2.2a).

It is not difficult to imagine these words to be Hosea's own, but as his speech progresses, taking up issues other than those within his own family, we begin to wonder: Is this Hosea speaking to Gomer? Or Yahweh speaking to Israel? The identity of the speaker remains uncertain until in verse 13 the words 'declares the LORD' send our eyes flitting back over the text a second time.

Another stylistic device that expresses how Hosea's life has become intertwined with God's is the divine point of view adopted by Hosea. Generally speaking, the prophets used enacted parables to dramatize the fate of the *people* as a warning to them (e.g. Eze 4–5), but Hosea's preoccupation is entirely with God's situation. Unlike Moses, Samuel, and Jeremiah, 'Hosea never tries to plead for the people or to dwell upon the reasons for the people's alienation from God. He has only one perspective: the divine partner.'[22]

In light of all this, the challenge posed by Hosea's prophetic spirituality seems rather foreboding, does it not? Can we really be God's hands and feet? Can we really make the Creator of the universe *visible* within the world and *known* to the world? Well, yes, actually that's exactly it, our great calling and even greater privilege! The Bible's claim that we were created in the image of God (Gen 1.27) suggests that the fundamental purpose of human existence is to reflect that image as accurately as humanly possible in order to make God known throughout the world. Like Hosea, each of us is called to 'play God' in an enacted drama that unveils, for all to see, the relentless love of God for a resistant people.

The Book of Common Prayer defines a sacrament as an 'outward and visible sign of an inward and spiritual grace.' Just as the water of baptism signifies our cleansing from sin, and as the bread we break together signifies our 'participation in the body of Christ' (1 Cor 10.16), so God's presence in the rudimentary details of our living makes each of us a sacrament, a visible sign to the world of the most profound gift of grace within, the very life of God.

I say more: the just man justices;
Keeps grace: that keeps all his goings graces;
Acts in God's eye what in God's eye he is—
Christ—for Christ plays in ten thousand places,
Lovely in limbs, and lovely in eyes not his
To the Father through the features of men's faces.[23]

Dig Deeper

■ How are sex and religion related in today's culture?

■ Think back through your day. If it were interpreted as an enacted parable, what was your message?

■ What 'Baals' impinge on your relationship with God?

■ Do you find it more natural to think of God as Father or Husband? What other metaphors enrich your understanding of God?

■ Read Romans 8.9-11. What does Paul suggest as a key to becoming a visible expression of God's life? (The word occurs six times in three verses.)

11

Prophetic Calling: Preaching to Divide

ISAIAH

This is why I speak to them in parables:
'Though seeing, they do not see;
though hearing, they do not hear or understand' (Mt 13.13).

Isaiah 6 – 7 (2 Kings 16)

Tough Call (Isaiah 6.1–5)

Not once in the Bible is a prophet appointed just because Israel is
running short on preachers. In every instance prophets are called
by God because particular situations need addressing. It is no
wonder they tended to squirm and make excuses in their moment
of summons. The call to represent Yahweh meant rocky times
ahead.[1] Moses' call sent him straight into enemy territory: 'So now,
go. I am sending you to Pharaoh to bring my people the Israelites
out of Egypt' (Exod 3.10). Likewise, young Samuel woke from a
disturbing night's sleep to immediately prophesy doom upon his
master's household. Amos left the tranquillity of life as a shepherd
and gardener to become one of the most direct spokesmen for
Yahweh on record and, to put it mildly, his sermons were not well
received: 'Get out, you seer! Go back to the land of Judah. Earn
your bread there and do your prophesying there' (Amos 7.12).

Isaiah, Jeremiah and Ezekiel were each given ample warning
of what lay before them when they were called. Jeremiah became

like 'a fortified city, an iron pillar and a bronze wall to stand against the whole land—against the kings of Judah, its officials, its priests and the people of the land' (Jer 1.18) and Ezekiel was likewise made 'unyielding and hardened' with a 'forehead like the hardest stone, harder than flint' (Eze 3.8–9). As for Isaiah, we will see that his response to the divine summons—'Who will go for us?'[2]—also segues into a prophetic confrontation with King Ahaz.

Even those prophets for whom we have no record of an initial summons were deeply involved in the conflicts of their times. Think of Deborah in the thick of battle, Nathan the dangerous liaison in the king's courts, Ahijah who gives and takes kingdoms at Yahweh's command, and John the Baptist who was imprisoned and beheaded for publicly condemning Herod's affair with his sister-in-law (Lk 3.19–20). Jesus was no exception either; after being affirmed from the heavens, he was immediately led 'into the desert to be tempted by the devil' (Mt 3.17–4.1).

Jonah's troubles were different (after all, he breaks the prophetic mould in every way) since it was his own resistance that led him from divine summons into a sequence of battles against a raging storm, his own anger, and even Yahweh himself. But his story conveys a critical message, however unwillingly transmitted, that provides a fitting introduction to Isaiah 6–7. After resisting God's call, Jonah was swallowed up by Sheol, the land of the dead, before being restored after three days to complete his mission.[3] The idea that Israel's stubbornness would lead to her own exile (death) in preparation for a fresh start (resurrection) is the key to understanding Isaiah's unusual call narrative.

The opening chapter of Isaiah speaks of purification, an appropriate image considering the nation's desperate need for a new beginning and the prophetic impulse to purge what is marred:[4]

> See how the faithful city
>   has become a harlot!
> She once was full of justice;
>   righteousness used to dwell in her—
>   but now murderers!

> Your silver has become dross,
>   your choice wine is diluted with water . . .
> I will turn my hand against you;
>   I will thoroughly purge away your dross
>   and remove all your impurities (Isa 1.21–22,25; see Jer 6.27–30).

The time had finally come for Jerusalem to be cleansed from her incessant idolatry, and the death of a king who had initially succeeded with God's help only then to become proud and blasphemous (2 Chr 26) further accents the purificatory nature of Isaiah's call. King Uzziah's death[5] (c.740 BC) meant uncertain times as the people awaited the policies of their next ruler. (Remember Rehoboam's foolish campaign in 1 Kgs 12 to rule with even greater force than Solomon had done.) Isaiah plays on these expectations by juxtaposing two phrases: 'In the year that King Uzziah died' and 'I saw the LORD seated on a throne'. For the prophets at least, the future did not depend on Uzziah's successor but on Creation's King, whose glory filled not just the Jerusalem temple but 'the whole earth', according to the testimony of the seraphs who attended him (Isa 6.3).

And what a vision it was! As Isaiah describes it, Yahweh is seated on a throne way up above the Jerusalem temple so that just the hem of his robe reaches down to the temple—and fills it! Looking beyond Yahweh's throne to the heavens, Isaiah sees the *seraphim* (literally, 'fiery ones') flying about, singing God's praises and shielding their faces from the magnificence of divine majesty. The sound of heaven's worship makes even the doorposts of Solomon's massive temple shake as the place fills with smoke, and because of the din we can scarcely make out the words on the terrified prophet's lips: 'Woe is me . . .'

Merciful Judgement (Isaiah 6.6–10)

There is a consistency in theme whenever God meets with his heavenly council. Such gatherings are very often related to matters of judgement in response to human choices,[6] and this seems especially to be the case when God invites his prophets to attend. Micaiah's vision, which we considered in chapter 8, not only illustrates this point particularly well, but has a great deal in common with Isaiah's vision in other respects, too.[7]

Neither Micaiah nor Isaiah were drawn into Yahweh's council to make judgements of kings or nations. They were summoned to understand judgements already made and to deliver them in their relevant earthly contexts. The question, Who will go? features in both visions, although in Isaiah's case it is the prophet and not a lying spirit who answers. Both accounts also refer to the stiff-necked resistance of those under judgement; in Micaiah's case deceit brings Ahab to his ruin, whereas for Isaiah it is his preaching that will harden his listeners! In light of the common themes between these and other visions of Yahweh's heavenly council, we may brace ourselves for what will inevitably be at the core of Isaiah's vision: divine judgement.[8]

Like Jeremiah and Ezekiel, Isaiah's mouth is consecrated for the words he will speak,[9] but as well as having his lips cleansed, Isaiah is also forgiven. The seraph proclaims that his 'guilt is taken away' and his 'sin atoned for' (Isa 6.7), leaving us to ponder why this might be necessary. Are we to think that Isaiah was an especially sinful fellow prior to his call? According to what follows, Isaiah is being set apart from the rest of the nation. His first words put him on equal footing with the rest of Judah, 'I am a man of unclean lips, and I live among a people of unclean lips' (Isa 6.5), but the priestly action of the seraph absolves Isaiah's sin to distinguish him from the people so that 'he is free to step forward and respond when God calls—something the nation is forbidden. He can hear and see; they can do neither.'[10] Only the prophet (and his readership) will be made privy to the mysterious workings of the heavenly council in order to grasp what God is doing through Judah's hardening. No wonder Isaiah's theophany is so breathtaking; it is hard to imagine how he would ever have come to accept God's paradoxical proposal otherwise. But before we can anticipate the solution proposed in Isaiah's vision, we must consider the problem.

In short, Israel (and Judah) could not have failed more drastically. God's people had indeed come to stand apart from other nations—but by their *wickedness* (Eze 5.7)! The nation elected to reflect God's image in the world had taken on the likeness of lifeless idols instead, thereby twisting and subverting her national calling (see 'You Are What You Worship' in chapter 7). Isaiah picks up the themes of Israel's spiritual deafness, dumbness and blindness,[11] adding to them dullness of mind. From its opening verses, the book of Isaiah speaks of Israel's failure to *understand* as a consequence of her rejection of Yahweh:

> Hear, O heavens! Listen, O earth!
>   For the LORD has spoken:
> 'I reared children and brought them up,
>   but they have rebelled against me.
> The ox knows his master,
>   the donkey his owner's manger,
> but Israel does not know,
> *my people do not understand*' (Isa 1.2–3).

The idea is developed further in Isaiah 44.12–20, where idolaters are mocked for not understanding how blatantly foolish it is to worship something carved from a block of wood (see also Hab 2.18–19). Just as the idolaters in Exodus 32 became as 'stiff-necked' as their golden calf, so the idolaters in Isaiah 44 are as 'thick' as the piece of wood they worship. By taking on the image of stupid idols, 'their minds [are] closed so that they cannot understand' the foolishness of their ways (Isa 44.18).

Human beings do not become independent by resisting God's love, but inept. We are more alive, more *real*, as the recipients of God's love (Marjory Williams' classic story *The Velveteen Rabbit* illustrates this idea beautifully), but equally, we lose spiritual sensitivity when our hearts become fixed on things other than the One in whose image we were made. Like the idols exalted before us, we grow spiritually numb until—for some at least—a major crisis is required to break our hardened shell and renew spiritual awareness.

This was precisely Israel's problem. Already half-dead in idolatry, only the burial of exile would allow for the possibility of resurrection. Therefore, the heavenly council's verdict was tough.

> Go and tell this people,
>   'Listen! Listen! (But don't understand.)
>   Look! Look! (But don't figure it out.)'

Make the minds of these people lazy![12]
   Make them hard[13] of hearing!
   Blind them!
For if they see with their eyes,
   hear with their ears,
   and understand with their minds,
     they will turn and be saved! (Isa 6.9–10; author's translation)

Yahweh's verdict does not simply foretell that Israel will resist Isaiah's message; it affirms that this is precisely the purification process Yahweh and his heavenly council have decided upon. (We are reminded again of King Ahab's obduracy and the judgement decided for him in the heavenly council of 1 Kgs 22.) Isaiah will preach and the people will look and listen, but their closed minds will not understand. The monotonous sequence of deep-sin-followed-by-shallow-repentance had already characterized the life of Israel for hundreds of years, and if she continued to sin and repent, sin and repent, as she had done in the days of the judges, the cycle could conceivably go on ad infinitum. Israel had arrived at a juncture where things were not going to get any better until they first became decidedly worse. Once we grasp this, we can begin to appreciate Israel's hardening as an act of merciful judgement.

It may be helpful at this point to briefly discuss the notion of hardening hearts.[14] Was it really a case of God acting 'behind the scenes' to *make* Israel resistant, or were things taking their natural course for an obstinate people who had repeatedly chosen to flaunt their idolatry 'on the stage'? On one hand, it is unimaginable that the hearts of the Israelites would have been hardened by Yahweh had they been obedient and cooperative with his purposes, but neither can we affirm that Israel's stiff-neckedness had nothing whatsoever to do with the meeting of God's heavenly council (who do gather for judgement, after all). Ultimately, if we are looking for whom to blame for Israel's hardness of heart, we must begin with Israel and only then go on to say something about God. That is to say, Israel hardened herself against God for a long time before he intervened to intensify that reality.[15] The bottom line for Judah at the time of Isaiah's call was that she had become irreversibly infected with sin (Jer 9.1–8) and trapped in a relentless cycle which Yahweh intended to break. She had become a laughing-stock to the nations and a disgrace to her Husband, who was now going to withhold his mercy for a time and abandon her to her senseless (i.e. blind and deaf) disobedience.

God's hardening of hearts for judgement may be understood as an absence of divine mercy, which leaves nations and their leaders to their own devices for a time (see Ps 81.11–12). The immediate result is judgement, but with fresh possibilities beyond the horizon. The point is not that God has lost interest in the nation's repentance, for that would directly contradict the prime purpose of every other prophet before and after Isaiah. But God must judge Judah for her idolatry so that he may begin to do 'a new thing' (Isa 43.8–9,18–19). The same pattern can be identified in the New Testament. When Saul was blinded on his way to persecute the church in Damascus, his idolatry was dealt with through an act of merciful judgement whereby his spiritual blindness became physical (Acts 9.1–19).[16] After three days in the dark, Paul's vision was restored and his new life began, 'proving that Jesus is the Christ' (Acts 9.22). Saul's loss of vision for a period did not ruin him completely, but rather enabled him to discover God's call on his life. Similarly, the exile did not signify the end for Israel, but only a necessary progression beyond what the Law could do for her (see Rom 5.20; 8.3). In time, salvation would rise from Israel's dusty bones (Eze 37), even if Isaiah did not live to see it himself.

Seeds and Stumps (Isaiah 6.11–13)

Isaiah was not asked to preach half-heartedly, or to be unclear so that the people *could not* understand. Rather, he was called to divide Israel with the kind of preaching that made no allowance for fence-sitters. Even so, no matter how convincing Isaiah's words were, they would be like water off a duck's back to Israel, who would remain stubborn and unresponsive. The only fruit of Isaiah's preaching would be Israel's judgement for her failure to respond. There would be no successful altar calls, and not a single parishioner would ever come forward for prayer—and yet, according to Isaiah's commission, this would mean that the prophet had served his purpose.

'How long?' Isaiah asks. How long must I preach without results?

It is a reasonable question, but God's answer is as disheartening as the call itself:

> Until the cities lie ruined
>   and without inhabitant,
> until the houses are left deserted
>   and the fields ruined and ravaged,
> until the LORD has sent everyone far away
>   and the land is utterly forsaken.
> And though a tenth remains in the land,
>   it will again be laid waste [NRSV: burnt again] (Isa 6.11b–13a).

What a bleak future! When God's judgement did come, even the few ('a tenth') that managed to survive the initial devastation would be 'burnt again' to ensure complete destruction!

> But as the terebinth and oak
>   leave stumps when they are cut down,
>   so the holy seed will be the stump [in the land][17] (Isa 6.13b).

The image of Israel being felled like a giant oak and the remaining stump[18] being burnt for good measure is consistent with one of Ezekiel's enacted parables in which his hair and beard, representing the nation, were shaved off and divided it into three parts, no doubt before an intrigued audience (Eze 5.1–4; see also Isa 7.20; Jer 7.29). One third was burnt, another struck with a sword and yet another scattered to the wind. Of the few remaining strands that Ezekiel kept in his robe, he was later commanded to 'take a few of these and throw them into the fire and burn them up.' Neither Isaiah's burnt stump nor Ezekiel's shaved head offered much hope for Israel. Whether Israel's identification as 'the holy seed' in verse 13 is taken as a hint toward the possibility of regrowth or as yet another word of condemnation (i.e. that even Israel's remnant would be idolatrous),[19] Isaiah's ministry had a grim outlook. That much was certain.

But one matter still remains unclear. Exactly how does a prophet go about preaching to an audience (for whom we can assume an average level of intelligence) without them understanding anything of his message? What form of communication might be used to *prevent* understanding? It would need to be something cryptic, a way of 'saying it sideways' . . . ah yes, a parable.

The Heart of Ahaz (Isaiah 7/2 Kings 16)

From Isaiah 6 to 7, we move from a surreal vision of the heavenly council to the immediate, life-threatening historical context of the prophet and his people. And what better to test the heart of Uzziah's grandson Ahaz[20] than an impending war?

> It is hardly co-incidental that Yahweh's commissioning of Isaiah to implement the divine verdict [Isa 6.9–10] is immediately followed by an encounter with the nation's ultimate leader, Ahaz (7:1ff). Ahaz's 'pious' rejection of Yahweh's word is not only paradigmatic, but also provides the archetypical illustration of how the prophet's message confirms the nation's unbelieving and idolatrous authorities in their blindness.[21]

In Isaiah 7.2 we read that 'the hearts of Ahaz and his people were shaken' at news of an alliance between Rezin of Aram (Syria) and Pekah of Israel (Ephraim), who had joined forces in response to Assyria's expanding presence in the north (see map). In response to the king's fear, Yahweh sent Isaiah and his son 'to meet Ahaz at the end of the aqueduct of the Upper Pool, on the road to the Washerman's Field' (Isa 7.3). It is quite possible that the king was checking on water supplies in anticipation of the impending siege on Jerusalem when Isaiah and his son met him to propose a solution (see 2 Kgs 16.5).

Ahaz's dilemma ultimately turned on the question of where to place his trust. Two options were laid open before him: Ahaz could plead for intervention from Assyria (the vastly greater power in the far north) to save him from the immediate threat of the Syro-Ephraimite coalition; or he could stand firm and trust in

Yahweh, as Isaiah implored him to do through spoken word and prophetic sign. God's word of assurance, 'Be careful, keep calm and don't be afraid' (Isa 7.4) was accompanied by the symbolic presence of Isaiah's son (see Isa 8.18), Shear-Jashub, whose name meant 'A remnant will remain'.

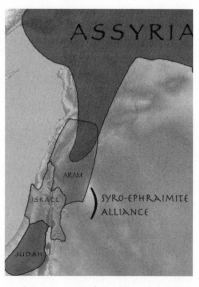

The interpretation of the boy's name that makes most sense of the immediate context is one where the 'remnant' refers not to Judah's future remnant (as it does in Isa 20.21), but to the scattered survivors of the Syro-Ephraimite alliance, so that when Isaiah's words are combined with the prophetic sign, God's message to Ahaz is, 'Be careful, keep calm and don't be afraid (Isa 7.4) . . . *for only a remnant will remain.*' Isaiah's prophetic sign (his son) complemented the spoken message.[22]

Isaiah's children, like Hosea's, functioned like parables by dividing the hearts of those who saw them: those who understood from those who did not (Isa 8.18). Ahaz was forced to choose sides by making a decision that would either crown Yahweh as King or expose his own idolatrous condition. Although few of us are in positions of such power, Ahaz's decision consisted of the same basic choice many of us face quite regularly: whether to trust in human resourcefulness or an unseen God.

According to Isaiah, both Ephraim and Syria were nothing more than 'smouldering stubs of firewood' compared to the Assyrian superpower that was approaching. Engaging in political negotiations with Assyria would be like opening the back door to a raging bushfire in order to escape from a few coals that had fallen from the hearth. Isaiah prophesied that the nations threatening Ahaz would be reduced to a remnant soon enough, and if the prophet's word and accompanying sign were not convincing enough, Ahaz was permitted to ask for a sign from God—*any* sign of his choosing!—to verify the prophecy.

Having made up his mind already, Ahaz refused to ask for any sign from God under the pretence of keeping the Law: 'I will not ask; I will not put the LORD to the test' (Isa 7.12; see Deut 6.16). Seeing past his farcical piety, Isaiah warned Ahaz against trying God's patience and declared that Yahweh himself would choose a sign for Ahaz; another parable in human form, this one named Immanuel ('God with us').[23] Note that the boy Immanuel in this context was not a symbol of hope, not the child we sing about at Christmastime! Rather, Isaiah's second child was God's response to Ahaz's lack of faith, a prophetic sign that he was going to manifest his presence in *judgement*. 'The LORD will bring on you and on your people and on the house of your father a time unlike any since Ephraim broke away from Judah—he will bring the king of Assyria' (Isa 7.17).[24] But like 'Shear Jashub', the meaning of the name needn't be tied down to only one possible interpretation. God can of course be 'with us' for blessing or judgement, depending on our response to him.

In Ahaz's case, the parabolic word did not take root. His decision to reject Yahweh and turn to Assyria proved him to be *deaf* to Isaiah's words, *blind* to Yahweh's power, and *unable* to *understand* precisely what was at stake, just as Isaiah had envisioned in the previous chapter (Isa 6.9–10). Ahaz is characterized in Isaiah 7 (and 2 Kgs 16) as an idolater of the worst kind, the epitome of Israel's problems that were addressed at Isaiah's commissioning. As the alliance moved against him, Ahaz wrote to Tiglath-Pileser III, referring to himself as the Assyrian king's 'servant and son' (2 Kgs 16.7 NRSV). The self-designation was a direct denouncement of his kingly role as Yahweh's servant and son (see 2 Sam 7.5), but the worst was still to come. After sacking his own temple and recommitting things that were created for Yahweh to the gods of Assyria, Ahaz travelled north to Damascus to visit his new lord. The gravity of his spiritual condition was cemented when, seeing an altar in Damascus that took his fancy, Ahaz aligned himself with Assyrian gods and their forms of worship by having the altar replicated in the Jerusalem temple (2 Kgs 16.10). In summary, 'King Ahaz is offered by the narrative as a quintessential non-truster'[23] and in his footsteps both Israel and Judah would follow.

In 732 BC, Hoshea assassinated Pekah and became the last king of northern Israel (2 Kgs 15.30; 17.1). He then made the same mistake as Ahaz by trusting in earthly power over Yahweh. In his seventh year, Hoshea stopped paying tribute to Assyria and secretly sought help from Egypt. When the Assyrian king found out, a siege followed, and in 722 BC Samaria[26] was conquered and Israel/Ephraim exiled from her land in accordance with the prophecy of Isaiah (Isa 7.8).

2 Kings 17 begins by outlining these events from a historical and political perspective (verses 1–6), but the remainder (and majority) of the chapter is given to the narrator's *theological* perspective: 'All this took place because the Israelites had sinned against the LORD their God' (2 Kgs 17.7). The Bible insists on interweaving theology with history because at the heart of these narratives is God's governance of human history. Once again we are reminded of the paradoxical truth that God neither forces his will upon us nor is limited by human action.

Planting Parables

Parabolic speech is an indirect way of proclaiming judgement on those whose priorities are upside down (idolaters). In chapter 5 we explored the function of Nathan's parabolic speech and it is worth pausing here to compare the responses of King David and King Ahaz. In 2 Samuel 12, when the morally blind King David had begun rewrite history to suit himself, Nathan's parable tested David's heart. The parable was understood and David yielded the fruit of repentance (2 Sam 12.13; see Ps 51). Prophetic speech saved him from the most dangerous and common form of idolatry: *self*-idolization. Ahaz, on the other hand, rejected Isaiah's prophecy and the parabolic sign accompanying it, showing a sense-less (i.e. blind and deaf) disregard for God's word. In the language of one of Jesus' parables, the heart of Ahaz was 'rocky' or 'thorny' ground in contrast to the good, receptive soil of David's heart (Mk 4.3–8).

Openness to the word of God is an obvious theme in Isaiah 6–7, where the severe implications of a hardened heart are made very clear. For Christian spirituality, this means keeping a watchful eye on the spiritual paralysis that takes us limb by limb when false gods take priority, diminishing our ability to hear and respond to God's voice. But for prophetic spirituality the implications are greater still. When Isaiah presented Ahaz with the ultimatum, 'If you do not stand firm in your faith, you will not stand at all' (Isa 7.9b), he spoke as a watchman for the house of Israel (see 'Watchmen' in chapter 4), thereby bringing the king to a moment of choice.

> To be a *nabi* [prophet] means to set the audience, to whom the words are addressed, before the choice and decision, directly or indirectly. The future is not something already fixed in this present hour, it is dependent upon the real decision, that is to say the decision in which man takes part in this hour.

Martin Buber's words remind us once again that the primary concern of prophecy is not future-telling, but with how *present* decisions impact on a yet-to-be-determined future. Such moments of choosing—for or against God—are at the heart of many memorable prophetic speeches:

> **Moses:** Choose life or death! (Deut 30.19)
> **Samuel:** Choose obedience or disobedience! (1 Sam 12.14–15)
> **Elijah:** Choose Yahweh or Baal! (1 Kgs 18.21)
> **Jesus:** Choose God or money! (Mt 6.24)
> **John of Patmos:** Choose to be hot or cold! (Rev 3.15)

Of course, there are a myriad of ways to go about presenting such a choice to others (see 'Poets of Persuasion' in chapter 5). Whether we are deep in conversation with someone at the local café, writing the lyrics to a song, or preparing a sermon for Sunday's congregation, we uphold the prophetic vocation of the church when we present others with a choice about where they will stand in relation to the one true God. And when decisions are made against idolatry, there follows a tingling in the bones as God's image-bearers return to their senses.

Let us, therefore, put false gods aside and give God his rightful place, so that the seed of God's word in fertile hearts may grow into 'oaks of righteousness, a planting of the LORD for the display of his splendour' (Isa 61.3).

Dig Deeper

■ Have you ever been appointed to do something you would rather have avoided?

■ Read John 12.34. Where do you see this dynamic at work?

■ Have you ever experienced 'merciful judgement'? What came of it?

■ 'If you do not stand firm in your faith, you will not stand at all' (Isa 7.9b). How is this verse relevant to you at the moment?

■ What choices have you had to make in the past week between human resourcefulness and trust in God?

■ Which type of soil in Mark 4.3-8 best describes your heart?

12

Prophetic Suffering: Exiled with God

JEREMIAH

Oh, my anguish, my anguish!
I writhe in pain.
Oh, the agony of my heart!
My heart pounds within me,
I cannot keep silent.
For I have heard the sound of the trumpet;
I have heard the battle cry (Jer 4.19).

Jeremiah 18 – 20; 26

Malleable Clay (Jeremiah 18)

Jeremiah was immensely unpopular in Jerusalem for his doom-and-gloom sermons. In his preaching the people were accused of being slaves (Jer 2.14), prostitutes (Jer 2.20), murderers (Jer 2.34), wayward children (Jer 3.19), ignorant fools (Jer 4.22), lusty adulterers (Jer 5.8), a wicked city (Jer 6.6) filled with hopeless idolaters (Jer 7.18). In spite of his desolate tone, however, Jeremiah affirmed that things *could* be different. Indeed, Jeremiah 18 contains a revelation of crystal clarity regarding the profound impact human decisions can have upon God's actions in the world.

Upon arriving at the potter's house in response to Yahweh's instruction, Jeremiah watches carefully as the artisan goes about his work. The first thing he notices, other than the use of a pottery wheel, is that the potter begins his work with a particular goal in mind. However, if a vessel loses its intended shape and becomes corrupted somehow, then the clay gets reworked and an alternative outcome is chosen for it (Jer 18.4). As Jeremiah stands by, observing the craftsman's movements, a word from Yahweh comes to him as promised: 'O house of Israel, can I not do with you as this potter does? . . . Like clay in the hand of the potter, so are you in my hand, O house of Israel' (Jer 18.6).

On first impressions, the metaphor appears to put everything in God's hands with little left to human responsibility. But even though other metaphors in Scripture seem more relational (Husband–wife, King–subjects, Father–child), the Potter–clay relationship is less unilateral here than in other contexts (e.g., Gen 2.7; Isa 64.8; Rom 9.21). The presence of a potter's wheel suggests that Israel is not simply inert matter in God's hands, for when clay is spinning on a wheel it generates a force of its own.[1] In fact, as Yahweh goes on to explain the significance of the metaphor, this is precisely the point he makes: even when God has foretold his *intentions* through a prophet, Israel's response to that prophetic word is taken seriously enough for God to genuinely reconsider and modify his proposed course of action. This, of course, is a dynamic we have seen at work on numerous occasions in previous chapters.

God's expressed intention to destroy the Israelites in Exodus 32 was a response to their idolatry, and his reconsideration of their fate a response to Moses' prayer. Barak's victory was made possible by Deborah's bold collaboration with Yahweh's battle-plans. Samuel explained Eli's loss of the priesthood and Saul's loss of kingship as the direct consequences of their disobedience. Ahijah made it perfectly clear that Yahweh was going to take back the kingdom of Israel from Jeroboam because of the foolish king's decision to operate by his own rules. Other examples could also be cited, but the point is clear enough: 'Both God and human beings are effective agents; God's activity is not all-determining.'[2]

Jeremiah's brief excursion down handicrafts lane reinforces the Potter's sovereignty without undermining the innate potential of the clay. The staggering truth is that God's decisions regarding the future, revealed through his messengers, are generally contingent upon human attitudes and actions in the present (see 'Engaging God' in chapter 2; also Eze 33.11–20). So while prophetic speech often resounds with certainty, it is actually conditional in many cases because God takes human behaviour seriously, and 'the prophets are not afraid to speak of God changing his plans in response to Israel's (or any nation's) response to him.'[3] In spite of Jeremiah's tendency to preach sermons of woe, Judah's future—like that of the clay—is still very much open, either for ruin or restoration.[4]

However, in spite of the emphasis placed on human responsibility in Jeremiah 18.1–12, the conversation does not end with much optimism. Just as Isaiah had been warned of the people's hardened disposition in Isaiah 6, Jeremiah is likewise warned that the nation will in all likelihood maintain her rebellious attitude. Indeed, Judah is a case in point for 'the pastoral reality that resistance to God practiced so long eventually nullifies the capacity to choose life'.[5]

> But they will reply, 'It's no use. We will continue with our own plans; each of us will follow the stubbornness of his evil heart' (Jer 18.12).

It is one thing for clay on a potter's wheel to generate a force of its own, but for clay to speak of asserting its 'own plans' is rather haughty, to say the least!

> You turn things upside down,
>   as if the potter were thought to be like the clay!
> Shall what is formed say to him who formed it,
>   'He did not make me'?
> Can the pot say of the potter,
>   'He knows nothing'? (Isa 29.16)

Judah's pride is chronic, and God laments her condition.

> Therefore this is what the LORD says:
>
> 'Enquire among the nations:
>   Who has ever heard anything like this?

A most horrible thing has been done by Virgin Israel . . .
My people have forgotten me' (Jer 18.13,15a).

How can anyone *forget* their marriage partner?
Even God finds it inconceivable that Israel could manage to forget her own Husband and turn to 'worthless idols' in his stead! A woman who prefers sex with strangers to intimacy with her own husband and who goes so far as to even pay them for it (Eze 16.32–34) has surely strayed beyond the reaches of forgiveness (see Jer 3.1). Time and again, God has relented (*niham*)[6] of his anger, but now—finally—enough is enough!

> You have rejected me, says the LORD,
>   you are going backwards;
> so I have stretched out my hand against you and destroyed you—
> I am weary of relenting [*niham*] (Jer 15.6 NRSV).

God's lament in Jeremiah 18.13–17 concludes with his desire to make an example of Judah to passers-by and to her enemies. She will be deserted by God in her day of need (just as Israel was) and her treasured land will become 'an object of lasting scorn'. She will be ravaged and left in disgrace, and those who look upon her will shake their heads in disgust (see Eze 16; 23).
But immediately following Yahweh's reaction to the rejection of his people, the pattern repeats itself as Judah reveals the same treacherous attitude towards Yahweh's prophet as well.

> Come, let's make plans against Jeremiah; for the teaching of the law by the priest will not be lost, nor will counsel from the wise, nor the word from the prophets. So come, let's attack him with our tongues and pay no attention to anything he says (Jer 18.18).

The people assume that since they will always have priests, sages and prophets, they may do away with this messenger who only ever speaks of the city's impending doom. They will 'pay no attention to anything he says' just as they have also 'forgotten' Yahweh. To hell with it! Let's shoot the messenger! After all, another prophet (with a more favourable message) will inevitably take his place.

Like the One he represents, Jeremiah has only ever had Judah's best interests at heart. He has stood between this sinful people and their angry God on numerous occasions to avert divine wrath from consuming them (Jer 18.20), even praying when Yahweh had commanded him not to! But now, reflecting God's exasperation, Jeremiah asks, 'Should good be repaid with evil?' and he too, expresses his desire for retribution. Yahweh's astounding 'Do not pray' (Jer 7.16; 11.14; 14.11) is mirrored in the prophet's equally troubling 'Do not forgive' (Jer 18.23). Even Jeremiah's desire to see Judah punished reflects the heart of a God who has resolved to purge Judah of her sin.

This juxtaposition of divine and prophetic lament is similar to that in Hosea 2, where the prophet's words became indistinguishable from God's. Bracketed on either side by metaphors comparing Israel to clay, these twin laments of Yahweh and Jeremiah reveal a shared experience of rejection.

A. Jer 18.1–12: ISRAEL = MALLEABLE CLAY
  B. Jer 18.13–15: Judah's rejection of Yahweh
    C. Jer 18.16–17: Yahweh's response
  B'. Jer 18.18–20: Judah's rejection of Jeremiah
    C'. Jer 18.21–23: Jeremiah's response
A'. Jer 19.1–15: ISRAEL = HARDENED CLAY

The logical sequence of the text goes from Israel as malleable (potentially responsive) clay, via the twin laments of God and his prophet, to Israel the hardened pot that must be smashed to be redeemed (see 'Merciful Judgement' in chapter 11).

Hardened Pots (Jeremiah 19)

In the next chapter, Jeremiah is instructed a second time to go to a potter's house, this time to buy an already-fashioned (hardened) pot. The metaphor of God's people as clay in his hands is present again, but where the earlier metaphor emphasized Israel's part in co-determining the future, the enacted parable of Jeremiah 19 announces that God is going to change Jerusalem forever. 'This is what the LORD Almighty says: I will smash this nation and this city just as this potter's jar is smashed and cannot be repaired' (Jer 19.11). God and his messenger have been rejected and Judah has chosen her path. She is as stubborn (Jer 18.12) and stiff-necked (Jer 19.15) as her sister Israel, and the image of clay is therefore altered to match her hardened resolve.

Our lives follow a similar pattern, do they not? As long as we are responsive to the nudging of God's Spirit we remain pliable in his hands, but when repeated acts of rebellion numb and harden us, we eventually find ourselves immobilized by pride. Often only a crisis can break us and wake us to be refashioned in God's image. The language of Jeremiah 18–19 provides us with two powerful symbols for reflection upon the course our life is taking.[7] What is the condition of our hearts? Are we closed off to future possibilities because we have become overly rigid in certain ways? Are we being moulded in the Potter's hands according to *his* will, or must we be broken to begin afresh?

For Jeremiah's part, in obedience to God's instruction, he takes the purchased pot to Potsherd Gate, where he proceeds to smash it and prophesy against Jerusalem as instructed. Since no appropriate response has been made by the people, God will act as he said he would and Judah will get her just desserts. But not before Jeremiah has suffered on account of his message.

You Deceived Me! (Jeremiah 20)

There are few who would not resent being told that their lives are about to go the way of a broken pot, and Pashhur, the priest and chief officer of the temple, is no exception. Having witnessed the prophet's street theatre, he seizes Jeremiah to have him beaten and put in stocks. He likely thinks that by tying down the messenger he can subdue the message (see 'The Final Word' in chapter 8). But God's word is not so easily muzzled, and apparently, neither is his spokesman. On the very morning of his release, Jeremiah announces further judgement against Pashhur, even assigning him a new name as an indication of his fate. Magor-Missabib, meaning 'Terror all around' (NRSV), will bring terror to all his family and friends, who will die in exile with him (Jer 20.4,6).

It doesn't take a genius to see the marked difference between Nathan's tact and Jeremiah's heavy-handedness. But Jeremiah's confident condemnation of Jerusalem and the priest Pashhur is by no means an expression of self-satisfaction. Jeremiah turns on his heels from the scathing indictment of Pashhur only to shake his fists at heaven:

> O LORD, you deceived[8] me, and I was deceived;
>   you overpowered me and prevailed (Jer 20.7).

The word translated here as 'deceived' (*patah*) is the same word that was used of the lying spirit sent to 'entice' Ahab in 1 Kings 22.20–22. But what deception is Jeremiah referring to? Does he fear he is being deceived in the same way Ahab's prophets were in Micaiah's day? Is he concerned that the reason none of his judgements have come to pass is because God is playing a cruel trick on him?

Undergirding Jeremiah's protest is the fact that he has *only* been given harsh words of judgement to speak against his people and his reputation is suffering for it, to say the least. But that's not all. Since none of his prophecies have (yet) been fulfilled, Jeremiah's authenticity as a prophet is under fire as well. The people keep questioning and mocking him, 'Where is the word of the LORD? Let it now be fulfilled!' (Jer 17.15) Perhaps he is even in danger of being treated like a false prophet. (Hananiah will certainly voice his doubts without reservation in Jer 28.) But isn't God partly to be blamed for the confusion? Why so many prophecies of judgement if none of them are being fulfilled? Jeremiah is the one who comes off as a fool, and his complaints, paraphrased below, are quite understandable:

> Whenever I speak, it's bad news (20.8), but I can't keep it in! (20.9) People are just waiting for me to make a false prophecy so they can get rid of me (20.10). LORD, vindicate me (20.11) by giving them what they deserve! (20.12)

Surely Jeremiah would not mind so much if at least *some* of his words proved true, for he could then at least say to those who accuse him, See? I warned you! But of all the words of judgement

God has put in Jeremiah's mouth, not one has come to fruition, and Jeremiah feels stuck between a rock and a hard place. Talk about vocational crisis! It is no wonder Jeremiah's prayer of protest has often been considered in light of its implications for pastors, whose calling can also bring with it a number of unexpected difficulties.[9] Perhaps part of Jeremiah's lament also stems from the fact that when God called him, he promised him protection (Jer 1.19), and Jeremiah has just been beaten and put in the stocks for faithfully speaking God's word!

But there is more to it than that. This is not simply a case of Jeremiah venting his frustration because he feels duped by God. Jeremiah feels God's concern for the Israelites so deeply that their rejection of him causes him to share in God's suffering. Indeed, that is part of what it means to be a prophet; it is because Jeremiah feels something of Yahweh's anguish and solitude that he is able to give voice to the suffering of God before the people.

You Must Die! (Jeremiah 26)

Early in Jehoiakim's reign, after the untimely death of King Josiah in 609 BC, the word of the Lord came to Jeremiah again, this time instructing him to go to the temple and preach as the people entered through the gates.

> This is what the LORD says: If you do not listen to me and follow my law, which I have set before you, and if you do not listen to the words of my servants the prophets, whom I have sent to you again and again (though you have not listened), then I will make this house like Shiloh and this city an object of cursing among all the nations of the earth (Jer 26.4–6).

To grasp just how scandalous these words were, one must understand that the inhabitants of Jerusalem believed that their temple made them untouchable. They seemed to think that even God could not harm them there because of his unconditional promises made to David. But as Jeremiah reminds them, their own history suggested otherwise. When the Israelites had become complacent in Samuel's day, trusting that the presence of the ark of the covenant in Shiloh would protect them, they were left dumbfounded and ashamed when one day the Philistines came, destroyed the tabernacle and stole the ark (1 Sam 4–6; Ps 78.60–61). And so, standing in the temple courts, Jeremiah appeals to the memory of Shiloh as a warning to Judah that her confidence in the temple is a misplacement of faith.

> Do not trust in deceptive words and say, 'This is the temple of the LORD, the temple of the LORD, the temple of the LORD!' (Jer 7.4)[10]

Reading this in the twenty-first century, we might ask what our own mantras have become. In what do we (mis)place our trust today? Good intentions? Baptism? Weekly church attendance? Daily Bible-reading? No doubt, if Jeremiah visited our pulpit on Sunday, he would remind us that none of these things ought to take God's place either, and then go on to preach about what the only worthy Object of our trust actually wants from us: 'Change your ways and your actions and deal with each other justly . . . do not oppress the alien, the fatherless or the widow . . . do not follow other gods to your own harm' (Jer 7.5–6).

As we might have expected, Jeremiah's message is not well received. To a crowd whose religious and political identity had become fused with weekly routines at the temple, Jeremiah's sermon is more than the people can bear. Even as he speaks, a crowd gathers around him to seize him and condemn him to death, led by the priests and prophets. The ones who feel most threatened by Jeremiah's words are those with too much invested in 'temple theology', and it doesn't take long for them to reach their verdict; 'You must die!' (Jer 26.8)

In his defence, Jeremiah has three things to say: (a) This is not my word against your city and temple, but God's word (Jer 26.12); (b) the purpose of my preaching is that you may still repent and receive God's mercy (Jer 26.13); (c) if you shoot the messenger, my blood will be on your heads, because I am only following Yahweh's orders (Jer 26.14–15). His third point seems to hit a nerve. Someone recalls that a hundred years earlier, when Micah of Moresheth gave a harsh prophecy (Jer 26.18/Mic 3.12), King Hezekiah responded in such a way as to change

Yahweh's mind (Jer 26.19 [*niham*]). And so, thanks to the memories of 'some of the elders', Jeremiah manages to escape the ordeal with his life intact.

The final five verses (Jer 26.20–24) appear as a kind of postscript, added to stress Jeremiah's fortune in surviving the whole ordeal. By way of comparison we are informed that another prophet named Uriah who 'prophesied the same things against this city and this land as Jeremiah did' was unable to escape Jehoiakim's henchmen, who dragged him all the way back from Egypt just to put him to death before the king. Jeremiah may have been persecuted, beaten and imprisoned, but he was still breathing.

The Suffering of God

When the words 'God' and 'suffering' are spoken about together, the context usually has something to do with why God *allows* suffering, questions like: Doesn't God care about human suffering? And isn't he powerful enough to rid the world of suffering? Our subject here is different, but not unrelated, since the suffering *of* God affects the way we perceive (and experience) human suffering.

But can we really speak of God suffering? Is such a notion just a mincing of words to make God feel more accessible to us? Can we truly claim that the Lord of history, the Maker of heaven and earth, has genuinely had his hopes dashed and experienced real pain? Well, what we can say with resounding certainty (and long before we come to the cross in the New Testament) is that the Bible does not shy away from saying so. As early as Genesis 6, when things didn't work out according to God's good intentions, we read that God's heart was 'filled with pain' (Gen 6.6). And the metaphor of the clay in Jeremiah 18 makes a similar point, does it not? When God's wonderful intentions for the clay are ruined by its propensity to resist, God must 'reconsider the good [he] had intended to do for it' (Jer 18.10). So *without* mincing words, God's vulnerability in love does indeed mean that he genuinely suffers, a reality that is often expressed in the Bible through questions that express God's anguish.[11]

How long will these people treat me with contempt? (Num 14.11a)

What can I do with you, Ephraim?
    What can I do with you, Judah? (Hos 6.4)

My people, what have I done to you?
    How have I burdened you? Answer me! (Mic 6.3)

Why should I forgive you? (Jer 5.7a)

Do these sound like the detached musings of a disinterested God? Of course not. Yahweh's deepest passion from the beginning has been to live among his people, as he did in the garden of Eden, in the desert tabernacle and in the Jerusalem temple. But at this juncture in history, in response to the insistent adultery of his beloved bride, Yahweh sadly withdraws his presence. Ezekiel describes God's withdrawal as gradual, occurring in stages, but certain.

> Then the glory of the LORD rose from above the cherubim and moved to the threshold of the temple. The cloud filled the temple, and the court was full of the radiance of the glory of the LORD (Eze 10.4).

> Then the glory of the LORD departed from over the threshold of the temple and stopped above the cherubim . . . They stopped at the entrance to the east gate of the LORD's house, and the glory of the God of Israel was above them (Eze 10.18,19b).

> The glory of the LORD went up from within the city and stopped above the mountain east of it (Eze 11.23).

Judah's rejection of Yahweh and his prophets finally led to the withdrawal of God's presence and the destruction of his home in Jerusalem. In light of God's desire to live among his people, we can be sure that the exile was nothing if not painful for God, a relinquishment of everything he had been working towards in collaboration with Israel and her prophets. Although it was not *the* end, the exile certainly brought *an* end to God's presence among his people, at least 'for a brief moment'.

For a brief moment I abandoned you,
>   but with deep compassion I will bring you back.
In a surge of anger
>   I hid my face from you for a moment,
but with everlasting kindness
I will have compassion on you (Isa 54.7–8a).

To Judah this 'moment' lasted half a century, and as the nation experienced godforsakenness in exile, no doubt she wondered whether Yahweh's compassion could ever be rekindled. But returning to our theme of God's suffering, we may rightly ask what happened in the life of God at this point.[12] Although God's distress over Israel's infidelity had been expressed repeatedly through the prophets for centuries, we cannot overlook the fact that at *this* moment in 587 BC the true King of Israel was finally exiled from his own people by their insistent rebellion against his rule. Of course, it is true that Jeremiah,[13] Ezekiel and Daniel also went into exile, and that God's people were abandoned to the imperial power of Babylon, but according to the preaching of Israel's prophets, these things were secondary to Yahweh being banished by his own people and 'forgotten' by them (Jer 18.15).

But even if we *can* affirm the suffering of God to be genuine, why also his prophets? Hosea's family life was a mess, Jeremiah was commanded to remain celibate (Jer 16.1–9), and Ezekiel was prohibited from mourning the death of his own wife, the 'delight of [his] eyes' (Eze 24.16). Given the frequency of demands like these, we are inclined to question God's habit of putting thorns in the flesh of his servants, to borrow Paul's phraseology. (But note that when the Corinthian church questioned Paul because they suspected his sufferings to be inconsistent with his status as an apostle, Paul defended his apostolic status using suffering as his evidence![14]) After Paul had asked God three times to remove his thorn, whatever it was, the answer he received from the Lord was that God's 'power is made perfect in weakness' (2 Cor 12.9). In fact, Paul became so convinced of this dynamic that he resolved to boast in his weaknesses in order to experience more of Christ's power! God's answer was obviously very meaningful to Paul, but many of us still want to ask *why*? Why must God-followers become weak to become strong? It all seems so backward!

Put simply, it is because God, whose image we reflect, has demonstrated the same 'foolishness' himself (1 Cor 1.18–31). God has revealed his glory to us not through self-actualizing power, but through self-emptying love (Php 2.5–11), quite literally suffering thorns in the flesh to achieve the greatest victory imaginable for us. Nowhere is the truth of Paul's claim more evident than in Gethsemane where Jesus prays three times, 'may this cup be taken from me' (Mt 26.39–44), until finally, acknowledging it to be the *only* way forward, he submits to a Roman cross and drinks the cup of suffering on behalf of 'all the kingdoms on the face of the earth' (Jer 25.26). It is there, suspended between heaven and earth, that Jesus bares the heart of God and reveals how the defeat of sin and death is accomplished through weakness. 'The punishment that brought us peace was upon him, and by his wounds we are healed' (Isa 53.5; 1 Pet 2.24).

It is not uncommon for Christians to experience a deeper awareness of God's presence in times of suffering, and perhaps this is because it is in suffering *with* God and forgiving *like* God that we fulfil our calling as his image-bearers, his living sacraments in the world.

> But we have this treasure [i.e. knowledge of God revealed in Jesus] in jars of clay to show that this all-surpassing power is from God and not from us. We are hard pressed on every side, but not crushed; perplexed, but not in despair; persecuted, but not abandoned; struck down, but not destroyed. We always carry around in our body the death of Jesus, *so that the life of Jesus may also be revealed in our body.* For we who are alive are always being given over to death for Jesus' sake, *so that his life may be revealed in our mortal body* (2 Cor 4.7–11).

Our comparatively simple lives ('jars of clay')[15] contain a treasure of infinite worth, the very life of Jesus as it is formed through our suffering, self-emptying and forgiving. And if all of this is beginning to sound rather defeatist, as though God has no real power to speak of, let us remember that the fruit of self-emptying is *resurrection life*, a life inspired by the Holy Spirit of God, here and now. Following in Jesus' footsteps, Paul learned to rejoice 'in weaknesses, in insults, in hardships, in persecutions, in difficulties' precisely because he experienced this profound truth: 'When I am weak, then I am strong' (2 Cor 12.10).

It is telling that these chapters (Jer 18–20; 26) reflect the suffering both of God and of his spokesman, Jeremiah. God loves the world to the point of suffering, but without the devotion of his prophets we can only wonder what God's extravagant love might look like as a tangible reality 'dwelling among us' (Jn 1.14). The lives of Hosea and Jeremiah in particular permit us to see God through the lens of prophetic suffering, pointing forward as they do to *the* incarnation, where the shared suffering of a Jewish prophet and his God will take the shape of the cross for the sake of the world.

Dig Deeper

■ Read Jeremiah 2.13. What do you think are today's 'broken cisterns'?

■ Do you think the greatest sins in the church are matters of (visible) action or (invisible) attitude?

■ How would a person know whether he or she is malleable or hardened?

■ How do you understand the relationship between the suffering of God and the suffering of people?

■ What does it mean to delight in difficulty? (2 Cor 12.10)

13

Prophetic Integrity: Imaging God

DANIEL & CO

So God created man in his own image,
in the image of God he created him;
male and female he created them (Gen 1.27).

> ## Daniel 1; 3; 6

Profile of a Prophet

As we near the end of the Old Testament in our survey of biblical prophets, it may be helpful to pause and outline the essential marks of a prophet, especially since Daniel's prophetic status is not a matter of general consensus. In Jewish tradition, the book of Daniel is not included among the Prophets but with the Writings (historical books), and even within Christian scholarship, Daniel is considered by some to be more at home with the sages of the wisdom tradition than he is with the prophets.[1] In Christian tradition, however, Daniel has been consistently regarded as a prophet because his life and message are consistent with the prophetic vocation, which may be summed up in these seven traits:

1. A prophet primarily *speaks God's word* into his/her immediate context (though their words may have implications for a more distant future as well).

2. A prophet *makes God known* through their lifestyle and message
   by means of poetic speech, direct rebuke, enacted signs, lived
   example, etc.
3. A prophet *intercedes boldly* for his/her people.
4. A prophet *has special insight* into God's purposes through direct
   revelation (e.g. prayer, visions, dreams).
5. A prophet *seeks to turn hearts* Godward.
6. A prophet *functions as an 'outsider'* to religious and political
   institutions.
7. A prophet *addresses God's people*, Israel.

That Daniel fulfils the first five of these conditions is clear
enough, but the last two give rise to questions, and therefore
require some clarification. The sixth point specifies that since
Yahweh's prophets claimed divine inspiration, they spoke to
human institutions not as established authorities within the temple or palace courts (as Daniel does), but from the *outside*.
However, we have already noticed at least two other prophets,
Nathan and Isaiah, who wielded their otherworldly authority
within the royal courts, so Daniel is not a unique exception in this
regard. Even though God's providence enabled Daniel to very
quickly take an insider position of political influence and even
religious authority in Babylon's courts (in Dan 5, he rebukes
Belshazzar for not acknowledging Yahweh), he remains an outsider in the sense that he cannot enforce Israel's Torah in Babylon.
We may therefore consider Daniel as both insider (due to his
position of authority in Babylon) and outsider (since he is not,
and refuses to become, a Babylonian).

The seventh trait identifies Israel as the target audience of
Yahweh's prophets, although there were exceptions in this
regard, too. A number of Israelite prophets besides Daniel spoke
on God's behalf to foreign nations: Elisha had numerous dealing
with Aram (Syria);[2] Jonah and Nahum were sent to Nineveh,
Assyria's capital; Obadiah addressed Edom; and various other
oracles were spoken against Egypt (Isa 19), Moab (Jer 48), and
other surrounding nations (Amos 1.3–2.1). Clearly, Daniel was
not the only Israelite prophet whose life and message made an
impact beyond Israel's borders, and besides, he had no choice but
to speak for God on foreign soil because of his unique (exilic) con-

text. Daniel may not have preached to Jewish exiles as his contemporary Ezekiel did, but the inspirational stories of his prophetic integrity continued to be a source of encouragement and strength for generations after him. In summary then, we may affirm Daniel's status as a prophet—or perhaps more precisely, as a missionary–prophet.

Identity Crisis (Daniel 1)

The Jason Bourne books and films begin with a simple but powerful premise. A young man is found floating in the Mediterranean Sea with gunshot wounds in his back and no memory of who he is, not even his own name. The stories follow Bourne's perilous endeavour to piece together his personal history, based on what clues he can gather and what help he can find along the way. As time passes, he becomes increasingly aware of various specialized skills he acquired before the amnesia, but with little sense of the *identity* that goes with them.

> I can tell you the license plate numbers of all six cars outside. I can tell you that our waitress is left-handed and the guy sitting up at the counter weighs two hundred fifteen pounds and knows how to handle himself. I know the best place to look for a gun is the cab of the gray truck outside, and at this altitude, I can run flat out for a half mile before my hands start shaking. Now why would I know that? How can I know that and not know who I am?

Memories are so vital to self-understanding that the notion of a fully grown adult starting again from scratch makes for a very compelling story. Without the identity markers of relationships, a job or a sense of home, Bourne is forced to reconsider who he is—and who he *will be*, given his fresh start.

Judah faced similar questions when deportation to Babylon began in 597 BC. Over a hundred years earlier, when the inhabitants of the northern kingdom (Israel) had been exiled to Assyria, Samaria had become a melting pot of pagan religious practices (2 Kgs 17.24–40). Now that Jeremiah's prophecies of doom had finally been fulfilled and the charred ruins of Solomon's temple no longer offered any assurance of Yahweh's presence, questions concerning the fate of Judah also hung in the balance. As the smoke of war dissipated, leaving Judah stripped naked of all her identity markers, a pivotal question lingered in the hearts of God's people . . . What now?

Did the Mosaic covenant, which God had established with such care, have any further relevance for them? If the temple had truly been God's home, why had it been ransacked and burnt to the ground? What did that say about Yahweh? Would it ever become a place for the soles of God's feet again (Eze 43.7)? And what of the land? Israel's distinct identity had been tied to the promised land of Canaan, which was now occupied by foreigners. Had God simply moved on? And what was to become of the monarchy? Hadn't God 'promised to maintain a lamp for David and his descendants for ever' (2 Kgs 8.19)? How could Judah reconcile that promise with the fact that King Zedekiah had been exiled and forced to watch his two sons, the final heirs to the kingdom, put to death before him (2 Kgs 25.7)? Such a massive defeat surely meant either that the Babylonian gods were more powerful than Yahweh, or that Yahweh had simply given up on Israel. Without Yahweh, who was Judah anyway? They had always been a people marked by his presence (Exod 33.16), but what good could it do to sustain faith in a God who had not only abandoned them, but had warned (repeatedly) through his prophets that he was going to do so? Too many questions and not enough answers!

The Bible rarely responds to such questions with philosophical meanderings about the impact trauma has on a person's sense of identity. Nor will you find a chapter anywhere in the Bible entitled, 'How to Re-establish National Identity after Exile'. Rather, concerns like these tend to be addressed through *stories*, stories about people responding to such crises in their times, stories about honourable characters showing integrity under pressure.

The book of Daniel opens with a brief report of Nebuchadnezzar's victory over Judah, followed by an edict demanding that some Israelites of noble blood be sent to Babylon to be trained for service in the king's court. Among these were

Daniel and three other men who had been handpicked for re-education and a fresh start—as Babylonians.

> . . . young men without any physical defect, handsome, showing aptitude for every kind of learning, well informed, quick to understand, and qualified to serve in the king's palace. [Ashpenaz the chief court official] was to teach them the language and literature of the Babylonians (Dan 1.4).

The new context should have changed Daniel completely. After all, he was immersed in a foreign culture, taught a new language, and even fed on a new diet so that he might, for all intents and purposes, lose his Hebrew identity. He was even given a Babylonian name, which included the replacement of *El* (meaning 'God') in Daniel with *Bel* (the chief Babylonian deity) in Belteshazzar (Dan 1.7; also 4.8). Daniel, God-is-my-judge, became Belteshazzar, Bel-protect-his-life. For a moment it seemed as though even Judah's best would lose their distinctive identity as believers in Yahweh.

> But Daniel resolved not to defile himself with the royal food and wine, and he asked the chief official for permission not to defile himself this way (Dan 1.8).

Daniel resists being Babylonized by holding fast to something that secures his identity as an Israelite. The official in charge is concerned that if the king loses his temper over Daniel's ill-health then the official may lose his head, but Daniel reassures him and manages somehow to negotiate an agreement. Daniel knows that he is in no position to confront or criticize the king since, unlike his prophetic predecessors, he is not on home territory. What he and his friends are in a position to do, however, is to serve King Nebuchadnezzar whilst maintaining loyalty to their true King. That way, Daniel and his friends may be able to sustain their Israelite identity (and their lives) without disrespecting their foreign context (see Jer 29.7).

Sure enough, 'at the end of the ten days they looked healthier and better nourished than any of the young men who ate the royal food' (Dan 1.15). What we have here is not an argument for vegetarianism, but rather Daniel's way of saying, I will not be shaped by my surrounds so easily. Ultimately, it is God who sets these men apart from the others (Dan 1.17) so that even in Babylon, or *especially* in Babylon, they may become a light unto the nations.

Image Problems (Daniel 3)

Daniel 3 begins by noting that 'King Nebuchadnezzar made an image of gold, ninety feet high and nine feet wide' (Dan 3.1), probably inspired by his dream in the previous chapter (Dan 2.31–33) and certainly an attempt to 'big himself up' in the estimation of the people.[4] Few people today would feel comfortable building massive, golden statues of themselves, but image problems prevail inside and outside of the church. Having the right image, whether it be beautiful, smart, busy, holy or otherwise, is a matter of great importance to many. Consequently, advertising campaigns no longer market products; they promote an image— *which could be* yours! This car will make you the talk of the town, that pair of jeans will flaunt your superior sense of fashion, and so it goes from cell phones to snack foods. Everything can be harnessed to alter your level of coolness. And despite the prophets' reputation for getting around in furry loincloths, they still had some pretty pertinent things to say about image.

Whether Nebuchadnezzar's statue was an image of himself or of a particular god the narrative doesn't specify. What is clear is that the image was to be worshipped by everyone—no exceptions!

> Whoever does not fall down and worship will immediately be thrown into a blazing furnace (Dan 3.6).

This posed an immediate problem for Shadrach, Meshach and Abednego, who knew the first and second commandments only too well (see 'You Are What You Worship' in chapter 7). Israel's Law stressed that no false idols were to be created under any circumstances. Even images of Yahweh were out of the question. Surrounding nations, however, created images of both gods and kings, and regarded them as much more than mere symbols.

Disrespect a king's statue and you disrespected the king himself. In ancient kingdoms such as Egypt, the king was considered to be the image or temporary incarnation of his god, so that there was less distinction between statues of pharaohs and statues of their gods than we might suppose.[5] So as soon as Shadrach, Meshach and Abednego were identified as foreigners failing to fit in, they were brought before the king to explain themselves.

The negative reaction of the Chaldeans (Babylonians) was possibly motivated by racism, since the Jews had managed to maintain their own cultural identity (Dan 1; see Esther), and exacerbated further by their promoted status (Dan 3.12). Even so, the charge against them was quite true: 'they neither serve your gods nor worship the image of gold you have set up' (Dan 3.12). Nebuchadnezzar was furious. He offered them one last opportunity to respond appropriately or they would die.

But Shadrach, Meshach and Abednego seemed unmoved by the gravity of their situation. The king's arrogant question, 'What god will be able to rescue you from my hand?' (Dan 3.15) elicited a carefree response from the three Jews, who responded rather candidly, We're glad you asked . . .

> O Nebuchadnezzar, we do not need to defend ourselves before you in this matter. If we are thrown into the blazing furnace, the God we serve is able to save us from it, and he will rescue us from your hand, O king. But even if he does not, we want you to know, O king, that we will not serve your gods or worship the image of gold you have set up (Dan 3.16–18).

Nebuchadnezzar is so infuriated by their defiance that he has the furnace heated to unthinkable temperatures (hot enough to kill members of his elite brute squad who get too close) and the three Jews are thrown in. The king of Babylon positions himself to enjoy the spectacle but soon finds himself squinting (and sweating) in disbelief, for not only are the men 'walking around in the fire, unbound and unharmed', but a fourth figure has also joined them (Dan 3.25)!

The story is simple in its details and narrated with plenty of repetition, lending itself to comedic retellings such as the popular church musical *It's Cool in the Furnace*. But its message is no less profound on account of its simplicity. The narrator's theology is expressed by contrasting the character of Nebuchadnezzar with that of the three Jews. While Nebuchadnezzar talks incessantly about the statue he has made (he is exceedingly image-conscious) and is described twice as being 'furious with rage' (Dan 3.13,19), Shadrach, Meshach and Abednego maintain their peaceful composure. Of even greater significance is the contrast between Nebuchadnezzar's giant, golden idol that stands mute at the story's edge and the flesh-and-blood images of God provided by Shadrach, Meshach and Abednego. What's more, they are joined in their act of protest by a fourth image of God, identified by Nebuchadnezzar as 'a son of the gods' (Dan 3.25) and an 'angel' (Dan 3.28). Unlike other gods in ancient times who were believed only to reside in kings, Yahweh's good intention was to fill creation with images of himself, who would reflect his nature by the way they exercised dominion over the earth.[6]

The narrative goes further still to suggest the importance of our bodies as flesh-and-blood images of the invisible God.[7] In contrast to some (still prevalent) schools of thought which consider the human capacities to *think* and *reason* as that which reflects the divine image, the Hebrew worldview affirms the fundamental importance of our physical bodies. It is worth quoting David Clines at length:

> The body cannot be left out of the meaning of the image; man [*sic*] is a totality, and his 'solid flesh' is as much the image of God as his spiritual capacity, creativeness, or personality, since none of these 'higher' aspects of the human being can exist in isolation from the body. The body is not a mere dwelling-place for the soul . . . In so far as man is a body and a bodiless man is not man, the body is the image of God.[8]

When the three men speak of being 'saved' from the furnace (Dan 3.17), they do not mean that their bodies may just as well perish since their souls are heaven-bound. On the contrary, the narrative affirms the salvation of the *whole* person by including some of the finer details: 'the fire had not harmed their bodies, nor was a hair of their heads singed; their robes were not scorched, and there was no smell of fire on them' (Dan 3.27). In short, the Bible affirms that a person's body is not something they *have*, but something they *are*, and the notion that they might one day be freed from it reflects a very serious image problem indeed.[9]

Safe in the Lions' Den (Daniel 6)

With the passing of time, Daniel is promoted to a position of extraordinary influence. In Daniel 6 the narrator reveals the big plans that Darius the Mede[10] has for him.

> Now Daniel so distinguished himself among the administrators and the satraps by his exceptional qualities that the king planned to set him over the whole kingdom (Dan 6.3).

When a person repeatedly excels at something (and happens to also be good-looking and intelligent; Dan 1.4) trouble is not far off. Unfortunately, success can sometimes lead to a proverbial lions' den where jealous colleagues and competitors lie in waiting. The problem for Daniel's antagonists (and they were many) was that they could not find a single legitimate reason to ruin Daniel since everything he touched turned to gold. But the plot begins to thicken when they realize that the very source of Daniel's success may well provide the means to undermining him. 'We will never find any basis for charges against this man Daniel unless it has something to do with the law of his God' (Dan 6.5).

Noting the steady rhythm of Daniel's prayer life, his opponents devise a plan to undo him by making those prayers contrary to 'the laws of the Medes and the Persians'. However, knowing that Darius would do anything to keep Daniel alive (Dan 6.14), they cannot simply point out his prayer life and leave it to Darius to punish him. Rather, they must create a situation where Daniel will break a rule and have to suffer its irrevocable—and deadly—consequence.

Before long, they have their plan: 'anyone who prays to any god or man during the next thirty days, except to [King Darius], shall be thrown into the lions' den.' And since the 'royal administrators, prefects, satraps, advisers and governors have all agreed', Darius signs the decree (Dan 6.7–9).

The trap is an interesting one, because Daniel is not caught between a law of the Medes and the Persians and a Jewish law. He is caught between his own integrity (which for him finds expression in three daily pauses for prayer) and a law designed for the sole purpose of ousting him for good. But even after hearing about the new law, Daniel continues to pray just as he had done before (Dan 6.10). Of course, Daniel *could* have altered his routine. The point is not that he wishes to cause a stir but that he has chosen to persist with a spiritual discipline that has become central to his way of life: prayer.

As we have been led to expect, Daniel gets caught in the act, and his antagonists proceed to stack the cards before playing their hand to the king.

> Did you not publish a decree that during the next thirty days anyone who prays to any god or man except to you, O king, would be thrown into the lions' den? (Dan 6.12a).

The king responds as they had anticipated, 'The decree stands' (Dan 6.12), and Daniel's adversaries proceed to accuse Daniel. Since even the king cannot tamper with the law, Darius reluctantly issues the order for Daniel to be thrown to the lions. But before they part ways, the king himself offers a kind of prayer: 'May your God, whom you serve continually, rescue you!' (Dan 6.16b)

Sure enough, that is precisely what happens.

After a restless night's sleep, 'the king got up and hurried to the lions' den' (Dan 6.19).

> 'Daniel, servant of the living God, has your God, whom you serve continually, been able to rescue you from the lions?' (Dan 6.20)

Daniel responds with a simple reason for his salvation, which may be paraphrased, 'The lions have done me no harm because I have done you no harm' (Dan 6.22).[11] His response not only vindicates himself but also proves Yahweh to be a God who sees everything and judges people in accordance with their deeds (Rom 2.6). And in fact, that is exactly what Darius proceeds to do. The satraps and their families are all cast into the lions' den because they, unlike Daniel, were not thinking in the best interests of the Babylonian kingdom. Daniel, by contrast, has succeeded in promoting the kingdom of Yahweh throughout the world.

> Then King Darius wrote to all the peoples, nations and men of every language throughout the land [NRSV: the whole world]:
>
> 'May you prosper greatly!
>
> 'I issue a decree that in every part of my kingdom people must fear and reverence the God of Daniel.
>
> 'For he is the living God
>   and he endures for ever;
> his kingdom will not be destroyed,
>   his dominion will never end.
> He rescues and he saves;
>   he performs signs and wonders
>   in the heavens and on the earth.
> He has rescued Daniel
>   from the power of the lions' (Dan 6.25–27).

What Daniel and his friends have done is indisputably prophetic, for 'the task of prophetic ministry is to nurture, nourish, and evoke a consciousness and perception alternative to the consciousness and perception of the dominant culture around us.'[12] These stories of conflict in the royal courts, played out in the context of competing laws, belief systems and gods, show how God's people living in exile can lead to opportunities for 'peoples, nations and men of every language' to recognize Yahweh as 'the living God'. Through their unshakable integrity, Daniel & Co turned the eyes of Babylon Godward. Their stories provide an inspiring model of mission, turning cultural displacement into an open door, through which the nations may enter and confess Yahweh's Lordship.[13]

Wholly in the Spirit

Although the Jewish exiles win the day in each of these chapters from the book of Daniel, their stories do not simply teach that all fares well for those who trust in God. Shadrach, Meshach and Abednego made it quite clear that while God was *able* to save them, he might equally have chosen not to do so. Either way, they simply refused to serve Nebuchadnezzar's gods or worship his image of gold (Dan 3.17). They went to the furnace willingly because of their *integrity*, not because Yahweh had guaranteed their safety.

But what exactly is integrity? When we speak of someone having integrity, are we referring to their honesty? Their morality? Their consistency? Their ability to hold their own in the face of harsh opposition? Perhaps all of these are true to some extent, but the word 'integrity' derives from the Latin word *integer*, meaning 'intact' or 'whole', suggesting that a person of integrity is in some sense 'complete'. (You may recall from a mathematics class that integers are 'whole numbers'.) How then, may those who desire such wholeness attain it? Perhaps a clue may be found in the characterization of Daniel in the book that bears his name.

Daniel's capacity to reflect the divine image is not presented as a mere by-product of his rugged resolve to live a disciplined life. Daniel owes much to being filled with the Spirit of God. As the narrator puts it, it is Daniel's 'excellent spirit' (*ruach*; Dan 6.3 NRSV) that sets him head and shoulders above the rest—or as Darius would have it, 'over the whole kingdom.' Between chapters 4 and 6, Daniel's spirit is recognized seven times as being exceptional and 'of the holy gods.'[14] His integrity (or wholeness) may therefore be understood to consist of two things: Daniel is an *image* of God filled with the *Spirit* of God.

This brings us back yet again to the idea of making God known in the world, though in a rather more profound sense wherein God's passion to live *among* us is ultimately fulfilled by the presence of his own Spirit *within* us. Numerous prophets point in this direction by the presence and power of God's Spirit in their lives, but none articulate it quite like Daniel's contemporary, Ezekiel (aka 'the prophet of the spirit').

So central to the book of Ezekiel is the theme of making God known that the phrase, 'then you/they will know that I am the Lord', occurs no less than fifty-four times! Ezekiel's central concern is that the world will come to know Yahweh as Lord by looking at Israel *in whom his Spirit dwells.*

> Then the nations will know that I am the LORD, declares the Sovereign LORD, *when I show myself holy through you* before their eyes.
>   For I will take you out of the nations; I will gather you from all the countries and bring you back into your own land. I will sprinkle clean water on you, and you will be clean; I will cleanse you from all your impurities and from all your idols. I will give you a new heart and *put a new spirit in you*; I will remove from you your heart of stone and give you a heart of flesh. And *I will put my Spirit in you* and move you to follow my decrees and be careful to keep my laws. You will live in the land I gave your forefathers; you will be my people, and I will be your God (Eze 36.23b–28).

How will the nations know that Yahweh is the one true God? By looking at his people. But how will Yahweh show his holiness through these people who have proven themselves to be distinctly *unholy*? By gathering them back from exile and washing them clean of sin and idolatry (see 'The Birth of Baptism' in chapter 14). And how will this New Israel be any different? She will have God's own Spirit within, moving her to obedience.

The much-repeated word *ruach*, meaning 'spirit/wind/breath', in Ezekiel's vision of the Valley of Dry Bones (Eze 37) not only anticipates the revival of God's people after the exile, but also promises the coming of Yahweh's Spirit so that as a holy nation, Israel will be empowered to make God known to the rest of the world. Ezekiel's great vision moves from an act of *creation* (prophesying to the bones and the breath) to a crescendo of *resurrection life*, the supreme form of human existence. But this imagined future, where God's image-bearers rise up together to represent God in the world, can only be fulfilled as God's people learn to live wholly in the Spirit.

Dig Deeper

- Have you ever known anyone you considered a prophet or prophetess?

- What are your identity markers? (relationships, activities, etc.)

- In what contexts do you feel you are on foreign territory as a Christian?

- Do you think of yourself, including your body, as an image of God?

- How conscious are you of the Holy Spirit's presence in your life?

14

Prophetic Humility: Becoming Less

JOHN

He must become greater; I must become less (Jn 3.30).

> # Matthew 3; John 3.22 – 30

Return to Me!

In answer to Daniel's prayer (Dan 9) and in fulfilment of Jeremiah's prophecy (Jer 51), Israel's exile came to an end in 539 BC with the decree of the Persian king Cyrus, who released worshippers of Yahweh to return home (see Ezra 1). But even this miraculous change in circumstances offered no easy resolution for Israel's identity crisis and unfulfilled prophecies of hope. Some decided to stay in Babylon where they had settled down (as Jeremiah had suggested; Jer 29.4–6), while others returned to Jerusalem only to be disheartened by the devastation there. The walls of the city and Solomon's Temple had been torn down by Nebuchadnezzar and the task of rebuilding seemed overwhelming. In addition, there was some opposition to the rebuilding (Ezra 4), and those who were old enough to remember the grandeur of Solomon's Temple doubted that this Second Temple[1] could ever be its equal (Ezra 3.12; Hag 2.3).

Almost twenty years later, God raised up two prophets, Haggai and Zechariah, to revitalize his people. Haggai's preaching contained a hopeful promise, 'I am with you' (Hag 1.13; 2.4), but with it also came a stern rebuke. The Israelites had prioritized the building of their own homes before Yahweh's, and as divine punishment for their neglect, their efforts had been sabotaged.

> I struck all the work of your hands with blight, mildew and hail, yet you did not turn to me,' declares the LORD (Hag 2.17).

Eventually, the Second Temple was completed (Ezra 6.14; c.515 BC), but even so there was no evidence that Yahweh had returned to dwell among his people. To Israel's accusation that God had been less than faithful, the response was simple:

> 'Return [*shuv*] to me, and I will return [*shuv*] to you,' says the LORD Almighty (Mal 3.7b; also Zech 1.3).

Of course the message was much the same as that delivered by other prophets before the exile. (Jeremiah in particular must have felt as though he was banging his head against a wall; see Jer 7.25; 25.4; 26.5–6; 29.19; 35.15; 44.4.) For centuries now, God's message through the prophets had not changed: 'Return to me! Return to me! Return to me!'

> Afterward the Israelites will return [*shuv*] and seek the LORD their God and David their king. They will come trembling to the LORD and to his blessings in the last days (Hos 3.5).

> Return [*shuv*], faithless people;
>   I will cure you of backsliding (Jer 3.22).

> Repent [*shuv*]! Turn [*shuv*] from your idols and renounce all your detestable practices! (Eze 14.6b)

> Return [*shuv*] to me, for I have redeemed you (Isa 44.22b).

> 'Even now,' declares the LORD
>   'return [*shuv*] to me with all your heart' (Joel 2.12a).

Hundreds of years after Israel's return from her Babylonian exile, very little had changed. Various empires had risen and fallen over the centuries,[2] but God's people (now living under Roman rule) still awaited the return of their King and the deliverance promised them by the post-exilic prophets. And although temple worship continued, Israel's religious practices were not yielding any *real* fruit, at least, not according to one Jewish prophet who had begun to cause a stir outside Jerusalem.

Prepare the Way! (Matthew 3.1–4)

The gospel writers all begin their accounts with the introduction of a lone prophet out in the desert of Judea. In many ways, John was no different from the prophets of the Old Testament. His message certainly had a familiar ring to it:

Repent [*metanoéo*], for the kingdom of heaven is near (Mt 3.2).

The Greek word for 'repent' (*metanoéo*) contains nuances of both the Hebrew words we've considered in previous chapters: *niham* (to change one's mind) and *shuv* (to turn around).[3] It is important to distinguish between repentance and regret; genuine repentance is a turning *from* one way of life *to* another that goes well beyond having guilty feelings. Essentially, John (like Jesus after him) was urging his hearers to reorient their hearts and start living in light of the fact that God's kingdom (his recognized rule) was close at hand. The restoration of God's good intentions for the world was fast approaching, said John, and the only appropriate way to respond was with revolutionary life-change.

Malachi had foretold the return of Elijah, who would prepare Israel for the day of the Lord's coming (Mal 4.5). Matthew's gospel hints at the fulfilment of that prophecy while singling out another verse from Isaiah as well:

This is he who was spoken of through the prophet Isaiah:

'A voice of one calling in the desert,
"Prepare the way for the Lord,
make straight paths for him"' [Isa 40.3].

John's clothes were made of camel's hair, and he had a leather belt round his waist [see 2 Kgs 1.8]. His food was locusts and wild honey (Mt 3.3–4).

Using language reminiscent of Israel's deliverance from Egypt, John the Baptist announces a *new exodus* through which God will deliver his people from their enemies and establish his rule forever by living among them. John's prophetic call to repentance is hardly novel, but his role in the bigger picture is of tremendous importance, for it has fallen to him to prepare the way for Yahweh's homecoming.

And what better place to announce such tidings than the desert? That was where the Israelites had been humbled as they came to understand what it meant to be God's people (Deut 8.2,16) and Hosea had also spoken of the desert as the place where Israel would one day renew her love and worship of Yahweh (Hos 2.14). So it was appropriate, in fulfilment of Isaiah 40.3, that John 'lived in the desert until he appeared publicly to Israel' (Lk 1.80). There on the banks of the Jordan River, John was summoning Israel back from exile to the place of her birth.

The Birth of Baptism (Matthew 3.5–6)

People went out to him from Jerusalem and all Judea and the whole region of the Jordan. Confessing their sins, they were baptised by him in the Jordan River (Mt 3.5–6).

So why baptism? Isn't it a bit odd, suddenly and without precedent, for a prophet to start dipping people's bodies into a river as a way of affirming their repentance? Where did John get the idea to baptize, presumably by immersion, in the Jordan River? Was baptism his innovation, or can its roots be traced elsewhere? We will briefly explore three background sources here: (a) a cleansing rite performed by Elisha, (b) the image-rich preaching of Israel's prophets, and (c) the religious ceremonies of Second Temple Judaism.

First, regarding the physical act of baptism itself, the clearest biblical antecedent to an immersion anything like John's is found in 2 Kings 5, where Elisha healed Naaman (an Aramean) of a skin disease by asking him to dip his body into the Jordan River seven times. Elisha's instruction was possibly a 'watered-down' version of an Israelite cleansing ritual described in Leviticus 14. It is significant that Naaman initially walked off in a huff, complaining angrily that the rivers from his own region were cleaner than those in Israel. Also, Elisha's means of purification seemed elementary and thereby, to Naaman's mind, illegitimate. Both excuses might have been expected from the 'commander of the army of the king of Aram', a man who took obvious pride in his position and who would therefore not bow easily to the odd methods of a foreign prophet. However, at the behest of his servants (who were for obvious reasons more humble than he), Naaman obeyed God's word and was cleansed. In light of his initial resistance, one commentator has suggested that the narrator's choice of words in saying that Naaman '*went down* and dipped himself in the Jordan' (2 Kgs 5.14) alludes to the Aramean warrior humbling himself prior to being healed.[4] In light of this, it may also be significant that the next verse speaks of Naaman 'turning' (*shuv*) to Elisha before declaring his faith in Yahweh: 'Now I know that there is no God in all the earth except in Israel' (2 Kgs 5.15). Naaman's resolve, following his baptism, to never worship any other god but Yahweh may reasonably be understood as 'an early example of conversion to Yahwism.'[5] As a cleansing rite in the Jordan River, this is the clearest parallel in the Old Testament to what John the Baptist was doing in the first century. But there were precedents of another kind to John's baptism as well.

A second source behind John's baptism was the preaching of Israel's prophets, who frequently made conceptual links between washing and new life. In Isaiah 1.16 (and Psalm 51.2) 'washing' entails a deep, spiritual cleansing, and in Ezekiel 36.25 'sprinkling' is suggested as the solution to Israel's idolatry.[6] In addition, the prophets also spoke of bathing or sprinkling as metaphors for forgiveness (Isa 4.4; Zech 13.1). And since baptism signifies not just death to a previous way of life (Rom 6.3), but also a rising to new life (Rom 6.4), the concept of resurrection may also have been linked to John's baptism (see Isa 26.19; Eze 37.1–14; Dan 12.1–3). Of course, John's presence in the desert was also suggestive in light of the exodus, Israel's momentous birth-event (Deut 32.18; Isa 46.3). Having been delivered from slavery, the nation had passed through the waters of the Red Sea to rise from the other side as God's new-born child. This exodus motif is prevalent in the opening verses of Isaiah 40, which all four Gospel writers quote to introduce John[7] (see above). In short, numerous images from the Old Testament provide the theological underpinnings for John's baptism.

Finally, the use of water to symbolize spiritual cleansing is not uncommon in religious contexts, and first-century Judaism was no exception. The terms of Israel's covenant relationship with God stipulated various types of symbolic cleansing rituals, including hand- and foot-washing (Exod 30.18–21), sprinkling (Num 8.7; 19.18) and bathing (Lev 15.1–13). All of these were generally self-administered, and in the first century, many of these self-cleansing rites (known as 'ablutions') were still being carried out at the temple in various forms.[8]

We can see, therefore, that John's baptism did not appear out of the blue, so to speak. Rather, it drew together a significant geographical setting, the metaphorical cleansing language of Israel's prophets, and key aspects of Israel's religious cultus. On one hand this is helpful for understanding how John's idea of baptism originated, but on the other, it raises a perplexing question. Since John's father, Zechariah, was a priest (see Lk 1), we can assume that John had an intimate knowledge of the priestly traditions and purity rituals associated with the temple, so why was he introducing an alternative purification rite?

Two thousand years ago, it was rather shocking for a young man not to follow in his father's footsteps career-wise.[9] It is even more astounding that John not only became a fur-wearing, desert-dwelling prophet, but that he also set up a 'practice' which seemed to directly challenge the priestly rites of purification. By administering the baptism *himself*, resulting in the nickname 'John the Baptist', John assumed a kind of priestly role. But how did John, the son of a priest, come to be living an ascetic lifestyle out in the desert?[10] And what on earth was he up to? Was John simply offering an alternative to the temple or was he trying to start a revolution?

In the eyes of the people, the temple represented Israel's privileged relationship with God, and since the temple was where

Yahweh resided, it was where forgiveness for sins also took place. But in John's eyes, Israel had become steeped in traditions that were not bearing any fruit, so he had begun to baptize the *truly* repentant as an act of criticism against the corruption of the temple. It was anything but a politically neutral act—and yes, he was starting a revolution.

The Coming Kingdom (Matthew 3.7–12)

In spite of considerable popularity (Mt 3.5), John understood his water baptism only as the means to a far greater end. Even with all its nuances of cleansing and forgiveness, death and resurrection, repentance and reorientation, water baptism was just a preliminary step. As many other prophets had said before him, God would return to his people when they returned to him (Zech 1.3), and John understood Israel's repentance to be the straightened path upon which Yahweh would make his arrival. God's coming kingdom was what the fuss was *really* all about.

Nonetheless, John's preaching and actions were causing some anxiety among those who understood the temple to be the locus of God's presence and forgiveness. Did John really think that God was present on the shores of some dirty river outside town? His actions certainly suggested as much. 'Anybody offering water-baptism for the forgiveness of sins was saying: you can have, here and now, what you would normally get through the Temple cult.'[12] So it wasn't long before the Pharisees and Sadducees came to investigate John's baptism. (The Sadducees were closely affiliated with the temple's official cleansing process; see Acts 5.17.) Even as they made their approach, however, John began to bark at them:

> You brood of vipers! Who warned you to flee from the coming wrath? Produce fruit in keeping with repentance. And do not think you can say to yourselves, 'We have Abraham as our father.' I tell you that out of these stones God can raise up children for Abraham. The axe is already at the root of the trees, and every tree that does not produce good fruit will be cut down and thrown into the fire (Mt 3.7b–10).

John's point was clear: If you want to avoid God's judgement, you'd better start bearing fruit, because being Jewish is not enough! He had already begun to distinguish ethnic Israel from true Israel, a distinction that his cousin would take up in due course (see Mt 12.33–34). Only the repentant could confidently regard themselves as *true* children of Abraham.

John's threat that the axe was already at the root of fruitless trees (Mt 3.10) implied with little subtlety that the Jewish temple system was failing in its task of preparing Israel for God's arrival. God's special vineyard, Israel, was not bearing any fruit (see Isa 5.1–7). John was essentially accusing the religious authorities of not doing their job properly, and his harsh words were consistent with his presence out in the desert, where he had quite literally taken the temple's purification rites into his own hands.

Jesus would be the one to fully announce and establish the kingdom as its King, but John was its forerunner, making sure people's hearts were right. After all, it wasn't the kind of kingdom where one needed to have a sword at the ready, but rather a kingdom made up of subjects who were habitually *turning* to face God and therefore able to 'produce fruit in keeping with repentance' (Mt 3.8).

John had begun the task of separating wheat from chaff, but Jesus would soon take over with 'winnowing[13] fork in hand' (Mt 3.12), telling parables to force decisions and pronouncing judgement upon the 'weeds' and restoration for the 'wheat' (Mt 13.24–30). Yes, John's baptism was just the beginning of a profound movement that would change the whole world. The still-to-be-recognized Messiah, who was more powerful than John, who would baptize 'with the Holy Spirit and fire' (Jn 3.11),[14] and whose sandals John didn't consider himself worthy to touch, was the one God had appointed to reign over his coming kingdom.

Becoming Less (John 3.22–30)

Some time later, after Jesus had been baptized by John, there was a period of overlap when both John and Jesus were baptizing disciples in the Jordan. John's followers, upset at the notion of someone poaching potential disciples upstream, came to speak with him.

They came to John and said to him, 'Rabbi, that man who was with you on the other side of the Jordan—the one you testified about—well, he is baptising, and everyone is going to him' (Jn 3.26).

While the loyalty of John's disciples is admirable, the Baptist perceives Jesus' success not as a threat to his ministry, but as its fulfilment. Indeed, Jesus stands over and above the temple's rites of purification as the one who has come to fulfil them (Jn 3.31).[15] Since John only ever intended to prepare the way for the Messiah (Jn 3.28), he is only too happy to step aside and make his joy complete by uniting Israel with her long-awaited groom (Jn 3.29). Taking up the language of Hosea and others,[16] John refers to Israel as Yahweh's bride and to himself as a kind of best man, extending the metaphor radically by calling Jesus, and not Yahweh, the bridegroom. He understands precisely the extent of his role in the story of God's love affair with Israel: 'The bride belongs to the bridegroom . . . [so] he must become greater; I must become less' (Jn 3.29–30). Jesus' growing reputation, John explains to his disciples, is in accordance with God's purpose, and true greatness is measured by the extent of one's witness to Christ (see Mt 11.11).

Even so, John pre-empted numerous aspects of Jesus' ministry, including the practice of baptism (Mt 3.1,6/Jn 4.1–2); the call to repentance in anticipation of God's coming kingdom (Mt 3.2,6/Mt 4.17); the challenge to the temple's purification rites (Mt 3.5–7/Mt 21.12); the use of parables and other particulars of speech;[17] and of course his death as a martyr (Mt 14.10).[18] One might even say that 'Jesus' vision, message, and tactics were shaped by John.'[19] Indeed, the evidence suggests, as more than a few scholars have recognized, that Jesus was initially a disciple of John's before he came to a fuller understanding of how his own prophetic vocation would play out.

The extent of John's influence on Jesus only makes John's humility all the more astounding. Even as 'the Baptizer' of Israel—surely a role of immense importance—John gladly put his reputation and successful ministry aside for the sake of a more important Word that simply had to be heard. He did everything so that Jesus 'might be revealed to Israel' as the Son of God (Jn 1.31–34). John did not come to plant new seeds himself, but to *turn* the hardened ground so that when the Gardener arrived, the land would be prepared to receive him.

Since baptism alone could neither absolve sin nor heal human resistance to God, John removed himself from the limelight in order to make Jesus all the more visible. Only Jesus could forgive wrongdoing and restore the human capacity to cooperate with God. Therefore, John was content with his function as a human signpost: 'Look, the Lamb of God, who takes away the sin of the world!' (Jn 1.29)

On a practical note, one mustn't equate humility with a low opinion of oneself. In fact, the opposite is quite true, for a humble Christian knows deep down that he or she was created to be God's ambassador in the world. Is a more esteemed calling even imaginable? Moreover, imaging God well does not require pushing and straining to greater heights, but an attitude of surrender so that whatever godliness is seen in us is actually *God with us*, the life of Jesus manifesting itself as we submit to his Kingship. As William Temple, former Archbishop of Canterbury put it:

> Humility does not mean thinking less of yourself than of other people, nor does it mean having a low opinion of your own gifts. It means freedom from thinking about yourself one way or the other at all.[20]

To grow in humility (if 'grow' is the right word) one must learn to resist natural impulses within and the way of the world without, both of which would have us grasping for greatness. But this is not to say that humility robs a person of their identity, either. Again, the opposite is true, for self-emptying permits us to *become* all that we were created to be: unique images of God filled with the Spirit of God (see 'Wholly in the Spirit' in chapter 13). It might even be helpful to think of humility as an antidote to idolatry. In stark contrast to the Babylonian King Nebuchadnezzar, who built an enormous statue of himself so that everyone in his kingdom would acknowledge his greatness, John's attitude was: 'He must become greater; I must become less.' As faith makes space for God in our lives, so humility prepares the way for his coming.

Dig Deeper

- Why was the desert an appropriate setting for John to call Israel to repentance?

- How do barren places cultivate humility?

- What do you think it means to repent of sin?

- Is humility something you value? Why/ why not?

- How can you become less so that Jesus might become greater?

- Commit John 3.30 to memory.

15

Prophetic Fulfilment: God with Us

JESUS (PART ONE)

The Word became flesh and made his dwelling among us (Jn 1.14a).

> John 1.1–5; Luke 2.40–3.22, 4.1–20; Mark
> 2.1–12, 7.1–23; Matthew 13.1–23; 21.1–9

Prophetic Fulfilment

Yahweh's prophets run a golden thread through the biblical tapestry, visible at every turning point of crisis and hope. But Jesus is the one who completes the rich embroidery of God's purposes by drawing together various loose ends from the Old Testament and sewing them into the fabric of God's grand plan. And as we shall see, the manner in which Jesus brings Israel's story to its climax is in many ways illuminated by our study of prophetic spirituality.

In this chapter, we will survey Jesus' ministry by picking up on seven of the spiritual virtues from previous chapters, and in chapter 16 (part two), the remaining six virtues will be explored in the context of Jesus' final week, his 'Passion'. The next two chapters will thereby reveal how each aspect of prophetic spirituality was intensified and amplified in the life of Israel's long-awaited Messiah.

As the gospels make quite clear, Jesus of Nazareth was regarded primarily as a prophet in his time,[1] although some of his prophetic actions also laid claim to kingly status as Yahweh's anointed, come to establish the kingdom of God once and for all. (Upon theological reflection, the church would later honour him with the title of great high priest as well; Heb 4.14.) But before we reflect on his life as a prophet, it will be helpful to put aside notions of Jesus as the second member of the Trinity walking around in human skin as though he were 'disguised' as one of us. To understand his mission and purpose, we must consider him as a fully human being within his own particular, historical context; Jesus of Nazareth, miraculously conceived and born of a human mother, grew up trusting deeply in God as he developed into a mature adult with a divine calling.[2] As is the case with any historical figure, Jesus' significance cannot be grasped without reference to the unfolding story in which he played his pivotal role.

The nation of Israel, descended from Jacob and his twelve sons, grew numerous in Egypt as slaves to Pharaoh. Under Moses' leadership, through an event remembered as the exodus, they were saved to become God's holy people. At Mount Sinai the Israelites received God's law so that they might reflect the nature of their King and establish his kingdom in the land of Canaan. God dwelt among them as promised in the tabernacle and in Solomon's Temple, but over time the Israelites developed a habit of rejecting Yahweh as their King along with his prophetic messengers, who sought to keep them in line with God's purposes. Eventually God withdrew his presence and left both Israel and Judah to suffer at the hands of their respective enemies, Assyria (722 BC) and Babylon (597 BC). In 539 BC, God raised up a Persian king named Cyrus who allowed Israel's remnant to return from exile in Babylon and rebuild their temple in Jerusalem. The temple was successfully completed, but Israel's remnant did not experience Yahweh's return. Even five hundred years later, as John the Baptist had begun to raise eyebrows by the Jordan River, the Jewish people were still waiting expectantly for Yahweh to send his Messiah (anointed one), who they believed would defeat their now Roman oppressors and establish God's kingdom forever.

Prophetic Wisdom (John 1.1–5/Luke 2.40–52)

John's gospel, which contains more explicit theological reflection than the Synoptics, introduces Jesus as the physical and temporal embodiment of God's eternal wisdom. Israel's prophets presented the words of God on his behalf, but Jesus is described as the very Word of God itself. By speaking of Jesus in this way, John means to clarify for his readers that the man who will feature in the following twenty-one chapters of his gospel is God's clearest word of Self-revelation, living among us (Jn 1.14). In the opening verses of his prologue, John borrows from the personification of Lady Wisdom in Proverbs to present Jesus as one who has been collaborating with God from the beginning of time.

> In the beginning was the Word [Prov 8.22–26], and the Word was with God [Prov 8.27–31], and the Word was God. He was with God in the beginning. Through him all things were made [Prov 3.19]; without him nothing was made that has been made. In him was life, and that life was the light of men [Prov 3.16–18]. The light shines in the darkness, but the darkness has not understood it [Prov 1.22–27] (Jn 1.1–5).

Luke's gospel also introduces Jesus with reference to his wisdom, which was apparent even from a young age. The story itself (the only one in the gospels about Jesus' childhood) is sandwiched between two interpretive clues, one stating that Jesus was 'filled with wisdom' even as a young child (Lk 2.40), and the other testifying that after the event Jesus continued to grow 'in wisdom and stature, and in favour with God and men' (Lk 2.52).

As God-fearing Jews, Joseph and Mary travelled from Nazareth to Jerusalem every year to celebrate the Passover. One particular year, when the festival had ended, Jesus' family and friends packed up and set off back to Nazareth, assuming that the twelve-year-old boy was among them. It wasn't until they had travelled for a full day that his parents realized he was missing. They immediately rushed back to Jerusalem, but Jesus was nowhere to be found. One can only imagine Mary's angst over the special son God had entrusted to her care!

Days later, still searching for any sign of their boy, Mary and Joseph heard a familiar voice as they were passing through the temple courts. Following the sound to its source, they were amazed to discover Jesus deep in conversation with the rabbis and with Jerusalem's most esteemed teachers of the law!

Suddenly Mary's relief gave way to disappointment, 'Son, why have you treated us like this? Your father and I have been anxiously searching for you' (Lk 2.48).

But young Jesus looked genuinely perplexed.

'Didn't you know I had to be in my Father's house?' (Lk 2.49)

Not only did Jesus demonstrate a profound understanding of the Scriptures from an early age, but he had already begun collaborating with the One he called Father, taking initiatives accordingly.

Prophetic Calling (Luke 3.21–22)

Many years later, having heard about the ministry of his cousin John, Jesus went down to the Jordan River to be baptized. And there, like his prophetic forebears, Jesus heard God's voice and experienced a heavenly vision during his moment of divine summons.

> When all the people were being baptised, Jesus was baptised too. And as he was praying, heaven was opened and the Holy Spirit descended on him in bodily form like a dove. And a voice came from heaven: 'You are my Son, whom I love; with you I am well pleased' (Lk 3.21–22).

On first impressions, the brief announcement from heaven doesn't seem to offer much detail about Jesus' calling, but the Old Testament texts undergirding these few words suggest that Jesus was simultaneously being commissioned as God's representative (Son of God) and Israel's representative (Messiah).[3] As we know from Moses' life, these twin roles are consistent with the prophetic vocation (see 'Living In-Between' in chapter 2). We will consider each of them briefly in the context of Jesus' baptism.

In the ancient world, kings were enthroned as earthly images of their gods (see 'Image Problems' in chapter 13), and Israel's hymnbook also included royal and enthronement psalms which esteemed their nation's king as a Son of God (e.g. Pss 2.4–9; 89.26–27). The words from heaven at Jesus' baptism draw on this tradition.

> I will proclaim the decree of the LORD:
> He said to me, '*You are my Son;*
>   *today I have become your Father*' (Ps 2.7).

With this enthronement language in mind, it is evident that Jesus was being commissioned as God's kingly image-bearer, followed by an anointing as the Holy Spirit alighted upon him. In the three years that followed, this young prophet would provide the Jewish people with a clearer image of God than any of their ancestors had ever seen; in Paul's words, 'the image of the invisible God' (Col 1.15).

The other dimension of Jesus' call lay in representing Israel. The Old Testament text behind this part of the heavenly affirmation comes from Isaiah:

> Here is my servant, *whom I uphold,*
>   my chosen one *in whom I delight* [am well pleased];[4]
> I will put my Spirit on him
>   and he will bring justice to the nations (Isa 42.1).

After his baptism, Jesus went on to claim that he had indeed been anointed with the Spirit of the Lord. In Luke's gospel, after returning from his testing in the wilderness, Jesus attended the synagogue in Nazareth, where he read from Isaiah:

> The Spirit of the Sovereign LORD is on me,
>   because the LORD has anointed me
>   to preach good news to the poor.
> He has sent me to bind up the broken-hearted,
>   to proclaim freedom for the captives
>   and release from darkness for the prisoners (Isa 61.1).

After reading these words, Jesus declared, 'Today this scripture is fulfilled in your hearing' (Lk 4.21). Believing himself to be Israel's

Messiah, Jesus sought to fulfil the calling that was Israel's before it became his;[5] to make Yahweh's kingdom an earthly reality. He gathered twelve disciples around him to signify the reconstitution of the twelve tribes of Israel and offered fresh interpretations of the Torah in his efforts to renew Israel's covenant with her true King.[6] In other words, Jesus proceeded to act like Israel's Messiah, albeit with a few critical differences to their expectations. Jesus had no intentions of asserting himself as a militant king in order to lead a Jewish revolt and conquer Roman oppressors (see Jn 6.15). Instead, he set out to defeat humanity's greatest enemies—sin and death. It was because of this alternative understanding of Messiahship that Jesus came to be rejected by Israel.

Prophetic Integrity (Luke 4.1–13)

Immediately following his baptism, Jesus 'was led by the Spirit in the desert, where for forty days he was tempted by the devil' (Lk 4.1b–2a). The details of his testing are strange to us—what is so sinful, after all, about turning stones into bread?—but the temptations you and I face don't begin with the words, 'if you are truly the Son of God . . .' (Lk 4.3,9). The most (and perhaps *only*) predictable thing about temptation is that it is always tailored to the individual. (C.S. Lewis makes this point with penetrating insight in *The Screwtape Letters*.) So even if the particulars of Jesus' temptations seem irrelevant to our lives, the fundamental question behind all such trials is whether one's first allegiance is to God or self, in other words, the choice between worship and idolatry.

The parallel between Israel's testing (in the wilderness for forty years after their watery rebirth) and that of Jesus (in the wilderness for forty days after his baptism) draws our attention to the far-reaching significance of Jesus' integrity. Deuteronomy 8.2 says that God tested and humbled the Israelites in the desert 'in order to know what was in [their] heart, whether or not [they] would keep his commands.' As the one called to take up Israel's mission on her behalf, Jesus succeeded precisely where Israel had failed.

The three temptations revolved around Jesus' designation as the Son of God, so that each of the devil's challenges was a variation on the same theme. If you are truly the Son of God (i.e. God's royal image-bearer), then you should act like it: provide food for yourself; take kingdoms for yourself; prove your identity through public spectacles. The devil's assumption was that if Jesus had the capacity to do such things (provide, take, prove) then surely he ought to do them. Jesus should have taken hold of what was rightfully his.

But Jesus, who discerned that being the Son of God meant something very different from exploiting opportunities for greatness, resisted these courses of action. For 'being in very nature God, [he] did not consider equality with God something to be grasped' (Php 2.6). Even before the devil had begun to tempt him, Jesus was already actively resisting any compulsion to provide for his own wants and needs by fasting, a discipline that prioritizes self-denial over self-gratification. In the same vein, Jesus' emphatic response to each temptation was to give God pre-eminence.[7]

> Jesus answered, 'It is written: "Man does not live on bread alone [but on every word that comes from the mouth of the LORD]"' (Lk 4.4; Deut 8.3).

> Jesus answered, 'It is written: "Worship the Lord your God and serve him only"' (Lk 4.8; Deut 6.13; 10.20).

> Jesus answered, 'It says: "Do not put the Lord your God to the test"' (Lk 4.12; Deut 6.16).

Through obedience and deep trust, Jesus held fast to his integrity as a 'complete' image of God. But his testing was by no means over. 'The possibility, the temptation, for Jesus to misconstrue his sonship and use God's power to his own advantage, remains to the very end.'[8]

Prophetic Mercy (Mark 2.1–12)

Jesus drew a lot of attention (and tension) by insisting on compassion and mercy. Not only did he spend a great deal of his time with sinners, tax-collectors, prostitutes, Gentiles, lepers, and other unclean outcasts and misfits (can you imagine Jonah ever doing such things?), but Jesus went even further—too far in the eyes of the Pharisees—offering people *forgiveness* for their sins as well.

On one such occasion, when a paralytic man was brought by his friends and placed before Jesus, Jesus did not respond to their faith with the words 'You are healed', but rather, 'You are forgiven'. This, of course, caused a huge stir among the teachers of the law, who accused Jesus of blasphemy, for 'who can forgive sins but God alone?' (Mk 2.7) Restoring a healed person to their community was one thing, but claiming to restore someone to God was quite another. So, to demonstrate that forgiveness and healing are twin expressions of the same divine mercy, Jesus spoke up again:

> 'But that you may know that the Son of Man has authority on earth to forgive sins . . .' He said to the paralytic, 'I tell you, get up, take your mat and go home' (Mk 2.10–11).

To those willing to receive it, Jesus extended God's mercy through healings, through the sharing of table fellowship and through explicit declarations of forgiveness. On another occasion, Jesus even healed the servant of a Roman centurion (Lk 7.1–10), surely an act of mercy that would have made Jonah's blood boil!

Such unrestrained acts of mercy are not politically innocent, for they entail a 'criticism of the system, forces, and ideologies that produce the hurt.'[9] The teachers of the law did not object to Jesus' declaration of forgiveness just because of the implicit claim to divine authority that came with it. There was *fear* behind their anger, too. As the ones who determined who was clean and who wasn't clean, who was in and who was out, they were afraid of losing that control. It was not surprising, then, that Jesus' prophetic mercy often led to conflict.

Prophetic Conflict (Mark 7.1–23)

Like Samuel, Jesus regularly came into conflict with the authority figures of his day, particularly with regards to the ways in which the central pillars of Judaism, Torah and temple, had been sucked dry of their God-given purpose. In Mark 7, the issue of purity in relation to food is tackled head-on.

Mark begins by setting the scene. Some Pharisees and teachers of the law had noticed that Jesus' followers were not following the Jewish customs concerning cleanliness (which Mark explains as an aside to readers in verses 3–4). They asked what was to them an obvious question. 'Why don't your disciples live according to the tradition of the elders instead of eating their food with "unclean" hands?' (Mk 7.5)

Rather than offering any explanation whatsoever for their 'unclean' hands, Jesus went straight to the heart of the matter: *man-made rules that grant power to the rule-makers*. He identified the Pharisees as hypocrites and the subjects of one of Isaiah's prophecies:

> These people honour me with their lips,
>   but their hearts are far from me.
> They worship me in vain;
>   their teachings are but rules taught by men (Mk 7.9; Isa 29.13).

And if that didn't stir the pot quite enough, Jesus continued, 'You have a fine way of setting aside the commands of God in order to observe your own traditions!' (Mk 7.9) He then illustrated his point by giving an example of the way their traditions took priority in order to meet selfish needs and circumnavigate the demands of the Torah (to honour one's parents).[10] Once a crowd had gathered to hear the debate, Jesus returned to the Pharisees' question, reinforcing a theme well known among Israel's prophets: the distinction between internal attitudes and external actions.

> Nothing outside a man can make him 'unclean' by going into him.
> Rather, it is what comes out of a man that makes him 'unclean' (Mk 7.15).

Later, when Jesus' disciples told him they still didn't get it, he broke the proverb down for them.

- *What goes in* (food) can't make you unclean because it only goes into your stomach before being excreted; food has little to do with your 'heart'.

- *What comes out* (premeditated actions) does determine whether or not you are unclean because the actions you choose have everything to do with your 'heart'.

This is the very principle that undergirded Samuel's various conflicts. What really matters, more than the keeping of rules, is the orientation of one's heart in order to accurately represent God's character (see 'Heart Reorientation' in chapter 4).

Prophetic Speech (Matthew 13.1–23)

Parables were Jesus' preferred mode of speech. Matthew even goes so far as to say that 'he did not say anything to them without using a parable' (Mt 13.34). When asked about this by his disciples, Jesus explained his bias for cryptic language with a quote from Isaiah's call narrative.

> This is why I speak to them in parables:
>
> > 'Though seeing, they do not see;
> >   though hearing, they do not hear or understand.'
>
> In them is fulfilled the prophecy of Isaiah (Mt 13.13–14a; see Isa 6.9–10).

In essence, Jesus was saying that his prophetic speech was designed to separate idolaters from true worshippers. 'He who has ears, let him hear,'[11] said Jesus, and the parable was left to do its subversive work. As a way of preaching to divide, open-ended parables were much more than just a clever rhetorical device on the lips of Jesus. Parables brought the kingdom of God near by evoking a decision, and those who proved their understanding by responding appropriately welcomed God's reign into their lives.

> The parables are not simply *information about* the kingdom, but are part of the *means of* bringing it to birth . . . They do not merely give people something to think about. They invite people into the new

world that is being created, and warn of dire consequences if the invitation is refused.[12]

For this reason the parables have been referred to as 'performative',[13] since the *experience* of hearing the story *is* the point. Whatever happens in a person's consciousness as they hear the story, *that* is the purpose of the parable, be it an extended story or a pithy proverb. The parables are left open so that they cannot be resolved in any other way than in the faith-response of listeners (see 'Filling the Gaps' in chapter 1). It is through *lived* responses to Jesus' world-making stories that God's kingdom (his recognized rule) is established in the world—and this is as much the case today as it was in their initial telling. Jesus plants parables in the hearts of his listeners in the hope of yielding 'a hundred, sixty or thirty times what was sown' (Mt 13.13–23). And if a parable evokes no response at all, then the audience evidently doesn't have what Jesus would call 'ears to hear'.

But as well as speaking on God's behalf, Jesus, like Hosea, is himself a parable of God (see 'Incarnate Word' in chapter 10). His undiscriminating love for sinners, his insistence on self-denial in the lives of his followers, his instruction about how many times one should forgive . . . all these things are rather difficult to digest, but they lead to the ultimate issue concerning how we will respond to Jesus *himself*. To be sure, the Christ-parable continues to sound like foolishness to some, just a made-up story without any bearing on reality (see Eze 20.49), but where the seed of God's Word takes root, it yields an abundance of good fruit (Gal 5.22–23).

Just as Isaiah confronted Israel and King Ahaz with a moment of choice (see 'The Heart of Ahaz' in chapter 11), Jesus set down a dividing line for his people.[14] What this meant in particular for Jews in the first century was that they could either put their faith in the kingdom of God and become the light of the world, or continue to trust in an earthly, militant kingdom and be consumed by the power of Rome[15] (see Lk 19.41–44).

Prophetic Signs (Matthew 21.1–9)

In much the same way that Jesus brought the kingdom of God to bear on Israel through parabolic speech, miracles were the prophetic signs that accompanied the return of Yahweh and the restoration of his people. Physical healings of lepers, demoniacs and the sick not only restored people to their communities, but they also signified a reversal of the dehumanizing power of idolatry (see 'You Are What You Worship' in chapter 7). Through prophetic signs, 'Jesus was not simply predicting or symbolizing, but *manifesting* the action of God.'[16]

But despite the excitement and drama associated with the miracles, not everyone grasped their significance. Even John the Baptist, locked in a prison cell, began to wonder whether Jesus' behaviour matched up to his expectations of Israel's Messiah. Eventually, he sent messengers to Jesus, who put the question to him directly, 'Are you the one who was to come, or should we expect someone else?' (Mt 11.3)

By way of response, Jesus gave this summary of his ministry:

> The blind receive sight, the lame walk, those who have leprosy are cured, the deaf hear, the dead are raised, and the good news is preached to the poor (Mt 11.5).

In other words, Jesus was doing the kinds of things the prophets had anticipated would be signs of God's coming kingdom (see Isa 29.18; 35.5; 42.7). Read the prophetic signs, says Jesus, and you will recognize me. (John's confusion was probably caused by the lack of prophetic *judgement* in Jesus' ministry, but we will come to that.)

The signs were obvious enough for those with eyes to see, but they were not given willy-nilly to authenticate Jesus' claims.[17] Nor were they to be treated as spectacles for curious observers with their hands in their pockets. Like the parables, they demanded a response. When, in the gospels, we witness Jesus eating with sinners before they have shown any hint of repentance (Lk 19.1–10), healing non-Jews in response to their genuine faith (Lk 7.1–10), washing the feet of his own disciples (Jn 13.3–17), and ultimately giving his life away in love, what we are seeing is a 'dramatic *embodiment* of the divine purpose.'[18] God is present *in* those actions, making himself known through Jesus.

One of Jesus' prophetic signs that invited a response from onlookers was the manner of his arrival to Jerusalem. Having established himself over three years as a prophet in Israel, Jesus made preparations to enter Jerusalem in accordance with the prophecy of Zechariah 9.9. From Bethphage, just east of Jerusalem, he sent two disciples ahead of him to fetch a donkey and her colt, so that his entrance to the royal city would unambiguously enact the return of Israel's long-awaited king.

> Rejoice greatly, O Daughter of Zion!
>   Shout, Daughter of Jerusalem!
> See, your king comes to you,
>   righteous and having salvation,
>   gentle and riding on a donkey,
>   on a colt, the foal of a donkey (Zech 9.9; Mt 21.5).

By fulfilling Zechariah's prophecy and entering Jerusalem on a donkey, Jesus claimed to be the heir to David's throne without verbally saying so. And judging by their response, the crowd knew exactly what was meant by the symbolic action (Mt 21.4–5).

> Hosanna[19] to the Son of David!
>
> Blessed is he who comes in the name of the Lord!
>
> Hosanna in the highest! (Mt 21.9; see Ps 118.25–26a)

On account of his wisdom and mercy, his authoritative speech and miraculous signs, Jesus was recognized by many as Israel's long-awaited messianic king, enacting Yahweh's triumphant return to Jerusalem.

But his story is not over yet . . .

Dig Deeper

■ Do you tend to think of Jesus as being primarily human or divine? Why?

■ What encouragement can we draw from Jesus' victory over temptation?

■ Read Mark 7.15. How does this verse apply to you?

■ How is mercy related to conflict? Have you ever experienced this dynamic?

■ What does it mean to have 'ears to hear' and 'eyes to see' the speech and signs of Jesus?

16

Prophetic Fulfilment: God with Us

JESUS (PART TWO)

Do not think that I have come to abolish the Law or the Prophets; I have not come to abolish them but to fulfil them (Mt 5.17).

Matthew 21.10–46; John 12.1–17;
Matthew 26.36–46; Mark 15.1–39;
Luke 23.33–24.7

Prophetic Judgement (Matthew 21.10–46)

After asserting himself as king by the manner of his arrival in Jerusalem, Jesus proceeded to proclaim judgement on the temple through prophetic signs and speech, as Jeremiah and Ezekiel had done before him.[1] Matthew narrates three events in close succession, two signs and a parable, which together issue a scathing indictment of the temple system's failure to bear real fruit in Israel.

In the city where Jeremiah had once smashed a pot and cried, 'I will smash this nation and this city just as this potter's jar is smashed and cannot be repaired' (Jer 19.11), Jesus overturned tables, scattering the profits of moneychangers and driving out buyers and sellers alike. He also evoked the context of Jeremiah's temple sermon by declaring that the temple had (again) become 'a den of robbers' (Jer 7.11; see 'You Must Die!' in chapter 12).

These dramatic words and actions hearkened back to Jeremiah's warnings, drawing historical conclusions from theological evidence; the fall of Jerusalem (in AD 70) would be the direct consequence of Israel's stubborn resistance against Yahweh and his prophets (Mt 24.1–2).[2]

Jesus' second prophetic sign that followed, the cursing of the fruitless fig tree, is also best understood in the context of judgement (Mt 21.18–22).[3] The enacted sign drew heavily on Old Testament prophecies (Mic 7.1–4; Jer 8.11–13) and on the notion that *'the fertility of the land bears a direct relationship to the spiritual fruitfulness of the people.'*[4] The strange miracle therefore provided further commentary (for the benefit of his disciples) on Jesus' criticism of the temple. The tree's lack of fruit was an indication that judgement loomed on Israel's horizon.

Following these prophetic signs came a question from the lips of the chief priests and elders, What gives you the right . . . ? (Mt 21.23), to which Jesus responded with a parable—and one with a sting in its tail. The parable is fairly straightforward once the allusions are understood. The landowner is God; the vineyard is Israel (see Isa 5.1–7); the tenants are Israel's religious leaders; the servants are Yahweh's prophets;[5] and the son is Jesus. Being a master of prophetic speech, however, Jesus did not immediately give away the parable's figurative meaning. Only after drawing the chief priests and elders into the story's plot did Jesus pose the question, 'Therefore, when the owner of the vineyard comes, what will he do to those tenants?' (Mt 21.40)

> 'He will bring those wretches to a wretched end,' they replied, 'and he will rent the vineyard to other tenants, who will give him his share of the crop at harvest time' (Mt 21.41).

The response of the temple authorities introduced new characters to the parable, 'other tenants', whom Jesus promptly identified as Gentiles, thereby turning the judgement of his hearers back upon themselves (see 'Nathan's Story' in chapter 5). Yes, Jesus affirmed, God will punish those who have not borne fruit with what has been entrusted to them. The parable's give-and-take punchline is reminiscent of Ahijah's prophetic judgement upon Jeroboam:

Therefore I tell you that the kingdom of God will be **taken** away from you and **given** to a people who will produce its fruit (Mt 21.43).

Having been drawn into Jesus' story, it quickly became apparent to the religious leaders that 'he was talking about them' (Mt 21.45). Jesus' actions in the temple and his (thinly) veiled accusation of the Jewish religious authorities had made the same point: Jewish worshippers, for all their pride in the temple, were failing to bear any real fruit (see 'The Coming Kingdom' in chapter 14).

By saying such things publicly, Jesus effectively signed his own death warrant. Any man game enough to reinterpret the Torah and speak brashly against Israel's temple could only live for so long. Just as the people had responded to Jeremiah in his day—'You must die!' (Jer 26.8)—so Jesus' judgement of the temple led directly to his arrest and crucifixion (Mt 26.66).

Prophetic Humility (John 13.1–17)

A couple of days later, on the eve of his arrest and just prior to the annual Passover celebrations, Jesus took time to be with his disciples. The opening verses of John 13 establish that the devil's plan was under way (Jn 13.2) and that Jesus knew for his part what had to be done (Jn 13.3). But in the events that followed, Jesus did not lecture his disciples to ensure that their theology was airtight, nor did he give them a pep talk on how best to tackle the task of evangelism. Rather, he showed them the way forward by kneeling to wash their feet and instructing them to do likewise.

In Jewish tradition, it was customary for a slave to bring a bowl of water to guests so they could wash their own feet upon entering the house (e.g. Gen 18.4).[6] But Jesus gives the foot-washing greater prominence by disrobing to wash his disciples' feet for them during the meal (Jn 13.4).[7] The amount of detail is telling.

He got up from the meal, took off his outer clothing, and wrapped a towel round his waist. After that, he poured water into a basin and began to wash his disciples' feet, drying them with the towel that was wrapped round him (Jn 13.4–5).

At a dinner which ought to have been in his honour, Jesus leaves the table and takes 'the form of a slave' (Php 2.7 NRSV). The notion of Jesus putting himself below his disciples feels completely wrong to Peter, who will have none of it, just as he had previously rejected Jesus' suggestion that being the Christ meant having to suffer (Mk 8.31–33). But Peter's resistance to having his feet washed actually helps to pinpoint the reason for Jesus' actions.

The washing of the disciples' feet does not symbolize forgiveness of sins; Jesus makes that quite explicit (Jn 13.9–11). Had that been his intention, Peter probably would not have objected, since Jesus would not have been the lesser figure in the exchange.[8] The point, rather, is that Jesus wishes to present himself to his own disciples as *their servant*.

After washing their feet and putting his robes back on, Jesus resumes his place at the table as Teacher and asks, 'Do you understand what I have done for you?' (Jn 13.12)

> You call me 'Teacher' and 'Lord,' and rightly so, for that is what I am. Now that I, your Lord and Teacher, have washed your feet, you also should wash one another's feet. I have set you an example that you should do as I have done for you (Jn 13.13–15).

Of course, the act of foot-washing has close ties with the Last Supper which follows. Self-emptying humility readies us to ingest the Bread of Life (Jn 6.53–56; see 'Digesting God's Word' in chapter 9) so that we may present Jesus to the world through acts of service.

Prophetic Prayer (Matthew 26.36–46)

After the Last Supper, Jesus went with his disciples to a familiar place where he could spend the night in prayer as he had done previously (see Lk 6.12). Once again, at the foot of a mountain, this time the Mount of Olives, Israel's representative prophet takes the strain between God and his people, expressing his angst openly before God (see 'Invitation to Prayer' in chapter 2). Since prayer was Jesus' faith-response to moments of crisis and decision,[9] it is not surprising that on the eve of his arrest, Jesus knelt in the garden of Gethsemane to plead with God for a way forward that did not involve drinking of 'the cup'.

The cup of God's wrath is a frequently used metaphor in the Old Testament. The prophets spoke of the cup to refer to God's impending judgement upon human rebellion, and various Old Testament prophecies extend the metaphor by speaking of the cup being drained of its wine, leading to inevitable drunkenness—and by implication, destruction.[10]

Earlier in Matthew's gospel, when James and John had asked to be given thrones on either side of Jesus when his kingdom was established, Jesus had simply replied, 'You don't know what you are asking . . . Can you drink the cup I am going to drink?' (Mt 20.22) He then went on to link suffering (the means) to glory (the end), saying, 'whoever wants to become great among you must be your servant, and whoever wants to be first must be your slave' (Mt 20.26–27). At that time Jesus had revealed to his disciples that the cup of God's judgement was one he himself would eventually have to drink. But now, in the eerie darkness of Gethsemane, Jesus begins to pray in earnest 'for this cup to be taken away' (Mt 26.42).

The narrative is a sombre reminder that Jesus' temptations and sufferings were genuine. Although his prayer in Gethsemane is often quoted for its 'Thy will be done' conclusion, it clearly entailed a wrestling with God before it became a prayer of submission. Not once or twice, but *three times* Jesus pleaded, 'My Father, if it is possible, may this cup be taken from me' (Mt 26.39–44). Only when he realized that there was no other way to fulfil God's purposes did Jesus concede, 'Yet not what I will, but what you will' (Mk 14.36). This is not to say that Jesus did his Father's will begrudgingly, but that the suffering of the cross was made no easier by his belief that resurrection awaited him on the other side of death.

Jesus made his way forward through prayerful engagement with God. His efforts to discern and obey the will of his Father were facilitated by the kind of praying that neither insisted on having things his own way (see Mt 26.53–54) nor resigned him passively to whatever might transpire. And as Jesus discerned that the way forward necessitated suffering, he stepped out, as each of us must do, in prayerful dependence upon God.

Prophetic Suffering (Mark 15.1–39)

After enduring a phoney trial to its foregone conclusion, Jesus was taken to Golgotha to die. With great sarcasm he was dressed in royal robes and crowned with thorns, hailed as 'King of the Jews' and crucified with an outlaw on either side (Mk 15.17–27). Some onlookers taunted him about his claims to rebuild the temple in three days while others ridiculed him for being unable to do for himself what he had done for so many others (Mk 15.29–31). But for all that may be said about Jesus' final moments, surely the worst of it was that God, like everyone else, had abandoned him.

> At the ninth hour Jesus cried out in a loud voice, *'Eloi, Eloi, lama sabachthani?'*—which means, 'My God, my God, why have you forsaken me?' (Mk 15.34; Ps 22.1)

The lament psalms were Israel's way of holding faith in tension with suffering, and although many of these psalms urge God not to abandon the psalmist, very few go so far as Psalm 22, which grieves a reality best described as 'godforsakenness'. The fact that Jesus chose to quote from *this* particular psalm in his dying moments on the cross has significance not just for his own experience of desolation, but for others who have felt abandoned by God as well.

By quoting from the psalmist, Jesus took up the plight of all those who are 'spoken for' by lament psalms such as this.[11] As a godforsaken man himself, he identified with those who feel ignored by God (Ps 22.2), with those who are mocked and hated for the foolishness of their faith (Ps 22.6–8) and with those who lie helpless at death's door (Ps 22.12–15). Perhaps most significantly, Jesus spoke for those who affirm the existence of 'my God' even while asking, 'why have you forsaken me?' For feelings of isolation are all the more acute when God, in whom the sufferer trusts, *allows* the pain and does nothing to help.[12]

How, then, are we to understand Jesus' horrible anguish? What can it have meant for this Jewish prophet, identified only moments later as the Son of God (by a Roman soldier no less), to have suffered such a lonely death?

Building on what we have learned from the suffering of other prophets like Hosea and Jeremiah, we are prompted to see Jesus' forsakenness as an expression of God's forgottenness[13] (see 'The Suffering of God' in chapter 11). Suspended on a cross between earth and heaven, Jesus provided the truest and most accurate image of God in human history. Suffering turns out to be central to Jesus' prophetic mission precisely because it reveals God most truly—naked and exposed—for who he is. By reaching out to the world's forsaken through Jesus' godforsakenness on the cross, God was, as Paul writes, 'reconciling the world to himself in Christ' (2 Cor 5.19a).

Ironically, in that very moment, Jesus was taunted to prove his identity with a sign. 'Let this Christ, this King of Israel, come down now from the cross, that we may see and believe' (Mk 15.32). What the priests and interpreters of the law failed to recognize was that the suffering of the Messiah was already the prophetic sign of a God who knows what it is to be forsaken by his own, but who offers himself in love nonetheless. The incarnate Word of God hung bleeding before their very eyes and they demanded a sign that they might 'see and believe'!

> See from his head, his hands, his feet,
> Sorrow and love flow mingled down!
> Did e'er such love and sorrow meet,
> Or thorns compose so rich a crown?

Prophetic Faith (Luke 23.44–24.12)

In Luke's gospel, Jesus' final words (again borrowed from the Psalms) testify to a relentless faith in the midst of torment. By appropriating the words of Psalm 31,[15] Jesus also aligns himself with those who choose to trust in God no matter how black the skies have become (Lk 23.44–45a).

> Jesus called out with a loud voice, 'Father, into your hands I commit my spirit.' When he had said this, he breathed his last (Lk 23.46; Ps 31.5).

The first eight verses of Psalm 31 follow a pattern in which God's answers to each petition do more than simply benefit the one praying. The psalmist's faith in God creates a context for Yahweh to prove his faithful character in answer to each petition. So, for instance, the deliverance of the psalmist proves the righteousness of Yahweh (Ps 31.1); the rescue of the psalmist confirms that God is a 'rock of refuge' and a 'strong fortress' (Ps 31.2); the redemption of the psalmist proves God's faithfulness (Ps 31.5) and so on. Similarly, in his dying moments, Jesus made space for God to prove himself faithful. Believing that his heavenly Father would vindicate his cause, Jesus committed his spirit into the hands of the very One whose calling had led him to the cross, and there, Jesus breathed his last.

* * * *

But there was no voice from heaven; only that of a Roman soldier, affirming the tragic death of an innocent man. Some waited, watching to see what might happen next, but there was no miracle. Joseph of Arimathea took the dead body down from the cross, wrapped it in linen and buried it in a tomb with the assistance of some women who had loved and followed Jesus. And as darkness fell on Friday evening, everyone returned home.

* * * *

One very long Sabbath later, the same women got up at the break of dawn to embalm the dead body of their beloved rabbi. But upon arriving at his tomb, they discovered the stone to have been moved and the body of Jesus gone. Confusion quickly turned to fear when two men, gleaming like angels, appeared out of nowhere, asking, 'Why do you look for the living among the dead? He is not here; he has risen!' (Lk 24.5b–6)

And then it began to dawn on them . . .

God was proving himself faithful.

Jesus had spoken of resurrection, but no one had really understood him (Lk 9.22; 24.7). Perhaps just another one of his cryptic parables; no one returns from the dead! But just as Elijah's faith in God on Mount Carmel had created an opportunity for God to reveal his glory to Israel, thereby 'turning their hearts back again' (1 Kgs 18.37), so Jesus' faith-full death on a hill outside Jerusalem opened the way for God to demonstrate his power over death through the resurrection, thereby proving his faithfulness—not just to Jesus, but to all those who pray with him, 'I trust in you, O LORD . . . You are my God' (Ps 31.14).

The faith *of* Jesus Christ has proven God's faithfulness once and for all, so that our faith *in* Christ makes us participants in his resurrection life (Rom 6.3–8). Such faith, however, should not be thought of as a once-off decision, but as a *way of living* that creates regular opportunities for God to prove himself worthy of our trust. Faith is essential to prophetic spirituality because it gives voice to God's character—which speaks volumes!

Prophetic Insight (Luke 24.13–27)

Christian pilgrims today still walk the road to Emmaus, our hearts a mix of wonder and confusion. Like Cleopas and his friend, we continue to seek answers to the quandary of Jesus' life and death. How did this impressive prophet come to such a sudden and bloody end? Why did Jesus not redeem Israel in the way his disciples had expected? And what of the hysterical nonsense from Jesus' female disciples that morning? Had they been telling the truth? (Lk 24.19–24)

As they travelled along, mulling these things over, Cleopas and his companion were joined by Jesus, although they were 'kept from recognizing him' (Lk 24.16). Between Jerusalem and Emmaus, Jesus offered them a prophet's insight into the ways of God by telling the larger story of Israel in relation to his own life (see 'Prophetic Fulfilment' in chapter 15).

> And beginning with Moses and all the Prophets, he explained to them what was said in all the Scriptures concerning himself (Lk 24.27).

For Jesus to tell his own story 'beginning with Moses and all the Prophets' says a great deal in itself. At the very least, it suggests that the answers to many of our questions are already present in the Old Testament, once we learn to read it in conjunction with Jesus' life, death and resurrection.

Perhaps the confusion of the disciples can be compared to watching a film that has an unforeseeable twist at the end. Once the surprise ending is revealed, it can be interesting to watch the whole film again to see whether its conclusion might have been anticipated.[16] The disciples describe something of this nature when, after being in conversation with Jesus for hours, they turn to one another and say, 'Were not our hearts burning within us while he talked with us on the road and opened the Scriptures to us?' (Lk 24.32) Their national history had just been reinterpreted in light of its (very recent) climax and their minds were struggling to catch up. But according to Jesus, the insight shared with them on the Emmaus road, the 'twist' if you like, was not something that could never have been anticipated, but in fact something they *should* have seen coming. 'How foolish you are, and how slow of heart to believe all that the prophets have spoken!' (Lk 24.25) Jesus' rebuke made it clear that previous prophets had also sought to communicate that which Cleopas and his companion had missed.

So what was Jesus driving at? What particular insight had the disciples failed to grasp?

The clue given in the narrative is brief—'Did not the Christ have to suffer these things and then enter his glory?' (Lk 24.26)— but it can be traced back to previous incidents in Jesus' life where he discerned the nature of his call and mission (Lk 4.18–21; see 'Prophetic Calling' in chapter 15). An especially notable incident is described in Luke 9.18–36, when Jesus asked his disciples how the crowds were perceiving him. On that occasion, after Peter had correctly identified Jesus as 'the Christ of God', Jesus went on to reveal something disturbing about what that title actually meant.

> The Son of Man *must* suffer many things and be rejected by the elders, chief priests and teachers of the law, and he *must* be killed and on the third day be raised to life (Lk 9.22).

In both narratives (Lk 9 and Lk 24) Jesus is referred to as 'the Christ'[17] and suffering is spoken of as something that 'must'[18] take

place in God's redemptive plan.[19] Of even greater significance is
the fact that both accounts speak of Jesus 'entering his glory'. One
text is linked to the transfiguration and the other to the resurrection, so both are clear instances of Jesus being exalted and recognized for who he truly is.

In light of these parallels, the profound truth which Jesus made
known on the Emmaus road is one we have already considered in
the sufferings of Jeremiah and the death of Jesus (see 'The
Suffering of God' in chapter 12; 'Prophetic Suffering' above): that
*God's glory is revealed not through self-actualizing power, but through
self-emptying love.* This insight became the heart of Paul's sermon
to the church at Philippi—written, significantly, from a prison cell:

> Your attitude should be the same as that of Christ Jesus:
>
> Who, being in very nature God,
>   did not consider equality with God something to be grasped,
> but made himself nothing,
>   taking the very nature of a servant,
>   being made in human likeness.
> And being found in appearance as a man,
>   he humbled himself
>   and became obedient to death—
>   even death on a cross!
> Therefore God exalted him to the highest place
>   and gave him the name that is above every name,
> that at the name of Jesus every knee should bow,
>   in heaven and on earth and under the earth,
> and every tongue confess that Jesus Christ is Lord,
>   to the glory of God the Father (Php 2.5–11).[20]

The orchestrations of the prophets finally reached their surprising crescendo in the resurrection of Jesus of Nazareth, who
turned the suffering of God into the victory of God. God's passion to dwell among his people was fully realized as Jesus
embodied Yahweh's return,[21] or in John's idiom, as the Word of
God 'pitched his tent'[22] among us (Jn 1.14). But that is not all.

Through his death and resurrection, Jesus opened the way for
God's passion to be shared most intimately with the church, a

body of Christ-like people into whom the Father breathes his own Spirit in order to dwell not just among them, but *within* them. Now who could have seen *that* twist coming?

Dig Deeper

■ How important is the Old Testament for understanding Jesus? Explain your thoughts.

■ How do acts of humble service affect the way a person sees him/herself?

■ What does Jesus' crucifixion say about God?

■ How, in the past week, has your faith provided God with opportunities to prove his character?

■ In what way(s) has God's passion to dwell among us been fulfilled in Jesus?

17

Prophetic Community: Passing On the Flame

THE CHURCH

*Indeed, all the prophets from Samuel on,
as many as have spoken, have foretold these days.
And you are heirs of the prophets (Acts 3.24–25a).*

Acts 2 – 3

The Spirit of Christ (Acts 2.1–41)

During the time between Jesus' resurrection and his ascension (a forty-day period according to Acts 1.3), Jesus commanded his disciples not to leave Jerusalem, but to wait for the Spirit-baptism John had spoken about (Acts 1.4–5). Sure enough, after the election of Matthias in Acts 1.15–26, the Twelve (signifying the tribes of Jacob; see Isa 49.6[1]) were indeed 'clothed with power from on high' (Lk 24.49). The Holy Spirit swept through the house, accompanied by two familiar symbols of Yahweh's presence: wind[2] and fire.[3] Both are described (as they are in OT texts) using similes; the disciples heard a sound *'like* the blowing of a violent wind' as 'what *seemed* to be tongues of fire' came to rest on each of them (Acts 2.2–3). Evidently, the experience was otherworldly and almost indescribable.

As an expression of God's empowering presence within, the disciples began to speak in a range of languages that even they themselves did not understand and, not surprisingly, a crowd soon gathered to investigate the noisy phenomenon (Acts 2.5,11). Peter immediately began to explain that the arrival of God's Spirit, which the people were witnessing, had been prophesied by Joel (Acts 2.17–21).

> In the last days, God says,
>   I will pour out my Spirit on all people.
> Your sons and daughters will prophesy,
>   your young men will see visions,
>   your old men will dream dreams.
> Even on my servants, both men and women,
>   I will pour out my Spirit in those days,
> and they will prophesy (Acts 2.17–18; Joel 2.28–29).

Previously, God had put his Spirit upon certain individuals in order to accomplish specific tasks,[4] but in accordance with Joel's prophecy—and Moses' wish (Num 11.29)—Peter now declared that *all* of God's people could be filled with his Spirit and prophesy, be they sons or daughters, young or old, slave or free, male or female (see Gal 3.28). But with his explanation for the bizarre event, Peter was just getting warmed up. With so many people gathered in one place, Peter proceeded to preach the good news, beginning (as one must) with the bad news: the intrigued crowd before him shared responsibility for the crucifixion of Jesus (Acts 2.23). Even so, since Christ's death had been part of a bigger plan, death did not have the final word.

> God has raised this Jesus to life, and we are all witnesses of the fact. Exalted to the right hand of God, he has received from the Father the promised Holy Spirit and has poured out what you now see and hear (Acts 2.32–33).

Even as Peter was speaking, the promised Spirit of God, so powerfully present among the disciples only moments earlier, began to also move among Peter's audience, who were 'cut to the heart' (Acts 2.37). Since God has made Jesus 'both Lord and Christ', announced Peter, the only appropriate response is to cease resisting God (repentance) and to begin one's life afresh (baptism), empowered by the astounding gift of God's Spirit (Acts 2.38).

According to Luke's records, three thousand people responded to Peter's invitation that very day (Acts 2.41)!

At Pentecost, in fulfilment of several Old Testament prophecies, the Spirit was finally put upon all the Lord's people, to borrow Moses' phrase (Num 11.29). This does not only mean that believers may now draw near to God in confidence (see Exod 20.19), but also that 'we are indwelt by the living God himself, in the person of God's Spirit.'[5] Once again, we are reminded of the way God fills his image with his Spirit in order to make a person whole (Gen 1.27; see 'Wholly in the Spirit' in chapter 13).

The Holy Spirit works within and among God's people to illuminate blind spots and bring conviction of our rebellion against God. While this may sound like a rather gut-wrenching process, an increasing awareness of sin is one of the Spirit's most generous, life-changing gifts. Without it, we would continue to stagger about, doing further damage to others and ourselves along life's way. The unveiling of our eyes, however, is just the beginning. The Holy Spirit won't reveal our desperate condition only to leave us feeling depressed about it. Not at all! When the Divine Breath[6] is invited to sweep through our lives, he not only exposes sin, but goes on to enable repentance, empower change, and equip us with spiritual gifts so that we may collaborate more effectively with God's purposes. As the Holy Spirit works within believers 'to will and to act according to [God's] good purpose' (Php 2.13; Eze 36.27), spiritual gifts are also given to members of the Christ-community 'just as the Spirit chooses' (1 Cor 12.11 NRSV). It is not up to church leaders to allocate gifts according to whomever they might think suitable; that is the Spirit's work. The tough task of church leadership is to identify each congregant's gifts and provide opportunities for them to be put into action.

Now if the stories we have been reading about biblical prophets are anything to go by, one might quickly come to the conclusion that prophetic spirituality does not lend itself easily to being part of a community. Other than 'the company of the prophets' that gathered under Elisha's leadership in 2 Kings,[7] nearly all prophetic tales in the Old Testament are about isolated men or women serving God against the tide. However, with the Holy Spirit uniting the church, prophetic spirituality can become more of a communal endeavour than an individual one.

The Community of Christ (Acts 2.42–47)

God does not wish to be invisible to his creation. That much is clear from the divine mandate for human 'images' to fill the earth and rule over it (Gen 1.27–28), from Israel's calling to reveal God's character to surrounding nations (Deut 4.6), and from the embodied testimony of his prophetic messengers, including its fullest expression in Jesus. But the task of enfleshing God on earth does not end with Jesus. Before entering the heavenly realm after his resurrection, Jesus commissioned his followers to carry on the somewhat daunting task of making God known to the world (Mt 28.19–20). Sent, filled and empowered by the Spirit of Christ, it has been left to the church to give tangible expression to God's character so that the world may 'see your good deeds and praise your Father in heaven' (Mt 5.16).

Acts 2.42[9] contains a taut summary of 'the four essential elements in the religious practice of the Christian church':[10] the teaching of the apostles; fellowship; the breaking of bread (reminiscent of the Last Supper; Lk 22.19; 24.35); and prayer. Significantly, this brief outline of the early church's inward practices concludes with a comment about its outward growth;[11] 'And the Lord added to their number daily those who were being saved' (Acts 2.47b). Sacraments, like prophetic signs that symbolize and intensify God's presence among his people, not only build up the church community from within, but also fuel the church's mission to the world by empowering believers to reveal God's good character.

Needless to say, this is not a task that can be done by individuals. Luke makes this clear in the book of Acts by presenting the disciples as a prophetic community who carry on Jesus' work in the power of the Spirit.[12] However, it should be acknowledged in a chapter entitled 'Prophetic Community' that there are many who would balk at the notion of a prophetic institution. An oxymoron, some might say. And they would have significant support from Scripture, considering the number of prophets in the Bible who speak to—or *at*—institutions from the outside (see 'Profile of a Prophet' in chapter 13). It is important, therefore, when using a phrase like 'prophetic community', to distinguish between a community made up of hundreds of individual prophets, and a community that is considered prophetic by virtue of its character and calling *as a body* of people.[13] The point in Acts is not that all Christians are individual prophets in their own right, but that the church is commissioned to take up the prophetic tasks of speaking on God's behalf and reorienting hearts Godward *as a body* of believers. The implicit answer to Paul's rhetorical question, 'Are all prophets?' in 1 Corinthians 12.29 is obviously negative. (By the same token, I would hesitate to call every believer a 'priest' despite the fact that Peter calls the church 'a holy priesthood' in 1 Pet 2.5.) In a similar vein, regarding the witness of the lampstands in Revelation, Richard Bauckham writes,

> Each Christian is not a lampstand. Only a church is symbolized by a lampstand. It is not primarily each individual Christian's witness to the world, but the church's witness to the world which is depicted as prophetic . . . Of course every Christian is called to participate in that witness, but this stops a little short of saying that each Christian is a prophet.[14]

Bauckham goes on to make it clear that the conflict between the church and idolatry stands in continuity with some of the epic battles in the Old Testament between the prophets and idolatry (e.g. Moses vs Pharaoh, Elijah vs Baal).[15] The church's prophetic witness is closely tied to its existence as a countercultural community that resists being Babylonized (see 'Identity Crisis' in chapter 13) or moulded into the image of 'the beast' (worldly power), but the call to stand apart becomes exceedingly difficult if one insists on doing it alone.

The spiritual qualities explored in this book are applicable to whole churches as well as individuals. Communities can of course learn to manifest spiritual traits like boldness in prayer, wise collaboration with God, heart reorientation, creative speech, and so on. 'God is not just saving individuals and preparing them for heaven; rather, he is creating *a people* among whom he can live and who in their life together will reproduce God's life and character.'[16] God's people are called to represent him as communities of Christ united by the Spirit, so that surrounding nations and neighbours will have no choice but to sit up and take notice—and 'glorify God on the day that he visits us' (1 Pet 2.12).

In His Steps (Acts 3)

The story of Peter and John healing 'a man crippled from birth' (Acts 3.2) is about the early church beginning to walk in Jesus' footsteps. 'Peter is able to do the kind of thing that Jesus did by acting in the name of Jesus: thus the continuity between the ministry of Jesus and the witness of the church is expressed.'[17] What Jesus began, his disciples now perpetuate, and although Peter takes most of the initiative, Luke seems intent on putting John in the picture too, so as 'to make the apostolic action communal.'[18]

After being miraculously healed, the well-known beggar from the temple gate clings to Peter and John and a crowd gathers to verify the rumours. Could it be true that this man, after being lame for forty years (Acts 4.22), has really found sufficient strength in his ankles not just to stand, nor even merely to walk, but to *leap* into the air in worship? Mirroring the pattern in Acts 2, the incident draws attention and is followed by a speech from Peter, who goes beyond explanation to evangelism.

Peter opens with a couple of rhetorical questions, 'Men of Israel, why does this surprise you? Why do you stare at us as if by our own power or godliness we had made this man walk?' (Acts 3.12) No doubt, Peter has their full attention, and the question on all their minds is one and the same. Peter goes on to answer it:

> By faith in the name of Jesus, this man whom you see and know was made strong. It is Jesus' name and the faith that comes through him that has given this complete healing to him, as you can all see (Acts 3.16).

Just as Jesus demonstrated his authority to forgive sins by the healing of a paralyzed man (Lk 5.24; see 'Prophetic Mercy' in chapter 15), so the apostles relate spiritual and physical wholeness to one another[19] in the name of Jesus. The lame man has not only found physical health through faith in Jesus' name, but his encounter with the 'author of life' (Acts 3.15) has implications for his wellbeing in every respect.[20]

As Peter again takes the opportunity to preach to the gathering crowds, his sermon takes an interesting turn—away, it would seem, from the healing that has just taken place. As he did previously (Acts 2.23,36), Peter informs the Jews gathered before him that they are responsible for the death of Jesus. But he does not say this to hold it against them; 'Now, brothers, I know that you acted in ignorance, as did your leaders' (Acts 3.17). Peter knows only too well from personal experience what it is like to fail and be graciously restored (Lk 22.61). The point is not to make his hearers feel guilty, but to let them in on the bigger picture. The death and resurrection of Jesus, Peter says, 'is how God fulfilled what he had foretold through all the prophets' (Acts 3.18). The only appropriate response, therefore, is to 'repent [*metanoéo*] . . . and turn to God, so that your sins may be wiped out' (Acts 3.19).

The crux of Peter's sermon is that this grand plan of God's has been moving for centuries toward its fulfilment in Christ. 'Indeed, all the prophets from Samuel on, as many as have spoken, have foretold these days' (Acts 3.24). There is a sense in which all of Israel's prophets, in their various shades and colours, have contributed to this message which culminates in Jesus. (Indeed, that is a central thesis of this book.) God's grand plan began with his promise to bless 'all peoples on earth' through Abraham's descendants, and he has been giving hints along the way through his prophets that the suffering of the Messiah would be necessary (e.g. Isa 53). Sure enough, says Peter, when the author of life came along, you crucified him. *But* . . . God raised him from the dead (Acts 3.15) and then poured out his Spirit, bringing 'times of refreshing' (Acts 3.19) in the present, even before God acts to fully restore everything—again, as the prophets have foretold (Acts 3.21).[21]

Peter tells the story of Israel in such a way as to show that all prophecy has been leading up to 'these days', when the Holy Spirit would be poured out freely upon God's people. The bottom line is that Peter's Jewish audience, the intended beneficiaries of God's special relationship with the prophets and his covenantal arrangements with Abraham, are being presented with an opportunity to inherit God's blessings and thereby become a blessing to others (Acts 3.25–26). As the story of God's relationship with his creation continues, declares Peter, *you* are invited to get on board with what God is doing!

To be 'heirs of the prophets' is to receive one's prophetic inheritance, just as being an heir of the covenant means receiving the
entitlements of that covenant. So in Peter's rhetoric, the prophets
(who were called to reveal God to Israel through speech and sign)
and the Abrahamic covenant (which appointed Israel to be God's
nation of ambassadors) lead to a common inheritance: the
immense task of making God known. Being 'heirs of the prophets
and of the covenant' means one and the same thing: 'Through
your offspring all peoples on earth will be blessed' (Acts 3.25b).

As we reach the end of our journey with the prophets, Peter's
challenge is most appropriate, for the mission of Israel and the
responsibility of the prophets has been bequeathed to the church.
The coming of the Spirit has brought about 'the renewal of
Israel's prophetic calling in the world',[22] an age in which *all* the
Lord's people may take up the prophetic task of speaking for
him. It is the vocation of the church, God's holy nation, to make
Christ known in the hope that one day all the nations of the earth
will welcome him to dwell in their midst. No doubt, the church
is another 'high risk mission strategy',[23] but with the empowering
presence of the Holy Spirit, everything is possible!

Dig Deeper

■ What does Acts 1.8 suggest about the purpose of Pentecost?

■ In what ways do you experience the Holy Spirit's activity in your life?

■ Read 1 Corinthians 12. What phrase or idea stands out most to you?

■ In what ways are your spiritual gifts being used in the church?

■ How do you feel about receiving your inheritance as an heir of the prophets?

You are invited to continue exploring the Bible
with Paul Hedley Jones at **textofmeeting.com**

The Tent of Meeting was the designated place for Moses and the
people of Israel to meet with God as they traveled through the
desert (Exod 33.7f.). It was God's portable dwelling place,
enabling him to remain close to his people as they made their
spiritual and physical pilgrimage from slavery in Egypt to freedom in the Promised Land. John picks up on this image in the
New Testament by introducing Jesus as God's revelatory Word
who 'tabernacled' among us (Jn 1.14) so that God might fully be
made known to humanity. Jesus is, as John puts it, the enfleshed
Word of God.

The Bible has served a similar purpose to the Tent of Meeting for
centuries now, as the *Text* of Meeting for God's people, presenting opportunities for us to encounter him regularly as we discern
the way. **textofmeeting.com** is an online space, devoted to
enabling fellow pilgrims to learn more about this special text
through which God desires to meet with us.

Endnotes

1. Introduction: Sharing God's Passion

[1] See also Exod 6.7; 7.16; 9.1,13; 10.3,7,17; 18.1; 32.11; Deut 7.6; 14.2,21; 27.9; 28.9; 29.13; 2 Sam 7.24; 1 Chr 17:21–22; Pss 33.12; 95.7; 100.3; Jer 7.23; 11.4; 30.22; 31:1,33 (Heb 8.10); 32.38; Eze 34.31; 36.28; 37.27; Dan 9.19; Hos 2.23; Joel 2.27; Zech 8.8; 9.16; 13.9; 1 Pet 2.9.

[2] The Hebrew words translated 'Adam' and 'Eve' may also be translated 'earth' and 'life'.

[3] See Terence E. Fretheim, 'Is Genesis 3 a Fall Story?' in *Word & World* 14/2 (1994): pp. 144–53.

[4] Cain's offering consists of 'some of the fruits of the soil', whereas Abel brings 'fat portions from . . . the firstborn of his flock' (Gen 4.3–4). Abel's offering to Yahweh is a priority; Cain's is an afterthought.

[5] Esau, when consumed by a similar desire to kill his brother Jacob (Gen 27.41), makes a better decision than Cain did in his moment of choice (Gen 32). Walter Moberly, *The Theology of the Book of Genesis* (New York: CUP, 2009), p. 98.

[6] Emphasis added. Throughout this book, all emphasis shown in Bible quotations has been added by the author.

[7] Gen 8.1 speaks of God sending a spirit/wind/breath (*ruach*) over the depths of the water, just as he did in Gen 1.2. For a more detailed examination of the textual similarities between these two creation accounts, see Warren Austin Gage, *The Gospel of Genesis: Studies in Protology and Eschatology* (Winona Lake, IN: Carpenter Books, 1984), pp. 7–15.

[8] See Janzen's insightful exploration of OT ethics, where the 'familial paradigm' is foundational to four other ethical paradigms that

uphold Israel's moral life. Waldemar Janzen, *Old Testament Ethics: A Paradigmatic Approach* (Louisville, KY: Westminster John Knox, 1994).

[9] Walter Brueggemann, 'The Trusted Creature', *CBQ* 31 (1969): p. 488 (original emphasis).

[10] Also Gen 15.4–5; 17.4–8; 22.17–18.

[11] By passing between the split animals, God commits himself to a similar fate if he fails to deliver on the promises of the covenant. See Jer 34.18–20.

[12] Terence E. Fretheim, *God and World in the Old Testament: A Relational Theology of Creation* (Nashville: Abingdon, 2005), p. 103. See also Christopher Wright's conclusive statement in *The Mission of God: Unlocking the Bible's Grand Narrative* (Leicester: IVP, 2006): 'It is God's mission in relation to the nations, arguably more than other single theme, that provides the key that unlocks the biblical grand narrative', p. 455.

[13] C. Wright, *Mission of God*, p. 258.

[14] See also Exod 9.12; 10.20,27; 11.10; 14.8.

[15] See ch. 11 (Isaiah) for further discussion on the hardening of hearts.

[16] The Chronicler interprets this event differently by ascribing the census to 'the satan' instead of God (1 Chr 21.1; see ch. 8 on the perspective of the narrator). In Hebrew, 'the satan' literally means 'the accuser' or 'the adversary'. It is used of human beings as well as spiritual beings in the Old Testament, and does not carry the same connotations as the proper name 'Satan' in the New Testament. For one treatment of the term, see Henry Ansgar Kelly's *Satan: A Biography* (CUP, 2006).

[17] See ch. 8 for a full treatment of 1 Kgs 22.

[18] See ch. 10.

[19] Jack Miles, *GOD: A Biography* (New York: Random House, 1995), p. 12. 'True, the Lord God of Israel is the creator and ruler of time, and the Psalms delight in repeating that he lives forever . . . And yet, contradictory as this may seem, he also enters time and is changed by experience. Were it not so, he could not be surprised; and he is endlessly and often most unpleasantly surprised.'

[20] Terence E. Fretheim, *The Suffering of God: An Old Testament Perspective*, OBT (Philadelphia: Fortress, 1984), p. 150. See esp. pp. 149–66.

[21] Terence E. Fretheim, *Exodus*, Interpretation (Louisville, KY: John Knox, 1991), p. 51.

²² See Jer 1.6; Jnh 1.3; 4.2 (compare Gideon in Jdg 6.15).

²³ See the first two chapters of Brueggemann's *Old Testament Theology: Essays on Structure, Theme and Text* (ed. Patrick D. Miller; Minneapolis: Augsburg Fortress, 1992), 'Structured Legitimacy' and 'Embrace of Pain' (pp. 1–44), where he suggests an approach to biblical theology based on this dialectic of self-assertion and self-abandonment.

²⁴ R.W.L. Moberly, *Prophecy and Discernment* (London: CUP, 2006), p. 1.

²⁵ Note that God's presence is manifested to Israel in a theophany (Exod 19.9–25) before he issues commands (Exod 20.1–17) and makes himself known via a mediator (Exod 20.18–21). Moses' prophetic call in Exod 3 follows the same pattern.

²⁶ See the discussion in Moberly, *Prophecy*, pp. 4–10.

²⁷ Deut 18.9–18 expands on the significance of this event by explicitly linking Israel's fearful request for a mediator with the raising up of future prophets to guide Israel after Moses. The mention of a prophet like Moses in Deut 18.18 is more likely to refer 'to a succession of prophets over time, raised up by YHWH as and when Israel needs appropriate guidance' (Moberly, *Prophecy*, p. 8, n. 21) than to one particular prophet, i.e. Jesus. The context outlines Israel's need for judges (Deut 16.18–17.3), kings (Deut 17.14–20), priests (Deut 18.1–8) and prophets (Deut 18.9–18) upon entering the promised land. See also Walter Brueggemann, *The Book of Exodus*, NIB, vol. 1 (Nashville: Abingdon, 1994), p. 854, n. 129.

²⁸ Abraham J. Heschel, *The Prophets* (New York: Harper Collins, 1962), p. 24.

²⁹ Compare Paul's exhortation in 1 Cor 14.1–5.

³⁰ See Moberly, *Prophecy*, p. 9. On this basis, I understand the narrative to cast Eldad and Medad in a positive light.

³¹ Isa 42.1–9; 49.1–13; 50.4–9; 52.13–53.12 (also see 61.1–3).

³² See John Goldingay, *God's Prophet, God's Servant: A Study in Jeremiah and Isaiah 40–55* (Toronto: Clements Publishing, rev. edn, 2002), p. 133.

³³ 'Prophetic activity by human persons signifies word. Priestly acts signify presence.' Walter Brueggemann, *Theology of the Old Testament: Testimony, Dispute, Advocacy* (Minneapolis: Fortress, 1997), p. 576.

³⁴ See, for example, 1 Cor 10.1–11.

³⁵ Leo Perdue, *The Collapse of History: Reconstructing Old Testament Theology* (Minneapolis: Fortress, 1994), p. 238.

[36] The novel by the same title, upon which the film is based, was written in 1979 by German author Michael Ende.

[37] I have borrowed this phrase from Stephen Crites's article, 'The Narrative Quality of Experience', *JAAR* 39/3 (Sept 1971): pp. 291–311.

[38] See J. Richard Middleton, Brian J. Walsh, *Truth Is Stranger Than It Used to Be* (Downers Grove: IVP, 1995), whose exploration of the biblical metanarrative is governed by these four worldview questions: Where are we? Who are we? What's wrong? and What's the remedy?

[39] Susan L. Nickerson, 'Book Review: Fiction (1983–10–15)', *Library Journal* 108 (R.R. Bowker Co, 1976).

[40] George Stroup, 'Theology of Narrative or Narrative Theology? A Response to Why Narrative?' *TT* 47/4 (Jan 1991): p. 432.

2. Prophetic Prayer: Living In-Between

[1] Fatalism is the belief that events are predetermined and therefore inescapable.

[2] The 1998 film *Run Lola Run* also provocatively explores how seemingly insignificant choices matter.

[3] According to a study of relevant biblical texts by Patrick D. Miller, only Yahweh's prophets were successful in praying for the remission of deserved punishment. Miller, *They Cried to the Lord: The Form and Theology of Biblical Prayer* (Minneapolis: Augsburg Fortress, 1994), p. 266.

[4] See Fretheim's 'Divine Dependence upon the Human: An Old Testament Perspective', *ExAud* 13 (1997): pp. 1–13.

[5] R.W.L. Moberly, 'How May We Speak of God? A Reconsideration of the Nature of Biblical Theology', *TynBul* 53/2 (2002): p. 198.

[6] The term 'stiff-necked' may have agricultural origins; a farmer's oxen would stiffen their neck muscles to resist their master's guidance.

[7] Brevard Childs, *The Book of Exodus* (Philadelphia: Westminster, 1974), p. 567. Childs is citing Benno Jacobs, *The Second Book of the Bible: Exodus* (Hoboken, NJ: Ktav, 1992), p. 944.

[8] Walter Brueggemann, *Old Testament Theology*, p. 28. Brueggemann has contributed significantly in highlighting the vital role of protest and lament in Israel's worship. Also see part II of his *Theology of the Old Testament*, pp. 317–406.

9 Donald E. Gowan, *Theology in Exodus: Biblical Theology in the Form of a Commentary* (Louisville, KY: John Knox, 1994), pp. 231–2.

10 Patrick D. Miller, 'Prayer and Divine Action', in *God in the Fray: A Tribute to Walter Brueggemann* (ed. Tod Linafelt and Timothy K. Beal; Minneapolis: Fortress, 1998), p. 217.

11 Ibid., p. 216.

12 Christopher Wright, *Deuteronomy*, NIBC (Peabody, MA: Hendrickson, 1996), p. 140 (original emphasis).

13 See Miller, *They Cried to the Lord*, 1996.

14 Patrick D. Miller, 'Prayer as Persuasion', *Word & World* 13/4 (1993): p. 357 (original emphasis).

15 John Goldingay, 'The Logic of Intercession', *Theology* (Jan/Feb 1998): p. 265.

16 Heschel, *Prophets*, p. 22. Heschel's comment does not have in mind a change in God's overall purposes, but a change in his intended, immediate course of action. On God's openness to be influenced through prayer, see also Samuel Balentine, *Prayer in the Hebrew Bible: The Drama of Divine-Human Dialogue* (Minneapolis: Augsburg Fortress, 1993).

17 Karl Barth, *Prayer* (Philadelphia: Westminster, 2nd edn, 1985), p. 13.

18 It would, of course, have been possible for God to begin again with Moses as he had done with Noah (Gen 6.13,18) and in fact the text indicates that this was God's intention. But because Moses was invited to share in the decision-making process (an opportunity Noah did not have), the prophet's response to the notion of being Israel's new patriarch becomes a critical factor (see Ps 106.23).

19 See Terence E. Fretheim, 'The Repentance of God: A Study of Jeremiah 18.7–10', *HAR* 11 (1987): pp. 81–92.

20 Exod 34.6; 2 Chr 30.9; Neh 9.17; Pss 86.15; 103.8; 111.4; 145.8; Joel 2.13; Jnh 4.2 (compare Eze 33.11). Only the books of Joel and Jonah add the phrase, 'who relents from sending calamity', and pose the question that follows: 'Who knows?'

21 Michael Widmer, *Moses, God, and the Dynamics of Intercessory Prayer* (Tübingen: Mohr Siebeck, 2004), p. 81.

22 The sin of the people affects Moses in more ways than one. In Deut 1.37, he blames them that he will never see the promised land.

23 Widmer, *Moses*, p. 104. See his excursus, 'Standing in the Breach', pp. 103–6.

[24] The narrative refers to Jacob's opponent initially as a 'man' (v. 25); only after the wrestling match does Jacob identify the mysterious figure as God (v. 30).

[25] See ch. 1, n. 16.

[26] In matters of discernment, however, it is not helpful to bemoan the past. Discerning God's will is something that must take *today's* reality into account, regardless of what might have happened yesterday, last week, or seven years ago, for that matter. See Gordon T. Smith, *Listening to God in Times of Choice: The Art of Discerning God's Will* (Downers Grove, IL: IVP, 1997).

[27] The first chapter of Thomas R. Kelly, *A Testament of Devotion* (New York: HarperCollins, 1992 [first pub. 1941]) contains some helpful reflections on learning to pray in 'simultaneity' with life, rather than alternating between times of passive prayer and active living.

3. Prophetic Wisdom: Collaborating with God

[1] Num 27.17; 1 Kgs 22.17; 2 Chr 18.16; Isa 13.14; Mt 9.36; Mk 6.34.

[2] See Walter Brueggemann's little book *Divine Presence amid Violence: Contextualizing the Book of Joshua* (Eugene, OR: Paternoster, 2009) for a helpful discussion of chariots as an indication of oppressive power in Scripture (chs 6–7).

[3] Female prophets in the Bible include Miriam (Exod 15.20), Deborah (Jdg 4.4), Huldah (2 Kgs 22.14), the anonymous prophetess of Isa 8.3, and Anna (Lk 2.36).

[4] New Zealand led the way in 1893.

[5] The phrase in Jdg 4.4, usually translated as 'the wife of Lappidoth', may also mean 'a woman of fire', which is certainly consistent with Deborah's spirited leadership. See Susan Niditch, *Judges*. OTL (Louisville, KY: John Knox, 2008), pp. 60–62.

[6] Wisdom is personified as a woman not only in Proverbs 1–9, but also in the apocryphal books of Sirach (esp. Sirach 24), Wisdom of Solomon, and Baruch.

[7] Bruce K. Waltke, 'Lady Wisdom as Mediatrix: An Exposition of Proverbs 1:20–33', *Presbyterion* 14/1 (1988): p. 14. James L. Crenshaw also refers to Lady Wisdom as a 'heavenly mediator'. See his *Old Testament Wisdom: An Introduction* (Louisville, KY: John Knox, 1998), p. 227.

[8] Meir Sternberg, *The Poetics of Biblical Narrative: Ideological Literature and the Drama of Reading* (Bloomington: Indiana University Press, 1985), p. 274.

[9] See Terence E. Fretheim, 'I Was Only a Little Angry: Divine Violence in the Prophets', *Interpretation* 58/4 (2004): pp. 365–75, for discussion concerning other human agents upon whom God also depends, including Moses, Nebuchadnezzar, and Cyrus.

[10] For more detailed analysis, see Niditch, *Judges*, p. 79.

[11] Nothing is known about the place called Meroz and it is mentioned nowhere else in Scripture.

[12] Fretheim, 'Divine Dependence', p. 6.

4. Prophetic Conflict: Heart Reorientation

[1] As a number of commentaries point out, the phrase 'give them warning from me' could equally (or perhaps better) be translated as 'give them warning *of* me', since Yahweh is the One approaching.

[2] Abraham J. Heschel, *The Insecurity of Freedom: Essays on Human Existence* (New York: Schocken, 1972), p. 11.

[3] Walter Brueggemman, *First and Second Samuel*. Interpretation (Atlanta: John Knox, 1990), pp. 25–6.

[4] Brueggemann, *Samuel*, p. 25.

[5] See Waldemar Janzen, *Old Testament Ethics*. Janzen identifies a familial paradigm at the centre of Israel's ethical life, with priestly, wisdom, and royal paradigms supporting it. The prophetic paradigm stands outside the other four as a corrective to them.

[6] Jacques Ellul, *The Politics of God and the Politics of Man* (trans. G.W. Bromiley; Grand Rapids, MI: Eerdmans, 1972), p. 18.

[7] See 1 Sam 12.3,5,7 for language suggestive of a legal context.

[8] Brueggemann, *Samuel*, p. 93.

[9] Paul D. Hanson, *The Diversity of Scripture: A Theological Interpretation* (Philadelphia: Fortress, 1982), p. 28. On the form-reform polarity between kings and prophets in the Old Testament, see pp. 27–36.

[10] This tension between prophets and kings features in the next four chapters (Nathan vs David; Ahijah vs Jeroboam; Elijah vs Ahab; Micaiah vs Ahab).

[11] See Isa 1.11–19; Jer 6.20; Hos 6.6; Amos 5.21–24; Mic 6.6–8. Israel's wisdom tradition also makes the same assertion: 'To do what is

right and just is more acceptable to the LORD than sacrifice' (Prov 21.3).

[12] The finality of the statement about God 'not changing his mind like men do' in 1 Sam 15.29 comes from the mouth of a prophet who knows all too well that God does in fact change his mind, since vv. 11 and 35 speak of God regretting (*niham*) his decision to anoint Saul. One way to understand the apparent contradiction or ambiguity here is to note the purpose and context each time the verb *niham* (relent) is used of God. In verses 11 and 35, God is responding to human choices whereas Samuel's statement in v. 29 concerns God's election of David, which he will never 'take back'. God relents in his personal interactions with the created order, but he is unchanging with regards to his redemptive will. Somewhat paradoxically, then, God may mercifully change a future course of action in order to remain constant in his fidelity to humanity (see 'Malleable Clay', ch. 12). For two fuller discussions, see Terence E. Fretheim, 'Divine Foreknowledge, Divine Constancy, and the Rejection of Saul's Kingship', *CBQ* 47/4 (Oct 1985): pp. 595–602, and R.W.L. Moberly, 'God Is Not a Human That He Should Repent: Numbers 23:19 and 1 Samuel 15:29', in *God in the Fray: A Tribute to Walter Brueggemann* (ed. Tod Linafelt and Timothy K. Beal; Minneapolis: Augsburg, 1998), pp. 112–23.

[13] For instance, 2 Sam 7.8 (NRSV) says of King David, 'I took you from the pasture, from following the sheep to be prince over my people Israel'.

[14] The Hebrew verb used in 1 Sam 15.33 literally means 'to chop into pieces'. The NIV makes it more palatable with 'Samuel put Agag to death'.

[15] The Urim and Thummim were a 'means of making decisions for the Israelites' (Exod 28.30). See also Lev 8.8; Num 27.21; Deut 33.8; Ezra 2.63; Neh 7.65. They are understood to have functioned much like dice, cast by a priest to discern between alternative courses of action.

[16] Also Lev 11.44–45; 20.7,26.

5. Prophetic Speech: Say It Sideways

[1] Micaiah in 1 Kgs 22; Hanani in 2 Chr 16.7–10; Jeremiah in Jer 20; 26; 28 (compare Amos 7.10–13.) Obadiah, though not a prophet, also feared being slain on the spot simply for announcing Elijah's arrival to King Ahab (1 Kgs 18.7–14).

2 Isaiah experienced a similar freedom, as did Daniel, in spite of his foreign context.

3 Some have questioned whether David's desire to build Yahweh a temple is truly (or only) a matter of piety. The notion of building a temple for Yahweh may also have been an expression of David's desire to 'plant' the divine presence in one place, in contrast to the ark of the covenant which could so easily be moved or even stolen (1 Sam 4–6).

4 The amount of attention given this chapter by biblical scholars testifies to its enormous importance within the books of Samuel and regarding the Davidic kingship. Walter Brueggemann, for instance, goes so far as to say, 'I judge this oracle with its unconditional promise to David to be the most crucial theological statement in the Old Testament.' Brueggemann, *First and Second Samuel*, p. 259.

5 Another possibility is that David sent Uriah to have sex with his own wife so that he could be executed for breaking the rules of holy war. So Randall C. Bailey, *David in Love and War: The Pursuit of Power in 2 Samuel 10–12*, JSOTSup 75 (Sheffield: JSOT, 1990), pp. 91–8.

6 The following verses are my own translation.

7 Similarly, see 1 Kgs 20.38–42.

8 Eugene Peterson, *First and Second Samuel* (Louisville, KY: John Knox, 1999), p. 187. Also see pp. 188–9 on the answer to David's prayer and the gift of Jedidiah.

9 Walter Brueggemann, 'On Trust and Freedom: A Study of Faith in the Succession Narratives', *Interpretation* 26/1 (1972): pp. 11–12.

10 Iain W. Provan, *1 and 2 Kings*. NIBC (Peabody, MA: Hendrickson, 1995), p. 24 (original emphasis).

11 Two lists of King David's children are given in 2 Sam: six children born in Horeb, all from different mothers (2 Sam 3.2–5); and eleven more in Jerusalem (2 Sam 5.13–16). The lists total seventeen children, but there were certainly more since the first list does not include daughters (e.g. Tamar).

12 See ch. 3, n. 2.

13 At this stage in Israel's history, the right of primogeniture (royal succession to the oldest male) had not yet been established. Saul was appointed on account of his impressive stature (1 Sam 9.2) and David was quite emphatically the youngest of eight brothers (1 Sam 16.11). Although Adonijah is David's eldest son (assuming Chileab is dead), he does not explicitly claim kingly succession on this basis.

[14] In 2 Sam 14, Joab's scheme with 'the wise woman of Tekoa' follows a similar pattern: questions are put into the mouth of a woman and directed at the king. But on that occasion, David sees through Joab's ruse.

[15] Keith Bodner, 'Nathan: Prophet, Politician and Novelist?' *JSOT* 95 (2001): p. 51: 'Nathan's machination is not to corroborate her witness or verify her story, but rather to rhetorically finish what she begins.'

[16] The name Bathsheba means 'Daughter of an oath'.

[17] In Hebrew this is actually a statement: 'My lord the king, you have declared that Adonijah will be king after you and that he will sit upon your throne', giving even greater force to the question that follows.

[18] It is worth noting that some scholars doubt the veracity of Nathan's mission and see him as 'a prophet who has sold himself out in a bit of court intrigue.' James Ackerman, 'Knowing Good and Evil: A Literary Analysis of the Court History in 2 Samuel 9–20 and 1 Kings 1–2', *JBL* 109/1 (1990): p. 53.

[19] Sternberg asserts that the art of indirection is the 'key strategy of the Bible's narrative discourse' (*Poetics*, p. 43). That is, the Bible makes sense for readers as they learn to wrestle with ambiguity and read between the lines.

[20] Hans Frei, *The Eclipse of Biblical Narrative: A Study in Eighteenth and Nineteenth Century Hermeneutics* (New Haven: Yale University Press, 1974), p. 280.

[21] See Fred B. Craddock, *As One Without Authority* (Nashville: Abingdon Press, 1971); Eugene Lowry, *The Homiletical Plot: The Sermon as Narrative Art Form* (Atlanta: John Knox, 1980).

[22] Walter Brueggemann, *The Prophetic Imagination* (Minneapolis: Fortress, 2nd edn, 2001), p. 40.

[23] Emily Dickinson (1830–86).

6. Prophetic Judgement: Give and Take

[1] For a more nuanced look at Solomon's characterization in Kings, see J. Daniel Hays, 'Has the Narrator Come to Praise Solomon or to Bury him? Narrative Subtlety in 1 Kings 1–11', *JSOT* 28/2 (2003): pp. 149–74.

[2] On the implications of Solomon's vision for Israel, see Brueggemann, *Prophetic Imagination*, pp. 21–38.

3 The use of the word 'cloak' (*salmah*) in 1 Kgs 11.29–30, instead of 'robe' (*me'il*) from 1 Sam 15.27; 24.11, is possibly due to the wordplay created between cloak (*salmah*) and Solomon (*sh'lomo*).

4 Astute readers will have noticed that 10+1≠12. The remaining tribe of Benjamin was subsumed into Judah in the south (to be ruled by Rehoboam).

5 The language also contains references to the Davidic covenant from 2 Sam 7. See John Gray, *I and II Kings: A Commentary*. OTL (Philadelphia: Westminster, 1970), p. 275.

6 Literally, 'My little one is thicker than my father's loins.' Translations generally diminish the vulgarity of the phrase, but the Hebrew wording reflects the tendency in young men to be preoccupied with genital size and to confuse machismo with political prowess. To his credit, Jeroboam at least has the sense to omit the offensive phrase from his answer to the people in v. 14.

7 Simon J. DeVries, *1 Kings*. WBC, vol. 12 (Waco: Word Books, 1985), p. 159.

8 See ch. 8 concerning the narrator's ability to expose the thoughts and motives of biblical characters.

9 See Moses Aberbach and Leivy Smolar, 'Aaron, Jeroboam, and the Golden Calves', *JBL* 86 (1967): pp. 129–40, for the many parallels established between Aaron in Exod 32 and Jeroboam in 1 Kgs 12.

10 D.W. Van Winkle, '1 Kings XII 25—XIII 34: Jeroboam's Cultic Innovations and the Man of God from Judah', *VT* 46/1 (1996): pp. 101–14.

11 The Hebrew in v. 26 reads, 'Jeroboam said in his heart . . .'

12 John Goldingay, *Old Testament Theology, vol. 1: Israel's Gospel* (Downers Grove, IL: IVP, 2003), p. 673.

13 Jeroboam's family is compared with human excrement twice in v. 10. First, through Ahijah's use of the phrase 'he who urinates against the wall' to signify 'every last male', and second, by the description of judgement that is coming: Jeroboam's rule reeks of idolatry and will be treated accordingly—like dung.

14 1 Kgs 13.34; 14.16; 15.30,34; 16.2,19,26,31; 21.22; 22.52; 2 Kgs 3.3; 10.29,31; 13.2,6,11; 14.24; 15.9,18,24,28; 17.22; 23.15.

15 Mark Leuchter, 'Jeroboam the Ephratite', *JBL* 125/1 (2006): p. 51.

16 Moberly, *Prophecy*, p. 237.

17 James K. Mead, 'Kings and Prophets, Donkeys and Lions: Dramatic Shape and Deuteronomistic Rhetoric in 1 Kings XIII', *VT* 49/2 (1999): p. 197f.

7. Prophetic Faith: Making space for God

[1] The NIV's use of quotation marks around the word 'gods' in these verses is an interpretive decision. The Hebrew suggests neither falsehood nor legitimacy.

[2] Yahweh appears in similar contexts in other parts of the Bible (Gen 1.26; Job 1.6–12; 2.1–7; 1 Kgs 22.19). Whether the so-called gods in Ps 82 are human rulers or pagan gods, the point is the same: they are unworthy of their title because they do not (and cannot) live up to it.

[3] Matitiahu Tsevat, 'God and the Gods in Assembly: An Interpretation of Psalm 82', *HUCA* (1969–70): p. 127.

[4] The verb *nitzav* (niphal form) in Ps 82.1, translated 'presides' (NIV) or 'takes his place' (NRSV) has the sense of 'taking a stand with a definite purpose in mind'. See Francis Brown, S.R. Driver, and Charles A. Briggs, eds, *The Brown-Driver-Briggs Hebrew and English Lexicon* (Peabody, MA: Hendrickson, 1996), p. 662.

[5] Asherah was a Canaanite fertility goddess whose name appears frequently in the Hebrew Bible, often in contexts condemning Israel's syncretistic practices (see Deut 16.21).

[6] Baal is presented throughout the Old Testament as Yahweh's greatest rival in the battle for Israel's trust. His worshippers hailed him as the 'storm god' with power over agricultural and sexual fertility (see ch. 10).

[7] Fretheim, *God and World*, p. 18. Also see C. Wright, *Mission of God*, pp. 136–88, for a helpful discussion of idolatry.

[8] The Hebrew word for 'idol' (*pesel*) may also be translated 'image', so that the commandment could be paraphrased, 'You shall not make for yourself an image of God in the form of anything other than that which I have chosen to bear my likeness upon the earth' (Exod 20.4).

[9] See Leah Bronner, *The Stories of Elijah and Elisha as Polemic against Baal Worship* (Leiden: Brill, 1968), pp. 35–49.

[10] Jezebel and her 450 prophets of Asherah never show up on Mount Carmel. This is not explained, but it confirms that Jezebel is a much stronger force to be reckoned with than Ahab, who folds before anyone who challenges him (Elijah, Naboth, Jezebel). The strength of Jezebel's character is also apparent in 1 Kgs 19.

[11] G.K. Beale makes the same point: 'The principle is this: if we worship idols, we will become like the idols, and that likeness will ruin us.' *We Become What We Worship: A Biblical Theology of Idolatry* (Downers Grove, IL: IVP, 2008), p. 46.

¹² See 'Narrators and Insight' in ch. 8 on the shared prophetic authority of prophets and narrators in the Bible.

¹³ These were typical manifestations of Baal's power as the storm god, according to Canaanite religious beliefs.

¹⁴ DeVries, *1 Kings*, p. 231.

¹⁵ Some scholars see ulterior motives behind Elijah's actions in 1 Kgs 18. See Paul J. Kissling, *Reliable Characters in the Primary History: Profiles of Moses, Joshua, Elijah and Elisha*, JSOTSup 224 (1996): p. 118f. 'Elijah does not simply represent Yahweh at Mt Carmel, he represents himself also' (p. 123).

¹⁶ See n. 10 above.

¹⁷ Provan, *1 and 2 Kings*, p. 147 (original emphasis).

¹⁸ What I have called 'confronting' and 'reorienting' (see ch. 4: Samuel) is in many ways similar to the pattern for prophetic ministry which Brueggemann calls 'criticizing' and 'energizing'. See his *Prophetic Imagination*, pp. 1–19.

8. Prophetic Insight: Discerning God's Ways

¹ Robert Alter, *The Art of Biblical Narrative* (New York: Basic Books, 1981), p. 184. So also Sternberg, *Poetics*, p. 51: 'The Bible always tells the truth in that its narrator is absolutely and straightforwardly reliable.' As Jews, neither Alter nor Sternberg would concur with an evangelical doctrine of inspiration, however. Also see David Gunn, who challenges Sternberg's position in 'Reading Right: Reliable and Omniscient Narrator, Omniscient God, and Foolproof Composition in the Hebrew Bible', in *The Bible in Three Dimensions* (ed. D.J.A. Clines et al.; Sheffield: JSOT Press, 1990), pp. 53–64.

² The books of the 'former prophets' (Joshua to 2 Kings) are so named in recognition of the fact that their authors discerned God's unfolding purposes in history.

³ Robert Polzin, *Samuel and the Deuteronomist: 1 Samuel* (Bloomington: Indiana University Press, 1993), p. 96.

⁴ Ibid., pp. 95–97.

⁵ Alter, *Art of Biblical Narrative*, p. 157.

⁶ Incidentally, in another incident of prophetic conflict, between Jeremiah and Hananiah (Jer 28), both prophets use props to substantiate their messages.

7 See Robert B. Chisholm Jr, 'Does God Deceive?' *BSac* 155 (Jan–Mar 1998): pp. 11–28.

8 The Hebrew in v. 24 infers something stronger than a slap on the cheek (NSRV). The same verb is translated elsewhere as 'beat', 'destroy', and even 'kill'.

9 Crites, 'Narrative Quality', p. 310.

10 An 'inner room' (in Hebrew, literally 'a room within a room') is a place of hiding; see 1 Kgs 20.30.

11 The best book I am aware of that addresses this question is Moberly's *Prophecy and Discernment* (2006).

12 Moberly, *Prophecy*, p. 81. Moberly also stresses moral integrity as a criterion for discerning between true and false prophecy, although he makes the point from Jeremiah's theology of discernment rather than from Micaiah's narrative context.

13 The death of Ahab sees the fulfilment of three distinct prophecies: of an anonymous prophet (1 Kgs 20.42); of Elijah (1 Kgs 21.19); and of Micaiah (1 Kgs 22.17,23).

14 Moberly places a greater emphasis on Micaiah's prophetic impulse to bring about repentance (*shuv*) in Ahab. Moberly, 'Does God Lie to His Prophets? The Story of Micaiah ben Imlah as a Test Case', *HTR* 96/1 (2003): pp. 1–23. While I certainly agree that reorientation is the primary purpose of prophetic speech, I see less evidence of it in this particular story than in the stories about Samuel, Nathan, Ahijah and Elijah explored in the last four chapters. Also see the discussions of Jer 19 and Isa 6 in chs 11 and 12 respectively.

15 On the implications of this narrative with regards to the power, foreknowledge and will of God, see Jeffries M. Hamilton, 'Caught in the Nets of Prophecy? The Death of King Ahab and the Character of God,' *CBQ* 56 (1994): pp. 649–63.

16 See J.J.M. Roberts, 'Does God Lie? Divine Deceit as a Theological Problem in Israelite Prophetic Literature', in *The Bible and the Ancient Near East: Collected Essays* (Winona Lake, IN: Eisenbrauns, 2002), p. 131.

17 The Hebrew word for 'entice' (*patah*) in Eze 14.9 is the same as that in 1 Kgs 22.20–21. See also Jer 20.7; 'You Deceived Me!' in ch. 12.

18 Moberly, 'Does God Lie?' p. 15.

9. Prophetic Mercy: Digesting God's Word

1. The twelve 'minor' prophets are so named simply on account of being shorter (not in height) than the three 'major' prophets, Isaiah, Jeremiah and Ezekiel. In the Christian canon, they are the books from Hosea through to Malachi.

2. For an imaginative series of letters peppered with fascinating insights written from the 'publishers' of the twelve minor prophets to Jonah in response to his 'book proposal', see Mary Katherine Deeley, 'The Shaping of Jonah', *TT* 34/3 (1977): pp. 305–10.

3. The use of parables and poems in Scripture does not mean those parts of the Bible contain less truth; it means that they do not claim to narrate events that actually happened. Jesus spoke a great deal of truth through parables (made-up stories), and of course poetry also conveys truth without having to refer to historic events. For instance, Isaiah's statement that 'the trees of the field will clap their hands' is a poetic way of anticipating that creation will voice Yahweh's praise (Isa 55.12).

4. Gordon J. Wenham, *Story as Torah: Reading Old Testament Narratives Ethically* (Grand Rapids: Baker, 2000), p. 7.

5. See John H. Stek, 'The Message of the Book of Jonah', *CTJ* 4/1 (1969): pp. 23–50, regarding Jonah's historical context.

6. A handful of the prophets did not address rebellious Israel, but rather foreign nations and cities. Obadiah's prophecies were against Edom while both Nahum and Jonah prophesied against Nineveh, Assyria's capital. Elisha also had various dealings with Aram/Syria (2 Kgs 5,8). See 'Profile of a Prophet' in ch. 13.

7. See 'Cycles of Sin' in ch. 3. See also 2 Kgs 13.1–5.

8. The term *Sheol* is translated in the NIV as 'the grave' throughout the OT. (NRSV retains 'Sheol'.)

9. v. 2 = Ps 18.6; v. 3 = Ps 42.7; v. 4 = Ps 5.7; v. 5 = Ps 18.4–5; 69.2; v. 6 = Ps 30.3; 103.4; v. 7 = Ps 107.5–6; 88.2; 5.7; 138.2; v. 8 = Ps 31.6; v. 9 = Ps 69.30; 61.8; 66.13; 42.4; 3.8; 37.39. Also see Athalya Brenner, 'Jonah's Poem out of and within Its Context', in *Among the Prophets* (ed. P.R. Davies and D.J.A. Clines; Sheffield: Sheffield Academic Press, 1993), p. 185.

10. Deeley, 'Shaping of Jonah', p. 309.

11. Danna Fewell and David Gunn note further points of comparison between Moses (in Exod 32) and Jonah. *Narrative Art in the Hebrew Bible* (New York: OUP, 1993), p. 141.

¹² Jesus' parable of the workers in the vineyard touches the same nerve: 'Are you envious because I am generous?' (Mt 20.1–16)

¹³ Miroslav Volf, *Exclusion and Embrace: A Theological Exploration of Identity, Otherness and Reconciliation* (Nashville: Abingdon Press, 1996), p. 74.

¹⁴ Volf, *Exclusion and Embrace*, p. 78.

¹⁵ Dietrich Bonhoeffer, *The Cost of Discipleship* (trans. R.H. Fuller; New York: Macmillan, 1963), p. 100.

¹⁶ L. Gregory Jones, *Embodying Forgiveness: A Theological Analysis* (Grand Rapids: Eerdmans, 1995), p. 22.

¹⁷ Miroslav Volf, *Free of Charge: Giving and Forgiving in a Culture Stripped of Grace* (Grand Rapids: Zondervan, 2005), p. 200.

10. Prophetic Signs: Enacted Parables

¹ James Luther Mays, *Hosea*. OTL (Philadelphia: Westminster, 1969), p. 25.

² Beale, *We Become What We Worship*, p. 244.

³ H.D. Beeby, *Grace Abounding: A Commentary on the Book of Hosea*, ITC (Grand Rapids: Eerdmans, 1989), p. 3.

⁴ *Baal* literally means 'lord' or 'master', but it came to be a proper name for this male Canaanite god.

⁵ Mays, *Hosea*, p. 26.

⁶ 'The misconduct was in one and the same act both infidelity and apostasy. Since everything points to her promiscuity as participation in the ritual sex acts of the Baal cult, it was doubly wicked, against both Hosea and Yahweh.' Francis L. Andersen and David Noel Freedman, *Hosea*, AB (Garden City, NY: Doubleday, 1980), p. 166.

⁷ See James Limburg, *Hosea-Micah*. Interpretation (Atlanta: John Knox, 1988), p. 22f.

⁸ See Raymond C. Ortlund Jr, *Whoredom: God's Unfaithful Wife in Biblical Theology* (Grand Rapids: Eerdmans, 1996), p. 49.

⁹ The book of Hosea is rich with metaphors, wordplays, parallelism and alliteration. There is an additional wordplay between the names Jezreel (*yizr'el*) and Israel (*yisra'el*), which sound almost identical in Hebrew.

¹⁰ Beeby, *Grace Abounding*, p. 34.

¹¹ Ortlund, *Whoredom*, p. 73.

12 For further reading, see Renita J. Weems, *Battered Love: Marriage, Sex and Violence in the Hebrew Prophets*, OBT (Minneapolis: Fortress, 1995).

13 Heschel, *Prophets*, p. 89.

14 Beeby, *Grace Abounding*, pp. 4–5, 140.

15 See H.F. van Rooy, 'The Names of Israel, Ephraim and Jacob in the Book of Hosea', *Old Testament Essays* 6 (1993): pp. 135–49.

16 Kazoh Kitamori considers God's experience of suffering to be caused by an internal conflict between his love and his wrath. *Theology of the Pain of God* (Richmond, VA: John Knox, 1965 [orig. 1946]), pp. 21–2.

17 As Hans Walter Wolff has noted, Hosea's speech abounds in metaphors. Yahweh is 'Israel's husband, lover, fiancé, father, physician, shepherd, fowler, and even lion, leopard, bear, dew, fruit tree, moth, and dry rot.' *The Old Testament: A Guide to Its Writings* (trans. Keith R. Crim; Philadelphia: Fortress, 1973 [1970]), p. 72.

18 Ulrich Mauser, 'God in Human Form', *ExAud* 16 (2000): p. 85.

19 Fretheim, *Suffering of God*, p. 151.

20 Mauser, 'God in Human Form', p. 82. Mauser focuses on Moses and Hosea, but refers also to the enacted parables of Isaiah, Jeremiah, and Ezekiel. See also Fretheim, *Suffering of God*, pp. 155–6.

21 Both the Hebrew (*ruach*) and Greek (*pneuma*) words for 'spirit' may also be translated 'breath' (or 'wind'). See Jn. 20.22; Acts 2.4.

22 Heschel, *Prophets*, p. 49.

23 Gerard Manley Hopkins, 'As Kingfishers Catch Fire'.

11. Prophetic Calling: Preaching to Divide

1 'Or perhaps it is better to say that the appearance and utterance of the prophets evokes a crisis circumstance where none had been perceived previously. That is, the prophets not only respond to crisis, but by their abrupt utterance, they generate crisis.' Brueggemann, *Theology of the Old Testament*, p. 624.

2 Because Isaiah's vision is not placed at the very beginning of the book, some regard it as an experience he had after his initial call to be a prophet. Whether or not this was the case, it is most certainly a call narrative, even if it constitutes a second calling to a very particular and somewhat confusing task. But see Norman Habel, 'The Form and Significance of Call Narratives', *ZAW* 77 (1965): pp. 297–323.

3 Jesus also preached about the necessity of death prior to the possibility of new life (Jn 12.24) before bearing out the full significance of 'the sign of Jonah' in his own death and resurrection (Mt 12.39–41; 16.4).

4 See Jer 9.7; Zech 13.9; Mal 3.3; Mk 9.49.

5 Uzziah (2 Chr 26; Isa 6) is also referred to as Azariah (2 Kgs 14.21; 15.1–7). The two names differ by a single consonant in the Hebrew.

6 See Pss 11.4–7; 18.6–15; 82; 97; Zech 3; Amos 9.1; Dan 7.9–11, and especially Job 1.6–12, where the role of the accuser (i.e. the satan) is to judge the character of Job.

7 For a more detailed comparison, see Edwin C. Kingsbury, 'The Prophets and the Council of Yahweh', *JBL* 83/3 (1964): esp. pp. 279–82.

8 On Isa 6 as both call narrative and judgement narrative, see Rolf Knierim, 'The Vocation of Isaiah', *VT* 18/1 (1968): pp. 47–68.

9 Jer 1.9; Eze 3.1–2.

10 Christopher Seitz, *Isaiah 1–39*. Interpretation (Louisville, KY: John Knox, 1993), p. 55.

11 See Beale, *We Become What We Worship*, pp. 36–70, on Isa 6 and the prophet's idolatrous audience.

12 Literally, 'Make the heart of this people fat'. I have translated 'heart' (*lev*) as 'mind' because the Hebrew notion of the heart as the place where decisions are made and our modern understanding of mind are very similar. We tend to think of the heart more in terms of emotion than decision, and the point here is an inability to *understand* and act.

13 The same form (hiphil) of the same verb (*kabed*) is used to speak of Pharaoh's hardened heart in Exodus.

14 On the subject of God hardening hearts, see Robert B. Chisholm Jr, 'Divine Hardening in the Old Testament', *BSac* 153/612 (1996): pp. 410–34; Gerhard von Rad, *Old Testament Theology, vol. 2: The Theology of Israel's Prophetic Traditions* (Louisville, KY: John Knox, 1960; trans. D.M.G. Stalker, 1965), pp. 151–5.

15 A similar dynamic may be seen in Moses' confrontation with Pharaoh in Exod 5–10. See the excursus in Fretheim, *Exodus*, pp. 96–103, where it is argued that 'God . . . intensifies Pharaoh's own obduracy' (p. 98).

16 I am grateful to Rikki E. Watts of Regent College for pointing out the context of idolatry (rejection of Jesus) behind Saul's blindness (private e-mail correspondence: May 6, 2010).

17 The words 'in the land' in the NIV are not present in the Hebrew.

18 The term for stump (*matzevet*) nearly always has cultic and idolatrous connotations, and Beale makes a good case for the same implication here: 'Isaiah 6:13a . . . metaphorically identifies Israel as idolatrous trees undergoing destruction.' Beale, *We Become What We Worship*, p. 55.

19 See Alec Motyer for the positive connotation, *The Prophecy of Isaiah: An Introduction and Commentary* (Downers Grove: IVP Academic, 1993), pp. 79–80; Beale for the negative, *We Become What We Worship*, pp. 59–63.

20 The events of Isa 7 (also 2 Kgs 16; 2 Chr 28) probably follow about ten years after Uzziah's death.

21 Rikki E. Watts, *Isaiah's New Exodus and Mark* (Grand Rapids: Baker Academic, 2000), p. 193.

22 This is not to say that the name could not also (positively) say of Judah that 'a remnant will remain'. We have already seen with Hosea's children that these parabolic names were intended to have more than one possible meaning.

23 Whether this prophecy in its own historical context (Isa 7.16) refers to Isaiah's second child, to Ahaz's son Hezekiah or to someone else is disputed among scholars. However, the gospel writers, with the benefits of hindsight and theological reflection, clearly understood its referent to be Mary's son, Jesus (Mt 1.23; Lk 1.31).

24 Isa 8.5–10 also places the name Immanuel (God-with-us) in a context of judgement.

25 Walter Brueggemann, *1 and 2 Kings* (Macon, GA: Smyth & Helwys, 2000), p. 473.

26 Samaria was the capital of the northern kingdom of Israel, but the name is also used to refer to the area between Galilee and Judea.

27 Martin Buber, *The Prophetic Faith* (trans. Carlyle Witton-Davies; New York: Macmillan, 1949), pp. 2–3 (emphasis added).

12. Prophetic Suffering: Exiled with God

1 Fretheim, 'The Repentance of God', p. 85.

2 Fretheim, 'I Was Only a Little Angry', p. 369.

3 C. Wright, *Mission of God*, p. 280.

4 I have borrowed this phrase from Beale, *We Become What We Worship*, pp. 16, 22, *passim*.

⁵ Walter Brueggemann, *A Commentary on Jeremiah: Exile and Home-coming* (Grand Rapids; Eerdmans, 1998), p. 169.

⁶ The verb *niham*, meaning 'to relent', occurs twenty-nine times in the Old Testament with Yahweh as its Subject. See also 'Persuading God' in ch. 2.

⁷ Study groups may wish to use a hardened pot and a lump of malleable clay as hands-on props for discussion and reflection.

⁸ The language here is unreservedly strong. Alternative translations for the verb *patah* include 'deceive/persuade' (NIV), 'dupe/trick' (NEB), 'push' (MSG), and even 'seduce/rape' (A.J. Heschel). The same Hebrew verb is elsewhere translated in the NIV as 'seduce' (Exod 22.16), 'coax' (Jdg 14.15), 'lure' (Jdg 16.5), 'entice' (1 Kgs 22.20), 'flatter' (Ps 78.36), 'deceive' (Prov 24.28), and 'persuade' (Prov 25.15).

⁹ See, for instance, Walter Brueggemann's sermon, 'The Secret of Survival: Jeremiah 20.7–13; Matthew 6.1–8', *Journal for Preachers* (Lent 2003): pp. 42–7.

¹⁰ Jer 26 is generally accepted to provide the context for the famous 'temple sermon' of Jer 7. Jer 7 emphasizes the sermon itself, Jer 26 the people's response.

¹¹ Fretheim, *Suffering of God*, pp. 113–26.

¹² Brueggemann addresses this question in *Old Testament Theology*, pp. 183–203.

¹³ Jeremiah disappears from historical records after being forced to go to Egypt because of the rebellion against Babylon. See Jer 43.

¹⁴ 'Paul's style of life and work is not just a pointer to what the true God is doing, but is actually an embodiment of it.' N.T. Wright, *The Resurrection of the Son of God* (Minneapolis: Fortress, 2003), p. 303. What I am saying in this chapter about Jeremiah's prophetic status is closely related to what Paul claimed regarding his apostolic status: that suffering proves authenticity. See Moberly, *Prophecy*, pp. 169–220.

¹⁵ We must be wary of taking 'jars of clay' to mean that our bodies are just temporary vessels, soon to be disposed of. See 'Image Problems' in ch. 13.

13. Prophetic Integrity: Imaging God

1 For further discussion, see Klaus Koch, 'Is Daniel Also among the Prophets?' *Interpretation* 39/2 (1985): pp. 117–30.

2 The 'anointing' of Hazael as king of Aram (2 Kgs 8.9–15) is a remarkable instance of prophetic authority on foreign soil.

3 Ralph W. Klein's *Israel in Exile: A Theological Interpretation* (Philadelphia: Fortress, 1979) explores six biblical responses to the theological problem of Israel's exile.

4 See Beale, *We Become What We Worship*, pp. 139–40, on the relation between huge statues and self-idolization.

5 David Clines, 'The Image of God in Man', *TynBul* 19 (1968): pp. 83–5.

6 This idea is very much behind the composition of Gen 1, where the author links the creation of human beings as images of God to the task of ruling (Gen 1.26).

7 Clines, 'Image of God', pp. 85–7.

8 Ibid., p. 86.

9 See N.T. Wright, *Surprised by Hope* (London: SPCK, 2008), pp. 159–76.

10 Dan 5.30–31 very briefly introduces Darius the Mede after the death of the Babylonian Belshazzar. Some believe him to have been the same person as Cyrus the Persian. For further details, see Joyce G. Baldwin, *Daniel: An Introduction and Commentary*. TOTC (Leicester: IVP, 1978), pp. 23–8.

11 This translation is suggested by Iain Provan in his Regent College lectures on Daniel (2009), based on a wordplay in the Aramaic.

12 Brueggemann, *Prophetic Imagination*, p. 13.

13 Similarly, Joseph (Gen 40–41) and Esther were two other Jewish exiles whose 'court tales' conclude with God being made known in foreign contexts.

14 Dan 4.8,9,18; 5.11,12,14; 6.3.

14. Prophetic Humility: Becoming Less

1 The 'Second Temple Period' refers to the period between the construction of the Second Temple (515 BC) after the Jews returned from exile and its destruction by the Romans in AD 70.

2 Babylon fell to Persia (430–332 BC) and Persia to Greece (331–167 BC), followed by a period of Jewish independence as a result of the

Maccabean revolt (the Hasmonean kingdom; 167–63 BC) before Rome conquered Palestine in 63 BC.

3   Johannes Behm and E. Würthwein, 'metanoéw, metanoia', in Gerhard Kittel, *Theological Dictionary of the New Testament*, vol. 4 (trans. Geoffrey W. Bromiley; Grand Rapids: Eerdmans, 1967), pp. 976–89, 1000–1001.

4   T.R. Hobbs, *2 Kings*, WBC 13 (Waco: Word, 1985), p. 65. Further to Hobbs's argument, Robert L. Webb notes other OT verses where *yarad* ('he went down') is understood to suggest humbling (Jer 13.18; Eze 30.6). *John the Baptizer and Prophet: A Socio-Historical Study* (Sheffield: JSOT Press, 1991), p. 104, n. 31.

5   Webb, *John the Baptizer*, p. 104.

6   Ezekiel, like John, came from a priestly family.

7   Mt 3.3; Mk 1.3; Lk 3.4; Jn 1.23.

8   See Webb, *John the Baptizer*, pp. 96–111.

9   Luke perhaps highlights the contradiction in John's circumstances in Lk 3.2: 'during the high priesthood of Annas and Caiaphas, the word of God came to John son of Zechariah in the desert.'

10   One possibility is that when John's parents passed away (they were already advanced in age at his birth; Lk 1.7), he was brought up in the desert by the Essenes, a group of dissident priests who had retreated from Jerusalem because of disagreements about purity laws and practices. This would explain his desert location, the priestly connection between his father's vocation and the Qumran community, and perhaps also the reasons for his decision to choose baptism as an appropriate ritual to complement his message. See J.A.T. Robinson, 'The Baptism of John and the Qumran Community', *HTR* 50 (1957): pp. 175–91.

11   See Webb, *John the Baptizer*, p. 197.

12   Wright, *Jesus and the Victory of God* (London: SPCK, 1996), p. 160.

13   Winnowing is the act of separating chaff/husks from the grain.

14   Opinions are divided over whether the 'spirit' and 'fire' in Mt 3.11 refer to Pentecost, or are symbols of judgement, or refer to something else.

15   John's gospel contains more explicit theological reflection than the Synoptics. Jesus is therefore presented as the New Temple more clearly in John than in the other gospels.

16   See Isa 49.14–26; 54.4–8; Jer 2.2; Eze 16.8–14; Hos 2.16–23.

17   In Matthew, John introduces various phrases which are later picked up by Jesus in the narrative (e.g. 'I tell you . . .' (3.9/5.20,22, etc.) and 'you brood of vipers!' in reference to Israel's religious leaders (Mt

12.34/23.33). It has also been suggested that Jesus follows John's lead by using parables to teach. See Ben Witherington III, *John's Wisdom: A Commentary on the Fourth Gospel* (Louisville, KY: Westminster John Knox, 1995), p. 109.

[18] John's untimely death is the result of his conflict with Herod Antipas (Mt 14.3–11). Like the prophets of old, he paid a heavy price for confronting compromise.

[19] Scot McKnight, *A New Vision For Israel: The Teachings of Jesus in National Context* (Grand Rapids: Eerdmans, 1999), p 4.

[20] William Temple, *Christ in His Church* (London: Macmillan, 1925).

15. Prophetic Fulfilment: God with Us

[1] E.g. Mt 13.57; Lk 24.19; Jn 4.19; 9.17. Over 300 pages of Wright's *Jesus and the Victory of God* (pp. 147–474) illustrate how Jesus fits the 'Profile of a Prophet'.

[2] E.g. Ben Witherington affirms that 'Jesus had a normal, progressive consciousness, and that awareness of what God wanted him to do did not come to him all at once at birth, or even at his baptism, but over the course of time.' *John's Wisdom*, p. 112.

[3] See N.T. Wright, *Jesus and the Victory of God*, p. 486.

[4] The Hebrew phrase (*ratztah nafshi*) could also be translated 'in whom I am well pleased'.

[5] Some scholars consider Isa 61.1–3 to be a fifth song of the Suffering Servant.

[6] See N.T. Wright, *Jesus and the Victory of God*, pp. 537–8.

[7] Luke Timothy Johnson, *The Gospel of Luke*, SP 3 (Collegeville, MN: The Liturgical Press, 1991), p. 74.

[8] Moberly, *The Bible, Theology, and Faith: A Study of Abraham and Jesus* (Cambridge: CUP, 2000), p. 223. Moberly identifies each of the temptations from Mt 4 again 'on the lips of the passers-by' in Mt 27 when Jesus is on the cross (pp. 201–5, 217–20.)

[9] Brueggemann, *Prophetic Imagination*, p. 89.

[10] The 'Corban' rule (Mk 7.11) enabled a son to maintain control of family funds by falsely claiming that money which should have been used to care for his parents in their dotage had been devoted to the temple. In this way their traditions ('rules taught by men') created ways to avoid the demands of the Torah (rules given by God).

[11] See also Mt 11.15; 13.9,43; Mk 4.9,23; Lk 8.8; 14.35.

[12] N.T. Wright, *Jesus and the Victory of God*, p. 176 (original emphasis).

[13] Ben F. Meyer, *The Aims of Jesus* (London: SCM, 1979), p. 162.

[14] Regrettably, there is insufficient space here to explore Jesus' masterful use of questions.

[15] N.T. Wright, *Jesus and the Victory of God*, p. 608.

[16] Richard A. Horsley, 'Popular Prophetic Movements at the Time of Jesus: Their Principal Features and Social Origins', *JSNT* 26 (1986): p. 23.

[17] The only sign Jesus promised his 'wicked and adulterous generation' was the cryptic 'sign of the prophet Jonah' (Mt 12.39–41). Jesus would follow Jonah's route (without the rebellion!), taking God's judgement upon himself in order to quench the power of evil forever with forgiveness.

[18] Morna D. Hooker, *The Signs of a Prophet: The Prophetic Actions of Jesus* (London: SCM, 1997), p. 39 (original emphasis).

[19] 'Hosanna' is derived from the Hebrew *hoshi'a na'*, meaning 'Save now!' or 'Please save!' encompassing both a cry of praise and a call for salvation.

16. Prophetic Fulfilment: God with Us

[1] These two actions—Jesus' royal claims (Mt 27.11,37) and his 'blasphemy' against the temple (Mt 26.61; 27.40)—were the central charges leading to Jesus' crucifixion.

[2] Within forty years of Jesus' prophecy, Jerusalem's Second Temple was destroyed (AD 70) when the Jews rose up against their Roman oppressors. Solomon's Temple had similarly been destroyed by Babylon only twenty years or so after Jeremiah's sermon. The events described in Mk 13 (also Mt 24; Lk 21) are often read as descriptions of 'end times' in some distant future, but they are almost certainly Jesus' response to the more immediate question about when the temple would fall (see Mk 13.30).

[3] In Mark's gospel, the temple judgement (Mk 11.12–14) comes between the cursing of the tree and its withered condition (Mk 11.20–21), making clear that the significance of these events is intertwined. Luke does not mention the event, though he does include a parable of similar substance (Lk 13.6–9).

⁴ William R. Telford, *The Barren Temple and the Withered Tree: A Redaction-Critical Analysis of the Cursing of the Fig-Tree Pericope in Mark's Gospel and its Relation to the Cleansing of the Temple Tradition*, JSNTSup 1 (Sheffield: JSOT Press, 1980), p. 138 (original emphasis).

⁵ The phrase 'my servants the prophets' is quite common in the OT: 2 Kgs 9.7; 17.13; Jer 7.25; 26.5; 29.19; 35.15; 44.4; Eze 38.17; Zech 1.6.

⁶ See John Christopher Thomas, *Footwashing in John 13 and the Johannine Community* (London: T&T Clark, 2004), p. 35f.

⁷ Herman Ridderbos, *The Gospel of John: A Theological Commentary* (Grand Rapids: Eerdmans, 1997), p. 459, n. 33.

⁸ Ibid., p. 460.

⁹ James D.G. Dunn, *Jesus and the Spirit: A Study of the Religious and Charismatic Experience of Jesus and the First Christians as Reflected in the New Testament* (London: SCM, 1975), pp. 20–21.

¹⁰ See Isa 51.17,22; Jer 25.15–17; 49.12; Lam 4.21; Eze 23.31–35; Hab 2.16.

¹¹ Richard Bauckham, *Jesus and the God of Israel: God Crucified and Other Essays on the New Testament's Christology of Divine Identity* (Milton Keynes: Paternoster, 2008), p. 256.

¹² Ibid., p. 257.

¹³ Isa 17.10; Jer 2.32; 3.21; 13.25; 18.15; Eze 22.12; 23.35; Hos 2.13; 8.14; 13.6.

¹⁴ Isaac Watts, 'When I Survey the Wondrous Cross' (1707).

¹⁵ The fact that Mark draws on Ps 22 and Luke on Ps 31 should not alarm readers. The two statements are by no means mutually exclusive. Taken together, they speak of profound faith in the midst of deep pain.

¹⁶ *The Sixth Sense* (1999) is one example that comes to mind.

¹⁷ 'Christ' (*Christos*) is the Greek translation of the Hebrew 'Messiah' (*mashiach*), both meaning 'anointed one'. See Jn 1.41; 4.25.

¹⁸ Luke also uses the Greek word *dei* ('must'; 'it is necessary') in other related contexts: Lk 2.49; 17.25; 22.37; 24.7,44.

¹⁹ The same story in Mark also includes Jesus' harsh rebuke to Peter, 'Get behind me, Satan!' when Peter attempted to steer Jesus away from the necessity of suffering in relation to his mission (Mk 8.32–33).

²⁰ In his preaching (Acts 3.18) and his writings (1 Pet 1.10–11), the apostle Peter also stresses how the prophets foresaw the inevitability of Christ's sufferings.

²¹ See N.T. Wright, *Jesus and the Victory of God*, pp. 612–53.

22 The Greek verb *eskenosen* in Jn 1.14 literally means 'to pitch a tent' or 'to dwell in a tent'. (NIV translates it 'made his dwelling'; NRSV as 'lived'.)

17. Prophetic Community: Passing On the Flame

1 This verse was almost certainly at the back of Luke's mind in his composition of the Luke–Acts saga (Lk 2.29–35; Acts 1.8; 13.47; 26.23; 28.28). See David L. Tiede, 'The Exaltation of Jesus and the Restoration of Israel in Acts 1', *HTR* 79:1–3 (1986): pp. 285–6.

2 2 Sam 22.16; Job 37.10; Eze 13.13,37.

3 Exod 3.2; 31.21; 19.18; Deut 4.24; 1 Kgs 18.38.

4 Num 11.25; 24.2; Jdg 3.10; 6.34; 11.29; 14.6,19; 15.14; 1 Sam 10.6,10; 11.6; 16.13; Eze 37.1; Mic 3.8; etc.

5 Gordon D. Fee, *God's Empowering Presence: The Holy Spirit in the Letters of Paul* (Peabody, MA: Hendrickson, 1994), p. 313.

6 Like the Hebrew word *ruach*, which may be translated 'wind', 'spirit', or 'breath', the Greek word pneuma has the same three possibilities for translation.

7 2 Kgs 2.3,5,7,15; 4.1,38; 5.22; 6.1; 9.1.

8 Many of Paul's metaphors for the Spirit emphasize unity, e.g. 1 Cor 12.13: 'we were all given the one Spirit to drink'; 2 Cor 3.3: 'you [plural] are a letter from Christ . . . written not with ink but with the Spirit'; 1 Cor 3.16: 'Don't you know that you yourselves are God's temple and that God's Spirit lives in you?'; Eph 1.13b: 'Having believed, you [plural] were marked in him with a seal, the promised Holy Spirit'; etc.

9 See also Acts 4.32–35.

10 I. Howard Marshall, *Acts*, TNTC (Leicester: IVP, 1980), p. 83. (See also Marshall, *Luke*, pp. 204–6).

11 Roger Stronstad, *The Prophethood of All Believers: A Study in Luke's Charismatic Theology* (Cleveland, TN: CPT Press, 2010), pp. 70–80.

12 Stronstad, *Prophethood*, pp. 28f., 60.

13 The final chapter and postscript of Brueggemann's *The Prophetic Imagination* (2nd edn) offer some helpful suggestions concerning the practice of prophetic ministry (pp. 115–25).

14 Richard Bauckham, *The Theology of the Book of Revelation* (Cambridge: CUP, 1993), pp. 119–20.

15 Ibid., p. 120.

16 Gordon D. Fee, *Paul, the Spirit, and the People of God* (Peabody, MA: Hendrickson, 1996), p. 66 (original emphasis).

17 Marshall, *Acts*, p. 86.

18 Luke Timothy Johnson, *Acts of the Apostles*, SP 5 (Collegeville, MN: Glazier, 1992), p. 65. See Acts 3.1,3,4,11; 4.1,3,7,13,19,23.

19 The Greek word *holokleria* ('whole and lacking nothing') is similar in meaning to the Latin word 'integer' explored in relation to Daniel's integrity (see 'Wholly in the Spirit', ch. 13).

20 The point is made with even greater force in Acts 4.9,12, where the Greek verb (*sozo*) suggests not just healing, but salvation for the crippled man.

21 See, for instance, Isa 43.6–7; Jer 31.7–9; Eze 36.24–28. For a sneak peek at the ending of the story we are currently living in, see Rev 21–22.

22 Tiede, 'The Exaltation of Jesus', p. 286.

23 C. Wright, *Mission of God*, p. 258.

Bibliography

Aberbach, Moses and Leivy Smolar. 'Aaron, Jeroboam, and the Golden Calves'. *Journal of Biblical Literature* 86 (1967): pp. 129–140.

Ackerman, James. 'Knowing Good and Evil: A Literary Analysis of the Court History in 2 Samuel 9–20 and 1 Kings 1–2'. *Journal of Biblical Literature* 109/1 (1990): pp. 41–60.

Alter, Robert. *The Art of Biblical Narrative* (New York: Basic Books, 1981).

Andersen, Francis L. and David Noel Freedman. *Hosea*. Anchor Bible (Garden City, NY: Doubleday, 1980).

Baldwin, Joyce G. *Daniel: An Introduction and Commentary.* Tyndale Old Testament Commentaries (Leicester: Inter-Varsity Press, 1978).

Balentine, Samuel. *Prayer in the Hebrew Bible: The Drama of Divine–Human Dialogue* (Minneapolis: Augsburg Fortress, 1993).

Bailey, Randall C. *David in Love and War: The Pursuit of Power in 2 Samuel 10–12*, JSOTSup 75 (Sheffield: JSOT, 1990).

Barth, Karl. *Prayer* (Philadelphia: Westminster John Knox, 2nd edn, 1992).

Bauckham, Richard. *Jesus and the God of Israel: God Crucified and Other Essays on the New Testament's Christology of Divine Identity* (Milton Keynes: Paternoster, 2008).

— *The Theology of the Book of Revelation* (Cambridge: Cambridge University Press, 1993).

Beale, G.K. *We Become What We Worship: A Biblical Theology of Idolatry* (Downers Grove, IL: Inter-Varsity Press, 2008).

Beeby, H.D. *Grace Abounding: A Commentary on the Book of Hosea.* International Theological Commentary (Grand Rapids: Eerdmans, 1989).

Bodner, Keith. 'Nathan: Prophet, Politician and Novelist?' *Journal for the Study of the Old Testament* 95 (2001): pp. 43–54.

Bonhoeffer, Dietrich. *The Cost of Discipleship* (trans. R.H. Fuller; New York: Macmillan, 1963).

Brenner, Athalya. 'Jonah's Poem out of and within Its Context.' Pages 183–92 in *Among the Prophets* (ed. P.R. Davies and D.J.A. Clines; Sheffield: Sheffield Academic Press, 1993).

Bronner, Leah. *The Stories of Elijah and Elisha as Polemic against Baal Worship* (Leiden: Brill, 1968).

Brown, Francis, S.R. Driver, and Charles A. Briggs, eds. *The Brown–Driver–Briggs Hebrew and English Lexicon* (Peabody, MA: Hendrickson, 1996).

Brueggemann, Walter. *A Commentary on Jeremiah: Exile and Homecoming* (Grand Rapids; Eerdmans, 1998).

— *1 & 2 Kings* (Macon, GA: Smyth & Helwys, 2000).

— 'The Secret of Survival: Jeremiah 20.7–13; Matthew 6.1–8'. *Journal for Preachers* (Lent 2003): pp. 42–47.

— *Finally Comes the Poet: Daring Speech for Proclamation* (Minneapolis: Fortress, 1989).

— *First and Second Samuel.* Interpretation (Atlanta: John Knox Press, 1990).

— *Divine Presence amid Violence: Contextualizing the Book of Joshua* (Eugene, OR: Paternoster, 2009).

— 'The Trusted Creature'. *Catholic Biblical Quarterly* 31 (1969): pp. 484–98.

— 'On Trust and Freedom: A Study of Faith in the Succession Narratives'. *Interpretation* 26/1 (1972): pp. 3–19.

— *Old Testament Theology: Essays on Structure, Theme, and Text* (ed. Patrick D. Miller; Minneapolis: Augsburg Fortress, 1992).

— *Theology of the Old Testament: Testimony, Dispute, Advocacy* (Minneapolis: Fortress, 1997)

— *The Prophetic Imagination* (Minneapolis: Fortress, rev. edn, 2001).

— *The Book of Exodus.* New Interpreter's Bible, vol. 1 (Nashville: Abingdon, 1994).

Buber, Martin. *The Prophetic Faith* (trans. Carlyle Witton-Davies; New York: Macmillan, 1949).

Buechner, Frederick. *Telling the Truth: The Gospel as Comedy, Tragedy, and Fairy-Tale* (San Francisco: Harper & Row, 1977).

Childs, Brevard, *The Book of Exodus* (Philadelphia: Westminster, 1974).

Chisholm Jr, Robert B. 'Does God Deceive?' *Bibliotheca sacra* 155 (Jan-Mar 1998): pp. 11–28.

— 'Divine Hardening in the Old Testament'. *Bibliotheca sacra* 153/612 (1996): pp. 410–34.

Clines, David J.A. 'The Image of God in Man'. *Tyndale Bulletin* 19 (1968): pp. 53–103.

Craddock, Fred B. *As One Without Authority* (Nashville: Abingdon Press, 1971).

Crenshaw, James L. *Old Testament Wisdom: An Introduction* (Louisville, KY: Westminster John Knox Press, 1998).

Crites, Stephen. 'The Narrative Quality of Experience'. *Journal of the American Academy of Religion* 39/3 (Sept 1971): pp. 291–311.

Deeley, Mary Katherine. 'The Shaping of Jonah'. *Theology Today* 34/3 (1977): pp. 305–10.

DeVries, Simon J. *1 Kings*. Word Biblical Commentary 12 (Waco, TX: Word Books, 1985).

Dunn, James D.G. *Jesus and the Spirit: A Study of the Religious and Charismatic Experience of Jesus and the First Christians as Reflected in the New Testament* (London: SCM Press, 1975).

Ellul, Jacques. *The Politics of God and the Politics of Man* (trans. GW Bromiley; Grand Rapids, MI: Eerdmans, 1972).

Fee, Gordon D. *God's Empowering Presence: The Holy Spirit in the Letters of Paul* (Milton Keynes: Paternoster, 1994).

— *Paul, the Spirit, and the People of God* (Peabody, MA: Hendrickson, 1996).

Fewell, Danna N. and David M. Gunn. *Narrative Art in the Hebrew Bible* (New York: Oxford University Press, 1993).

Frei, Hans. *The Eclipse of Biblical Narrative: A Study in Eighteenth and Nineteenth Century Hermeneutics* (New Haven: Yale University Press, 1974).

Fretheim, Terence E. 'I Was Only a Little Angry: Divine Violence in the Prophets'. *Interpretation* 58/4 (2004):pp. 365–75.

— 'Is Genesis 3 a Fall Story?' *Word & World* 14/2 (1994): pp. 144–53.

— 'Divine Foreknowledge, Divine Constancy, and the Rejection of Saul's Kingship'. *Catholic Biblical Quarterly* 47/4 (Oct 1985): pp. 595–602.

— *God and World in the Old Testament: A Relational Theology of Creation* (Nashville: Abingdon, 2005).

— *The Suffering of God: An Old Testament Perspective. Overtures to Biblical Theology* (Philadelphia: Fortress, 1984).

— *Exodus*. Interpretation (Louisville, KY: John Knox Press, 1991).

— 'Divine Dependence upon the Human: An Old Testament Perspective'. *Ex Auditu* 13 (1997): pp. 1–13.

— 'The Repentance of God: A Study of Jeremiah 18.7–10'. *Hebrew Annual Review* 11 (1987): pp. 81–92.

Gage, Warren Austin. *The Gospel of Genesis: Studies in Protology and Eschatology* (Winona Lake, IN: Carpenter Books, 1984).

Goldingay, John. 'The Logic of Intercession'. *Theology* 99 (Jan/Feb 1998): pp. 262–70.

— *God's Prophet, God's Servant: A Study in Jeremiah and Isaiah 40–55* (Toronto: Clements Publishing, rev. edn, 2002).

— *Old Testament Theology, vol. 1: Israel's Gospel* (Downers Grove, IL: Inter-Varsity Press, 2003).

Gowan, Donald E. *Theology in Exodus: Biblical Theology in the Form of a Commentary* (Louisville, KY: John Knox Press, 1994).

Gray, John. *I and II Kings: A Commentary*. Old Testament Library (Philadelphia: Westminster, 1970).

Gunn, David M. 'Reading Right: Reliable and Omniscient Narrator, Omniscient God, and Foolproof Composition in the Hebrew Bible.' Pages 53–64 in *The Bible in Three Dimensions* (ed. D.J.A. Clines et al.; Sheffield: JSOT Press, 1990).

Habel, Norman. 'The Form and Significance of Call Narratives'. *Zeitschrift für die Alttestamentliche Wissenschaft* 77 (1965): pp. 297–323.

Hamilton, Jeffries M. 'Caught in the Nets of Prophecy? The Death of King Ahab and the Character of God'. *Catholic Biblical Quarterly* 56 (1994): pp. 649–63.

Hanson, Paul D. *The Diversity of Scripture: A Theological Interpretation* (Philadelphia: Fortress, 1982).

Hays, J. Daniel. 'Has the Narrator Come to Praise Solomon or to Bury Him? Narrative Subtlety in 1 Kings 1–11'. *Journal for the Study of the Old Testament* 28/2 (2003): pp. 149–74.

Heschel, A. J. *The Prophets* (New York: Harper Collins, 1962).

— *The Insecurity of Freedom: Essays on Human Existence* (New York: Schocken, 1972).

Hobbs, T.R. *2 Kings.* Word Biblical Commentary 13 (Waco: Word, 1985).

Hooker, Morna D. *The Signs of a Prophet: The Prophetic Actions of Jesus* (London: SCM Press, 1997).

Horsley, Richard A. 'Popular Prophetic Movements at the Time of Jesus: Their Principal Features and Social Origins'. *Journal for the Study of the New Testament* 26 (1986): pp. 3–27.

Jacobs, Benno. *The Second Book of the Bible: Exodus* (Hoboken, NJ: Ktav, 1992).

Janzen, Waldemar. *Old Testament Ethics: A Paradigmatic Approach* (Louisville, KY: Westminster John Knox Press, 1994).

Johnson, Luke Timothy. *The Gospel of Luke.* Sacra Pagina 3 (Collegeville, MN: The Liturgical Press, 1991).

— *Acts of the Apostles.* Sacra Pagina 5 (Collegeville, MN: Glazier, 1992).

Jones, L. Gregory. *Embodying Forgiveness: A Theological Analysis* (Grand Rapids: Eerdmans, 1995).

Kelly, Henry Ansgar. *Satan: A Biography* (Cambridge University Press, 2006).

Kelly, Thomas R. *A Testament of Devotion* (New York: HarperCollins, 1992 [first pub. 1941]).

Kingsbury, Edwin C. 'The Prophets and the Council of Yahweh'. *Journal of Biblical Literature* 83/3 (1964): pp. 279–86.

Kissling, Paul J. Reliable *Characters in the Primary History: Profiles of Moses, Joshua, Elijah and Elisha.* JSOTSup 224 (Sheffield Academic Press, 1996).

Kitamori, Kazoh. *Theology of the Pain of God* (Richmond, VA: John Knox Press, 1965).

Kittel, Gerhard. *Theological Dictionary of the New Testament*, vol. 4 (trans. Geoffrey W. Bromiley; Grand Rapids: Eerdmans, 1967).

Klein, Ralph W. *Israel in Exile: A Theological Interpretation* (Philadelphia: Fortress, 1979).

Knierim, Rolf. 'The Vocation of Isaiah'. *Vetus Testamentum* 18/1 (1968): pp. 47–68.

Koch, Klaus. 'Is Daniel Also among the Prophets?' *Interpretation* 39/2 (Apr 1985): pp. 117–130.

Leuchter, Mark. 'Jeroboam the Ephratite'. *Journal of Biblical Literature* 125/1 (2006): pp. 51–72.

Limburg, James. *Hosea–Micah*. Interpretation (Atlanta: John Knox Press, 1988).

Lowry, Eugene. *The Homiletical Plot: The Sermon as Narrative Art Form* (Atlanta: John Knox Press, 1980).

McKnight, Scot. *A New Vision for Israel: The Teachings of Jesus in National Context* (Grand Rapids: Eerdmans, 1999).

Marshall, I. Howard. *Acts*. Tyndale New Testament Commentaries (Leicester: Inter-Varsity Press, 1980).

Mauser, Ulrich. 'God in Human Form'. *Ex Auditu* 16 (2000): pp. 81–100.

Mays, James Luther. *Hosea*, Old Testament Commentary (Philadelphia: Westminster, 1969).

Mead, James K., 'Kings and Prophets, Donkeys and Lions: Dramatic Shape and Deuteronomistic Rhetoric in 1 Kings XIII'. *Vetus Testamentum* XLIX/2 (1999): pp. 191–205.

Meyer, Ben F. *The Aims of Jesus* (London: SCM Press, 1979).

Middleton, J. Richard and Brian J. Walsh. *Truth Is Stranger Than It Used To Be* (Downers Grove: Inter-Varsity Press, 1995).

Miles, Jack. *GOD: A Biography* (New York: Random House, 1995).

Miller, Patrick D. *They Cried to the Lord: The Form and Theology of Biblical Prayer* (Minneapolis: Augsburg Fortress, 1994).

— 'Prayer and Divine Action.' Pages 211–32 in *God in the Fray: A Tribute to Walter Brueggemann* (ed. Tod Linafelt and Timothy K. Beal; Minneapolis: Fortress, 1998).

— 'Prayer as Persuasion: The Rhetoric and Intention of Prayer'. *Word & World* XIII/4 (1993): pp. 356–62.

Moberly, R.W.L. 'Does God Lie to His Prophets? The Story of Micaiah ben Imlah as a Test Case'. *Harvard Theological Review* 96:1 (2003): pp. 1–23.

— 'God Is Not a Human That He Should Repent: Numbers 23:19 and 1 Samuel 15:29.' Pages 112–23 in *God in the Fray: A Tribute to Walter Brueggemann* (ed. Tod Linafelt and Timothy K. Beal; Minneapolis: Augsburg, 1998).

— *Old Testament Theology: The Theology of the Book of Genesis* (New York: Cambridge University Press, 2009).

— 'How May We Speak of God? A Reconsideration of the Nature of Biblical Theology'. *Tyndale Bulletin* 53/2 (2002): pp. 177–202.

— *The Bible, Theology, and Faith: A Study of Abraham and Jesus* (Cambridge: Cambridge University Press), 2000.

— *Prophecy and Discernment: Cambridge Studies in Christian Doctrine* (New York: Cambridge University Press, 2006).

Motyer, J. Alec. *The Prophecy of Isaiah: An Introduction and Commentary* (Downers Grove: IVP Academic, 1993).

Nickerson, Susan L. 'Book Review: Fiction (1983–10–15)'. *Library Journal* (R.R. Bowker Co, 1976).

Niditch, Susan. *Judges*. Old Testament Library (Louisville, KY: John Knox Press, 2008).

Ortlund, Jr, Raymond C. *Whoredom: God's Unfaithful Wife in Biblical Theology* (Grand Rapids: Eerdmans, 1996).

Perdue, Leo. *The Collapse of History: Reconstructing Old Testament Theology* (Minneapolis: Fortress Press, 1994).

Polzin, Robert. *Samuel and the Deuteronomist: 1 Samuel* (Bloomington: Indiana University Press, 1993).

Provan, Iain W. *1 and 2 Kings*. New International Bible Commentary (Peabody, MA: Hendrickson, 1995).

Peterson, Eugene H. *First and Second Samuel* (Louisville, KY: Westminster John Knox Press, 1999).

Ridderbos, Herman. *The Gospel of John: A Theological Commentary* (Grand Rapids: Eerdmans, 1997).

Roberts, J.J.M. 'Does God Lie? Divine Deceit as a Theological Problem in Israelite Prophetic Literature.' Pages 123–31 in *The Bible and the Ancient Near East: Collected Essays* (Winona Lake, IN: Eisenbrauns, 2002).

Robinson, J.A.T. 'The Baptism of John and the Qumran Community'. *Harvard Theological Review* 50 (1957): pp. 175–91.

Seitz, Christopher. *Isaiah 1–39*. Interpretation (Louisville, KY: John Knox Press, 1993).

Smith, Gordon T. *Listening to God in Times of Choice: The Art of Discerning God's Will* (Downers Grove, IL: Inter-Varsity Press, 1997).

Stek, John H. 'The Message of the Book of Jonah'. *Calvin Theological Journal* 4/1 (1969): pp. 23–50.

Sternberg, Meir. *The Poetics of Biblical Narrative: Ideological Literature and the Drama of Reading* (Bloomington: Indiana University Press, 1985).

Stronstad, Roger. *The Prophethood of All Believers: A Study in Luke's Charismatic Theology* (Cleveland, TN: CPT Press, 2010).

Stroup, George. 'Theology of Narrative or Narrative Theology? A Response to Why Narrative?' *Theology Today* 47/4 (Jan 1991): pp. 424–32.

Telford, William R. *The Barren Temple and the Withered Tree: A Redaction-Critical Analysis of the Cursing of the Fig-Tree Pericope in Mark's Gospel and its Relation to the Cleansing of the Temple Tradition*. JSNTSup 1 (Sheffield: JSOT Press, 1980).

Temple, William. *Christ in His Church* (Macmillan, 1925).

Thomas, John Christopher. *Footwashing in John 13 and the Johannine Community* (London: T&T Clark, 2004).

Tiede, David L. 'The Exaltation of Jesus and the Restoration of Israel in Acts 1'. *Harvard Theological Review* 79.1–3 (1986): pp. 278–86.

Tsevat, Matitiahu. 'God and the Gods in Assembly: An Interpretation of Psalm 82'. *Hebrew Union College Annual* 40–41 (1969–1970): pp. 123–137.

Van Rooy, H.F. 'The Names of Israel, Ephraim and Jacob in the Book of Hosea'. *Old Testament Essays* 6 (1993): pp. 135–49.

Van Winkle, D.W. '1 Kings XII–XIII 34: Jeroboam's Cultic Innovations and the Man of God from Judah'. *Vetus Testamentum* 46 (1996): pp. 101–14.

Volf, Miroslav. *Exclusion and Embrace: A Theological Exploration of Identity, Otherness and Reconciliation* (Nashville: Abingdon Press, 1996).

— *Free of Charge: Giving and Forgiving in a Culture Stripped of Grace* (Grand Rapids: Zondervan, 2005).

Von Rad, Gerhard. *Old Testament Theology, vol. 2: The Theology of Israel's Prophetic Traditions* (Louisville, KY: John Knox Press 1960; trans. D.M.G. Stalker, 1965).

Waltke, Bruce K. 'Lady Wisdom as Mediatrix: An Exposition of Proverbs 1.20–33'. *Presbyterian* 14/1 (1988): pp. 1–15.

Watts, Rikki E. *Isaiah's New Exodus and Mark* (Grand Rapids: Baker Academic, 2000).

Webb, Robert L. *John the Baptizer and Prophet: A Socio-Historical Study* (Sheffield: JSOT Press, 1991).

Weems, Renita J. *Battered Love: Marriage, Sex, and Violence in the Hebrew Prophets* (Minneapolis: Fortress, 1995).

Wenham, Gordon J. *Story as Torah: Reading Old Testament Narratives Ethically* (Grand Rapids: Baker, 2000).

Widmer, Michael. *Moses, God, and the Dynamics of Intercessory Prayer* (Tübingen: Mohr Siebeck, 2004).

Witherington III, Ben. *John's Wisdom: A Commentary on the Fourth Gospel* (Louisville, KY: Westminster John Knox Press, 1995).

— *The Gospel of Mark: A Socio-Rhetorical Commentary* (Grand Rapids: Eerdmans, 2002).

Wolff, Hans Walter. *The Old Testament: A Guide to Its Writings* (trans. Keith R. Crim; Philadelphia: Fortress, 1973 [1970]).

Wright, Christopher J.H. *Deuteronomy*. New International Bible Commentary (Peabody, MA: Hendrickson, 1996).

— *The Mission of God: Unlocking the Bible's Grand Narrative* (Leicester: Inter-Varsity Press, 2006).

Wright, N.T. *Surprised by Hope* (London: SPCK, 2008).

— *Jesus and the Victory of God* (London: SPCK, 1996).

— *The Resurrection of the Son of God* (Minneapolis: Fortress, 2003).

General Index

Scripture Index

Genesis (Gen)

1–11	**2–6**
1.1	1
1.2	6
1.27	4, 19, 143, 175, 229–230
1.28	5, 230
2.7	161
3.8	1
4.7	3
4.12	3
4.24	4
5.3	4
6.5	4
6.6	33, 169
6.6–7	4, 106
6.7–8	8
6.9	4
9.1	5
9.7	5
11.4	5
11.7	5
11.8–9	5
12.2–3	7
15.8–21	7
18	141
18.4	216
18.16–33	32
18.25	26, 32, 62
19.29	32
20.7	24
25.22, 26	32
32.11	28
32.24–32	32
48.13–20	141

Exodus (Exod)

1.7f.	8
3	134
3.8	12
3.10	12, 146
4.10	121
5.22–23	12
7.1	12, 30
10.1–2	9
15.13–16	13
15.20–21	43
17.8–16	57
18	40
19.4–6	16–17
20.3	67
20.3–6	95
20.18–19	14, 229
20.21	14
23.9	78
24	25
30.18–21	194
32	84, 125–126, 150, 161
32.1–10	**25–26**
32.7–14	29, 35, 83
32.11–14	**27–29, 35**
32.12	62
32.14	30, 35, 125
32.15–35	**29–30**
32.25	69
32.32	127
33.11	26

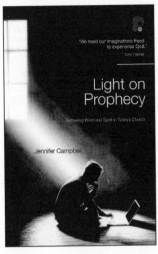

Light on Prophecy

Retrieving Word and Prophecy in Today's Church

Jennifer Campbell

The author correlates the vision and thinking of two powerful prophetic leaders: Hildegard of Bingen, a twelfth-century enclosed nun/mystic, and Dietrich Bonhoeffer, the twentieth-century German pastor/theologian executed by the Nazis. With a view to recovering a balanced and rounded theology of prophecy for the church today, she discusses the closely related workings of both the Word of God (viewed as Christ and the Scriptures) and the Holy Spirit in the works and lives of these famous Christians.

'Rarely do we encounter maturity, depth and wisdom when the subject at hand is the prophetic gift. Jenny Campbell's book is the exception. With rare insight she offers us a workable and thorough theology of Prophecy' – **Mike Breen, 3DM Global Leader.**

Jennifer Campbell is a lecturer in Christian Doctrine at Westminster Theological Centre, Cheltenham, UK. She is also the leader of Eaglesinflight.

978-1-84227-768-3

No More Law!

A Bold Study in Galatians

Bruce Atkinson

No More Law! is an accessible commentary on Paul's letter to the Galatian church. In it Bruce Atkinson concentrates on the work of the Holy Spirit in the Christian life; walking in the Spirit, how this brings freedom and produces godliness. He maintains a good theological balance between the Word and the Spirit, the gospel and the place of the Mosaic Law, freedom from that Law, but with an emphasis upon our responsibility to live godly lives in today's world.

'Bruce Atkinson offers a singularly pure treatment on the triumph of grace over law based on the book of Galatians. Powerful and convincing, his written exposition reflects his bold preaching style. *No More Law!* is first Century truth effectively applied to twenty-first Century hearts. A joy to read' – **Colin Dye, Senior Minister of Kensington Temple and a member of the National Leadership Team of the Elim Pentecostal Churches.**

Bruce Atkinson is the Associate Minister of Kensington Temple Elim Pentecostal Church, Notting Hill Gate, London.

978-1-84227-747-8

Understanding Jesus

Five Ways to Spiritual Enlightenment

Peter Williams

Peter Williams examines the Gospel accounts of Jesus' life from an apologetic perspective clearing the ground from preconceived ideas and prejudices and opening up five ways to consider the claims of Jesus' life and ministry. Williams encourages readers to take Jesus seriously and gives serious reasons why we should. Understanding Jesus helps readers to make their own informed response to the historical Jesus.

> 'Aquinas offered five ways to God; Peter Williams gives five powerful reasons for thinking that God revealed Himself in Jesus Christ. While the new atheists recycle nineteenth century doubts about the historicity and divinity of Jesus, Williams appeals to the most recent work of qualified scholars, including secularists and Jewish scholars as well as Christian authorities. He shows the evidence is stronger than ever for the New Testament account of Jesus' life and works, and that Jesus continues to transform lives today – **Angus J. L. Menuge Ph.D., Professor of Philosophy, Concordia University Wisconsin, USA.**

Peter S. Williams is a Christian philosopher and apologist. He is an Assistant Professor in Communication & Worldviews, Gimlekollen School of Journalism and Communication, Kristiansand, Norway.

978-1-84227-739-3

Paternoster:
thinking faith

We trust you enjoyed reading this book from Paternoster. If you want to be informed of any new titles from this author and other releases you can sign up to the Paternoster newsletter by contacting us:

Contact us
By Post: Paternoster
52 Presley Way
Crownhill
Milton Keynes
MK8 0ES

E-mail:paternoster@authenticmedia.co.uk

Follow us: